PUBLIC POLICY AND
MEDIA ORGANIZATIONS

Public Policy and Media Organizations

DAVID BERRY
Southampton Solent University, UK

CAROLINE KAMAU
Birkbeck, University of London, UK

ASHGATE

Published by
Ashgate Publishing Limited
Wey Court East
Union Road
Farnham
Surrey, GU9 7PT
England

Ashgate Publishing Company
110 Cherry Street
Suite 3-1
Burlington, VT 05401-3818
USA

www.ashgate.com

British Library Cataloguing in Publication Data
Berry, David, 1960–
  Public policy and media organizations.
  1. Social policy – Decision making. 2. Social policy – Public opinion.
  3. Social policy – Press coverage. 4. Mass media – Political aspects.
  5. Mass media and public opinion. 6. Journalism – Social aspects. 7. Journalism –
  Political aspects. 8. Social psychology. 9. Crime in mass media.
  I. Title II. Kamau, Caroline.
  361.6'1–dc23

Library of Congress Cataloging-in-Publication Data
Berry, David, 1960–
  Public policy and media organizations / by David Berry and Caroline Kamau.
      p. cm.
  Includes bibliographical references and index.
  ISBN 978-1-4094-0275-6 (hardback)—ISBN 978-1-4094-0276-3 (ebook) 1. Political
  planning—Case studies. 2. Policy sciences—Case studies. 3. Mass media—Case studies.
  I. Kamau, Caroline. II. Title.
  H97.B474 2012
  320.6—dc23

                                                                2012021240

ISBN 9781409402756 (hbk)
ISBN 9781409402763 (ebk – PDF)
ISBN 9781472404343 (ebk – ePUB)

Printed and bound in Great Britain by the
MPG Books Group, UK.

Contents

List of Figures and Tables

Figures

Tables

About the Authors

David Berry gained his PhD in Media Communication at the University of Glamorgan and currently works at Southampton Solent University, England. Publications include *Ethics and Media Culture: Practices and Representations* 2000, *The Romanian Mass Media and Cultural Development* 2004, *Radical Mass Media Criticism: A Cultural Genealogy* 2006, and *Journalism, Ethics and Society* 2008, which is currently being translated into Arabic by the King Saud Center, King Saud University, Saudi Arabia. His most recent publication is *Revisiting the Frankfurt School: Essays on Culture, Media and Theory*, published by Ashgate Publishing, 2012.

Caroline Kamau obtained her PhD in Social Psychology and BSc (Hons) in Psychology with Clinical Psychology from the University of Kent in England. She is a lecturer in Organizational Psychology at Birkbeck, University of London. She conducts experimental and applied psychology research on group processes. Her recent publications include an article reporting a laboratory study on group initiations and an article on intergroup emotions.

Preface

In modern Western systems public policy issues are wide and varied, but whatever the range the rationale behind public policy implementation by incumbent government is based on maintenance of power and the introduction of social benefits to society. This latter point has however complex motives attached and benefits that are not always universal in scope. For instance, reducing pay levels for public service workers in the name of a 'national interest' – to reduce debt perhaps – is one example. Taxation in general to invest in health care is seen to bring benefits to all – except those who believe that tax is a discreet form of theft. The reasoning behind public policy implementation is indeed extremely complex and multi-faceted – but we cannot deny that in social democratic systems, governments that are elected to power have a right to implement public policy according to their respective political philosophies. However, philosophical thinking can be subject to varying influencing factors such as media that help to condition or re-shape public policy thinking and implementation.

This book sets out to examine public policy and the influence news media organizations have in the production and implementation of public policy. Part of the reasoning behind this is to examine the impact that media organizations have on the democratic process: after all the public elect political parties to govern based on their respective policies outlined in manifestos which are conditioned by various types of political philosophy: this is essentially a democratic moment and to what extent media organizations can re-shape thinking is to ponder on the issue concerning the democratic moment of individual freewill to elect and legitimate rights to govern.

In principle, the news media have a right to free speech – limited by legal restraint sometimes – to hold government to account; for if capitalism was so perfect there would be no need for a news media in the first place. However, the influence media have over public policy-making is of interest when we consider the limited size of the mainstream media itself. In other words, ownership of most news organizations is limited to a small number of powerful individuals or institutions such as the BBC that is governed by historical class values. The most influential news media organization over recent years is Rupert Murdoch's News Corporation and Murdoch's connections with both the Labour Party and Conservative Party are legendary and thus influence over public policy is a serious matter of concern in the way it impacts upon the democratic process. During the Tony Blair-led government it was once claimed by a high-ranking police officer that Murdoch's *News of the World* dictated public policy on law and order, not the governing Labour Party. Whilst these are legitimate concerns, we do however recognize that the process of public policy thinking and implementation is extremely complex but fascinating in trying to understand how implementation as a process impacts upon society.

The book is divided in two parts: Part I, titled 'Theorizing Public Policy and News Media Representations', is a combination of political philosophy and sociology which examines some of the historical concepts that are central to public policy thinking. It then examines public policy in more broad detail before assessing the role of news media representations and discourse in relation to public policy issues.

Part II, titled 'Group Processes and the Media as a Referee in Public Policy-Making', is written from the perspective of psychology. Using theories about social cognition, Part II explains the psychological factors governing thinking within and between policy-makers, media organizations and the public. Chapter 4 critically examines the realism of the moral ideal of the 'common good' as the driving force for public policy. Chapter 4 investigates the hypothesis that group processes explain public policy decision-making. Chapter 5 then assesses the role of media organizations and media workers as referees in the process of public policy decision-making. Chapter 5 then reviews the psychological characteristics of policy dilemmas that make policy-makers susceptible to group influences. Chapter 6 then assesses the socio-cognitive group processes among media workers that create faulty decision-making and influence public opinion about policy issues.

Acknowledgements

We would like to express our thanks to Abigail Spong for her role in collecting, coding and inputting the data from Hansard (UK Parliament records) for Chapter 4, and for her excellent work on the index. We would also like to say thank you to Claire Jarvis at Ashgate for her patience and to Sadie Copley-May for her close attention to detail.

David Berry and Caroline Kamau

PART I
Theorizing Public Policy and News Media Representations

David Berry

Introduction
Some Notes on Public Policy and Media

The ideas that form the basis of public policy – referred to also as 'social policy' – are rooted in Western philosophy dating back to the ancient Greeks. In general, public policy thinking historically and in modern times is partly based on the idea of producing benefits for society, and concepts such as the 'common good' or 'public good' are used to rationalize and legitimize judgements on policy implementation. Besides the Ancient philosophical influence, there are historical roots of public policy that lay in the great legal charter of the United Kingdom – the Magna Carta (Great Charter of Freedoms) – produced in 1215.

When we think about public policy today, perhaps it is not unusual to focus more on the actual implementation rather than the philosophical-intellectual process that seeks to justify and rationalize implementation – this process of philosophical thinking effectively underpins public policy decision-making. Today, public policy in social democracies is the product of government elected by the people. Different political parties set out key objectives on public policy in their respective manifestos that reflect their political, ideological and moral views of society and its functioning mores – often attempting to differentiate from one another, although in contemporary times with the global dominance of capitalism, such differences are often blurred, limiting actual differences. The public elect parties to government based on their respective policies outlined in manifestos which are conditioned by various types of political philosophy, based broadly within a social democratic context, which in Britain is dominated by a combination of Liberal and neo-Liberal political and economic contexts.

Political philosophy shapes public policy thinking, and in contemporary times what I term as *government perceptions* of the public, equally shape thinking and decision-making. Such perceptions come to fruition through market research, polls, social surveys and social networking sites, and may impact upon the political philosophy that form the basis for decision-making in the first instance and the subsequent narrative and political positions detailed in manifestos. Political thinking is however subject to change from a variety of social pressures and influences, which in turn impact upon prevailing government perceptions of public opinion in relation to public policy and the actual implementation of policy itself. One such influential medium on political philosophy and public policy is the mainstream news media – particularly the relationship between news representations and government thinking on public policy issues and one important part of this book overall and in Chapter 3 of Part I is to consider whether news influences political thinking on public policy.

Chapter 1 assesses the role political philosophy has in underpinning and conditioning modern day thinking on public policy. The chapter discusses ancient and medieval philosophers such as Plato, Aristotle, Aquinas and the relatively unknown Marsilius of Padua whose works have all contributed in one way or another towards theorizing public policy in relation to theories of the 'common good', the 'good life', 'happiness' and 'well being', all of which feature prominently in this chapter. These concepts have always been central to liberal political philosophy, but they re-emerged with vigour in 2010 in the United Kingdom with the election of the Conservative-led coalition government along with the Liberal Democrats, where the idea of the 'Big Society' was introduced as a campaign objective to re-engage the public with the aforementioned ideas that concern how best society can develop in an environment suffering from economic recession. An additional concept is equally discussed in this present chapter in relation to the aforementioned concepts, which is the 'public interest', where the works of two prominent modern philosophers feature; Robert Nozick and John Rawls.

The second chapter begins with a discussion on public policy, reviewing debates over definition and meaning and then continues to discuss public policy in relation to the Conservative Party's idea of Big Society – a form of public policy – utilizing a combination of philosophical and ideological objectives to sustain governance. The chapter assesses the Big Society idea as a form of bureaucratic authority in relation to the English riots that occurred during the summer of 2011 in England mainly to address the issues of how conflict impacted on political discourse, public policy thinking and public policy initiatives. The chapter also assesses public policy as an instrument of social democracy and introduces a discussion on public policy in relation to the construction of civil society. It also addresses the idea that public policy is often formed on *perceptions* of community sometimes in relation to a limited understanding of public opinion and the political philosophy that underpins authority.

The third chapter is concerned with news representations and news discourse in relation to social concerns and public policy issues. The chapter begins with a discussion on news and the public interest and assesses a number of empirical examples of news representations of public policy issues that builds on the previous chapter by providing examples of news representations of the riots in 2011. The chapter offers some analysis on the theory of representation and further provides an assessment of the conceptual frameworks that constitute the production of news representations and news discourse, such as 'news frames', 'news values', 'news sources' and 'typifications'. Finally, it presents a discussion on methodology to assess the attempt by media to influence public policy thinking through news discourse.

Chapter 1
Political Philosophy

Theorizing Public Policy

Political philosophy underpins all thinking on public policy, but it may not always attain a detached-prominent position of dominance and absolutely, purely condition all thinking in its entirety, particularly when economic realities concerning historical circumstances are taken into consideration. Today as I write in 2012, various governments throughout Europe have implemented severe cutbacks in public spending and welfare programmes in many European countries as the debt burden and budget deficits increase. What has become known as economic determinism – the theory that the economy (base) determines all other aspects of life (superstructure) – is not to be understated in this context, despite the frequent claim that such thinking is crude and materialistic; but we may justifiably ask: what is the point of political philosophy if it is determined by the power and influence of 'economic realities'?

One could further ask what is meant by 'economic reality'? For even in times of supposed 'economic prosperity', government thinking on public policy initiatives such as health and welfare can be limited; the USA is an historical case in point and where today the current reduction in public spending and welfare is equally acute, and exacerbated by social housing and health problems with many domestic homes left abandoned across the USA, and almost 50 million people remain without health insurance as the USA continues to fail to provide universal healthcare for all. This situation, whilst not identical, was also evident during the free market ideological period of Thatcherism as the state was 'rolled-back' from its social and moral responsibilities.

National debt and budget deficits are apart from the total wealth generated in national and/or trans-national contexts and the debate here concerns whether private wealth should be redistributed in order to satisfy public policy strategies. The debate over the redistribution of wealth, particularly during present times with such debt and deficit burdens, is about political philosophical differences and approaches towards strategies for change. However, such differences are underpinned by key concepts that aide public policy thinking particularly in social democracies, which will be discussed in more detail below and which form the basis of this chapter; such concepts are 'happiness', 'well-being', the 'good life', the 'common good' and the 'public interest'. There's no doubt that the crisis in capitalism beginning in 2008 with the banking collapse has effectively reshaped thinking in political philosophy towards public policy initiatives across a broad range of political perspectives. But it is not difficult or entirely unreasonable to empathize with the view that the economy is such a determining factor in many aspects of our lives, particularly in the way it shapes public policy thinking in an economic climate that has steadily worsened since 2008.

Political philosophy differs substantially from political science, because the latter is non-normative and is solely about facts, whilst political philosophy is normative, always involving a moral imperative. To abandon political philosophy to the whims of the market is in itself a derogation of duty and humanity; some even argue that the most that political philosophy can achieve against the ravages of a global economic downturn – a political fact and reality of capitalism – is to subdue it; to cushion the blow against the possibilities of increasing poverty and inequalities above the levels already in existence – another fact political science can highlight. A clear example of how political philosophy is used to cushion the blow of an economic slump and to maintain the present social and political system in the United Kingdom is the Conservative Party's introduction of the 'Big Society' idea and despite the fact that it has been met with a healthy degree of cynicism, it nevertheless indicates how the history of ideas is encapsulated within a modern broader context, governed by economic realities. Whatever one may think of the 'Big Society' as an idea, it does contain many of the concepts central to the political philosophy of public policy that are deeply entrenched in Western philosophical traditions, which are central themes of this present chapter, such as the common good, the good life, happiness, well-being and the public interest.

At its core, political philosophy in this present context is primarily about theorizing public policy. Part one of Goodin's (1982) book titled 'The Need for Theory' is a defence of theorizing public policy and partly a critique of *incrementalism* which is seen in the US at least as *the* model for determining or shaping public policy although Schulman (1975) adds the 'divisibility' model as the other dominating paradigm.[1] Goodin argues that incrementalism is 'atheoretical' (1982: 3) and 'is a doctrine which … maintains that theoretical understanding of the social system is unnecessary and probably undesirable for policymaking'[2] and goes on to critique the notion of separating fact and value when deliberating on policy initiatives, stating: 'Empirical and ethical theory ought both to be used, and used in tandem, to guide public policymaking' (ibid: 4). The discussion on separating value from fact – and its concomitant usefulness – is well established, but it's true that some facts intervene and subsequently affect or obscure the discourse of value and ethics. For instance, economic conditions transgress constantly in the realm of political and moral philosophizing, impacting on the value of public policy narratives. This has long been viewed as unacceptable because it means that the normative discussion on value, associated with the free will of individuals is contaminated by exogenous material economic forces. Values are of themselves remarkably complex considering the degree of difference between individuals and

---

1   See Schulman (1975) for a full explanation of both 'incrementalism' and the 'divisibility' model.

2   See Chapters 1, 2 and 3 specifically.

political parties over the meaning of what is morally acceptable, as value, and when we discuss the relationship with facts – wise or otherwise – we witness an inextricable increase in complexity and validity.

With complete disregard for separating value from fact, Lewin (2007) begins his paper titled 'Facts, Values and the Burden of Proof' thus: 'I examine here the connection between facts, values, and the burden of proof, and I suggest a relationship that is always present, though seldom acknowledged' (ibid: 503). Lewin's paper assesses the arguments and debates concerning value and facts and specifically analyses this debate within the context of economics and economic-scientific inquiry:

> Students of economics are told from the start that good scientists are careful to separate facts and values. Positive economics deals with 'facts' about how the world works. Normative economics deals with what we ought to do with knowledge of those facts. There is a widely shared conviction that good scientists, as such, ought to keep their moral sensibilities out of the analysis. In any case, we know from David Hume that one cannot get an 'ought' exclusively from an 'is', so it behoves the good scientist to be forthcoming about the values introduced in the derivation of any policy conclusion (ibid.).

For the purposes of this present chapter Lewin's account is informative because it addresses both normative (moral) perspectives indicative of thinking about how society can best function in economic terms in relation to the notion of the common good. Indeed, two of the terms central to this present chapter briefly referred to above namely happiness and the good life are referred to (ibid: 509–510) in the context of thinking about ethical concerns in relation to economic policy assessment, although by referring to Yeager, Lewin argues both terms are problematic in terms of securing and identifying coherent and rational meanings, preferring Yeager's term 'social cooperation' as a normative criteria and basis for thinking about economic policy. I shall address some of the issues raised here further below in this chapter, but for the time being if both happiness and notions of the good life – two traditional and deeply embedded historical concepts in terms of thinking about morality and society – are problematic how exactly does 'social cooperation' compensate for their lack of pragmatic meaning?

Political philosophy is a discipline concerned with many areas of human life including but not restricted to the role of the state, political economy, justice, liberty, society and in relation to the establishment and justification of resources to support public policy initiatives – 'government legitimacy' – in decision-making which in social democracies is based on acting on behalf of the people by elected means. Today it is taken as a given – for right or for wrong – that government is or at least *should be* the sole arbiter for making decisions on public policy, but what political philosophy hasn't fully explored is the role of an un-elected and unaccountable body that may influence the political decision-making process on public policy. Therefore, theorizing public policy becomes increasingly important today to understand what, if any role, the news media play in influencing government decision-making which impacts upon the lives of people.

Generally speaking political parties are elected on the basis of promises and principles detailed in their respective manifestos; therefore a degree of trust is awarded by the people towards parties to carry out such promises. Such promises are routinely broken and in 2010 the coalition government in the UK between the Conservative Party and the Liberal Democrats, although unusual, was nevertheless another example of broken promises. The justification to 'rip up' their respective manifestos was according to them based on an 'economic reality' of an overburdening debt problem and budget deficit in the UK. To what extent the news media help to maintain and justify such political views is an issue of power to influence the public and to what extent in certain circumstances the news media influence government decision-making with respect to policy becomes an issue of importance that goes right to the heart of democracy and the rights of political citizenship, for the media are unaccountable despite the fact of their power and influence. Perhaps paradoxically the news media are essential also for democracy to function despite the unaccountability. There is another aspect to consider here which is the influence the Internet may have on government thinking which ranges from online journalism, social media and social networking sites. Media communication therefore is important to study in relation to public policy because it may alter the principle of what Plato termed a 'just society' and this is central to theorizing public policy within the tradition of political philosophy.

History informs us of how humans have sought to establish the principle of social development in written texts since the Ancient Greek period beginning with the writings of Plato and then Aristotle. The official formation much later in Western historical development of governmental initiatives known today as public policy is merely an extension of the philosophical writings of the early Greek writers and the value we invest today is not merely based on that historical tradition alone; the value also directly reflects those early philosophical traditions. The introduction of universal education or healthcare known in the UK as the National Health Service (NHS) was also a part of the struggle over ideas and the creation of a just society that had its earliest appearance in the writings of Plato and its survival today, in the face of harsh economic realities, will once again reflect early philosophy on how to better society, and at the heart of that discussion is a vision of humanity, ideology and political advancement. Today at the time of writing, the British coalition government is cutting public sector funding despite the fact that it was the private sector (banking collapse) which was the cause of the damage and government in the UK and the USA spent huge sums bailing out failed banks with public money. Ironically, the private sector collapse was the result of less state intervention and regulation, but Tory politics are based on less public spending that equals even less state intervention and this is purely an ideological assault on public policy that is government-led.

The Common Good

> Every art and every inquiry, and similarly every action and pursuit, is thought to aim at some good; and for this reason the good has rightly been declared to be that at which all things aim.

Thus begins Aristotle's *Nicomachean Ethics* (Book I, Chapter 1), a work that inspired the medieval theologian and philosopher Thomas Aquinas much later in the 12th century which formed the basis of much of Aquinas' ideas on the theory of the common good, which will be examined shortly. Public policy is seen to be a means to achieving what is termed the 'common good'. For Max Horkheimer in his book the *Eclipse of Reason* such thinking of the common good was a part of what would become known and established as 'reason'; the norm, despite the fact – and to use Kant – that such concepts are philosophical categories devised by humans, but appearing as 'natural' and 'right'. Later in Aristotle's work in Book VIII, he refers to the common good in relation to education which is a product of the 'just' thinker as opposed to the 'unjust' who is more selfish or in Aristotle's words 'grasping'. Aristotle was building an argument on how ruling should proceed and be morally justified based on the premise he formulated that 'man is a social and political animal' and one in which went beyond self-interest. Aristotle thus states: 'The just, then, is the lawful and the fair, the unjust the unlawful and the unfair' and therefore establishing a principle of a common good is not only fair but legal and legitimate. Moreover, 'a ruler is necessarily in relation to other men and a member of a society', so thinking and acting for the common good is to act unselfishly. In *Politics* Aristotle set out to defend what he termed the 'Common Good of All', which had multiple meanings beyond policy and extended to political citizenship.

In relation to Aristotle's work the contemporary writer and academic Noam Chomsky discusses a number of issues in an interview given in *The Common Good* with David Barsamian, and under the subheading 'That Dangerous Radical Aristotle' states:

> Aristotle took it for granted that a democracy should be fully participatory ... and that it should aim for the common good. In order to achieve that, it has to ensure relative equality, 'moderate and sufficient property' and 'lasting prosperity' for everyone (Chomsky 1998: 6).

Chomsky reminds us that 'Aristotle felt that if you have extremes of poor and rich, you can't talk seriously about democracy' and that today democracy in this Aristotelian context would be akin to developing a 'welfare state' (ibid.). Aristotle's notion of the common good serves as crucial basis on which to discuss public policy, however, what constitutes the common good today, or what is held to be in the public interest, is much wider than in Aristotle's usage mainly because of the complexities of modern-day societies. For example, the issue over environment and global climate change and how that impacts on the well-being of citizens to lead a good life is complicated by the fact that global issues are at times out of the control of national states, but nonetheless require government intervention to produce national policy and influence other states to implement policies for the benefit of humankind. This also could in theory be applied to other global issues such as poverty, human rights and terrorism to mention a few.

But equally, Chomsky uses Aristotle's insights to discuss the relationship between the common good and democracy, particularly in relation to wealth inequalities and disparities over rights to property. Chomsky reminds us that many rights issues are often bundled together and often seen as having equal status, but rightly disputes this, arguing that rights to free speech cannot be seen in equal terms to rights to property. The former, in the US at least, is granted to all as detailed in the US Constitution but the latter (property) depends on wealth and power. What this means is that government-led public policy initiatives regarding property turn into ideological objectives, such as the introduction of social housing to compensate for disparities in property ownership or even to house the homeless. This intervention was introduced in post-Second World War Britain under the leadership of Clement Attlee's Labour Party, and was a decisive moment in establishing a relationship between the common good and democracy.

The work of Thomas Aquinas (1227–1274) is clear evidence of the continuation of the history of ideas in Western philosophy concerning society rooted in earlier Greek philosophy. As stated above, Aquinas based his theory of the common good on the works of Aristotle and argued that the organization of politics was a natural act of humans in order to preserve society and life. Aquinas recognized that there was a potential conflict between individual self-interest and the common good for all within any given social system and his solution to quell such conflicts was to advocate a Ruler who worked on behalf of the common good which would equally quell the Ruler's inclination towards becoming a tyrant pursuing his own self-interest. Aquinas maintained that God was purposeful in that He reflected man's 'natural instincts' to help each other, to be good and dutiful and furthermore, loving God was security to act out in good ways. The Ruler could only secure his legitimacy to govern when he clearly acted or served the common good. Even though there is quite clearly a spiritual dimension to the works of Aquinas, nevertheless, it still informs us of the relationship between government today in a secularized society, and people, which we call a mandate to govern legitimately and properly. The first or primary good was then spiritual, but there were additional or secondary goods to be attained to ethical ruling and these included knowledge, culture and morality. For Aquinas the common good for all was something to be achieved, not yet realized, and in this context it was a goal or an end to actively pursue, so his idea of a just ruler would simply fulfil this role, but the important point for our purposes was the fact that the common good was greater in moral value than individual self-interest demonstrated by the following 'the good of the multitude is greater than the good of one who belongs to the multitude'[3] and,

---

3   From *Summa Theologica, II–II, q. 39, a. 2, ad 2.*

if a great number of people were to live, each intent only upon his own interests, such a community would surely disintegrate unless there were one of its number to have care for the common good: just as the body of a man or of any other animal would disintegrate were there not in the body itself a single controlling force sustaining the general vitality of all the members (Aquinas in Cottingham 1996: 478).

Aquinas also spoke of the 'political community' as a form of 'unity' (*Commentary on Ethics 1, c.)* and of the 'common welfare' of society (*Summa Theologica, I–II, q. 96, a. 4, c)*. The most perfect condition which life could be ordered was the City State, which could 'provide the things which are sufficient by themselves for human life' (*Commentary on Politics, prologus*).

Similarly, in Chapter 1 of the *Rules* titled 'Purpose and Basis of Common Life' St. Augustine, otherwise known as Augustine of Hippo, also infers a common good theory by stating: 'Those who owned something in the world should freely wish it to be shared amongst all'[4] and that poverty restricted health, making it morally acceptable and legitimate for health to be made better by those who suffered. Augustine also spoke in terms of the rich contributing their wealth to the 'common life' and that in doing so one must neither be 'elated ... nor take pride in sharing their riches'. This was clearly not a duty to perform but rather an appeal to social responsibility to create a welfare system based on a common good for all.

Both Aquinas and Augustine were Catholic theologians and the theory of the common good remains today a central tenet of Catholic social teaching. Indeed the *Catholics in Alliance for the Common Good*,[5] a lay organization, promotes public policies in the USA in relation to the theory of the common good. In the encyclical *Caritas in Veritate* issued in 2009, Pope Benedict XVI also spoke of the importance of the common good and in true Aristotelian language spoke of how the political community can take responsibility for achieving the common good, stating:

> *Caritas in veritate* is the principle around which the Church's social doctrine turns, a principle that takes on practical form in the criteria that govern moral action. I would like to consider two of these in particular, of special relevance to the commitment to development in an increasingly globalized society: *justice and the common good* (Point 6).[6]

Even though Pope Benedict XVI was emphasizing 'love' and 'charity' he also spoke of the secular and of the political in helping to attain common good goals. Moreover, in Chapter 3 titled 'Fraternity, Economic Development and Civil

---

4   http://www.norbertines.co.uk/Rule.htm, accessed 10 July 2010.

5   http://www.catholicsinalliance.org/, accessed 12 July 2010.

6   http://www.vatican.va/holy_father/benedict_xvi/encyclicals/documents/hf_ben-xvi_enc_20090629_caritas-in-veritate_en.html, accessed 15 August 2010.

Society' he outlined the Catholic Church's social doctrine in relation to the capitalist market. This has particular poignancy considering the banking collapse and the debt crisis that began in 2008:

> Economic activity cannot solve all social problems through the simple application of *commercial logic*. This needs to be *directed towards the pursuit of the common good*, for which the political community in particular must also take responsibility. Therefore, it must be borne in mind that grave imbalances are produced when economic action, conceived merely as an engine for wealth creation, is detached from political action, conceived as a means for pursuing justice through redistribution (Point 36).

The responsibility that the Pope is alluding to, amongst other matters, is the way in which the political community pursues public policy matters that seek to protect citizens in general, but in particular the vulnerable or the poor emphasized by the following:

> The Church's social doctrine has always maintained that *justice must be applied to every phase of economic activity*, because this is always concerned with man and his needs. Locating resources, financing, production, consumption and all the other phases in the economic cycle inevitably have moral implications. *Thus every economic decision has a moral consequence* (Point 37).

The Catholic Church does recognize the legitimacy of the market in relations of production as outlined by Pope Benedict XVI: 'The Church has always held that economic action is not to be regarded as something opposed to society' (Point 36) but it justifies government intervention in order to secure the common good for all, detailed also by *The American Catholic* in an article titled 'Socialism, Catholicism & The Common Good'.[7] It highlights the similarities and differences between Socialism and Catholicism, which stands in contradistinction to Pope Benedict's predecessor Pope John Paul VI vehement 'anti-communist' views. The article defends 'higher taxes and more wealth distribution', defends the right to private property which is at odds with Socialist views but defends the moral right of government to exercise power and restraint over excesses: quoting the Catechism the author states: '*Political authority* has the right and duty to regulate the exercise of the right to ownership for the sake of the common good'.

This Catholic viewpoint isn't dissimilar to many points expounded on politics, economy and society in *Judaism*. For instance in *Radical Then, Radical Now*, the British Jewish Chief Rabbi, Jonathan Sacks, although not using the term common good, refers to social welfare which in-turn is, depending on your view, either synonymous with, intrinsic to or a key component of. Sacks begins Chapter 10

---

7   http://the-american-catholic.com/2009/02/01/socialism-catholicism-the-common-good/, accessed 14 September 2010.

titled 'Covenantal Society' thus: 'Judaism has not one political theory but two. Not only does it have its own theory of the state, possibly the earliest of its kind, but it also has a political theory of society' (2000: 118). The theory of the state is determined by the Israelites insistence to Samuel that a powerful King is required for 'Without government, life and liberty would be impossible to defend' (ibid: 119). The theory of the state is based on a 'social contract' which as Sacks rightly points out was central to both Thomas Hobbes' and Jean Jacques Rousseau's theory of society. Missing from the account however is Thomas Aquinas who as detailed above defended the notion of a King who worked tirelessly for the common good of all, although there seemed to be no guarantees. In Judaism, the second theory of society is not rooted in the social contract of the state but rather is 'created by a social *covenant*' and that the 'state exists to serve society and not vice versa' (ibid.).

A keyword or indeed concept is '*Tzedek* or *tzedakah*' (ibid: 120) which normally Sacks states, translates into 'charity' where in fact 'it means social and distributive justice' further stating: 'In biblical law it involved a whole series of institutions that together constituted the first ever attempt at a welfare state' (ibid.). Finally, Sacks draws comparisons with capitalism and socialism which results in similar if not identical conclusions to the discussion above relating to Catholicism:

> One way of understanding *tzedek* is to contrast it with two other political theories: capitalism and socialism ... Unlike socialism it believes in the free market, private property and minimum government intervention. Unlike capitalism it believes that the free market, without periodic redistributions, creates inequalities that are ultimately unsustainable because they deprive some individuals of independence and hope (ibid: 121).

Likewise other religions such as the Anglican Communion of Churches and Islam also refer to the common good, perhaps more so in the former than the latter, but the latter refers to common good elements such as social justice. All these religions are inspired by faith in God but equally all, to varying degrees perhaps, relate God's will to society and moral and legal actions to promote public policies that reflect God's wishes. This dualist position between faith and politics is deeply rooted in Christianity for instance dating back to Augustine's *City of God* and since become a tradition. The fact that as a secular thinker I can disagree with God's intervention is immaterial; the fact that public policy is actualized in legal terms through discussions on the common good inspired by God is to recognize that public policy transcends differences. What is in common however between the secular and the religious is a belief in a governing body to enact policy irrespective of inspiration and in both, the governing body has a legitimacy to act on behalf of a common good.

In the 13th century the Italian scholar Marsilius of Padua wrote the *Defensor Pacis* (*The Defender of the Peace*), which is also rooted in the *Politics* of Aristotle and equally emphasized the authority of the state, which for Marsilius should be governed by citizens for the pursuit and completion of the common good. The state is greater than the authority of the Church and thus the common good is clearly rooted in material existence, although clearly defined by Christian practice. Citizens were best placed to decide how the common good could be materially realized but only in relation to belief, but nonetheless, his work emphasized how policy is central to achieving the good life. An important extract from the *Defensor Pacis* is the following: 'The whole body of citizens or its majority alone is the human "legislator"' and this work is an early commentary on citizenship, political representation and the decision making process. At the time it was extremely controversial material, seen by Pope John XXII as heretical, not simply because it called upon the separation of church from state and the legitimacy of the latter over the former, but also for its radical policies on empowering citizens to make decisions on welfare. Reading Marsilius today is extremely important for understanding which body should decide policy in the name of the common good or to use that other closely related term, the 'public interest'. But the real reason for Marsilius to publish his works, which in my view has a profound impact on policy initiatives today is written into the title of the book the 'defender' of the peace. It was a work to reconcile the social needs and requirements of citizens with established power and to avoid strife and conflict, hence the production of the common good, whereby citizens are mostly content, because he also favoured majority rule, which for Marsilius, would induce harmonic relations. In today's language public policies that are clearly effective may help to reduce the prospect of conflict which in Marsilian terms upsets the harmony of the state, which Aristotle so promoted as the *means to the common good* and as Nederman (2003: 395) states in relation to Marsilius and his contribution towards the common good:

> Marsiglio of Padua presents an extended argument for the compatibility of the material advantage of individuals with civil association by basing his conception of community on the benefits that accrue to human beings from realizing their 'natural' self-interests.

This latter point is very much open to various interpretations because it appears to contradict the social dimension of the common good that reflect both the works of Aristotle and Aquinas. Realizing, 'natural self-interests', appears to be more closely associated with the work of Robert Nozick who argued for a minimal state, so individuals could pursue their interests without state authority interfering into decision-making. Whatever we are to make of it, it is probably one reason why modern day Catholics prefer to reference Aquinas as a source for the common good, because his work can be more strongly and legitimately contrasted with what we today call 'individualism', which is historically associated with liberal philosophy. It's for this reason perhaps that the Catholic Worker Movement places emphasis on the contribution of Aquinas to help construct modern conceptions of the common good:

A compelling alternative to this individualism assumed by both liberal and conservative party politics is St. Thomas Aquinas' doctrine of the common good. The doctrine of the common good teaches that the individual person is a member of a larger body. Just as the goal, or end, of each individual member of a community is the common good of that larger community, so also the goal, or end, of each organ and muscle in our body is the common good of the overall person.[8]

The Good Life, Happiness and Well-Being

Three related concepts to the common good theory are, ideas of the good life, happiness and well-being, although the latter is mostly inferred as a consequence of the former which is more commonly referred to in texts. For instance in Book VII of *Politics*, Aristotle says 'happiness is the highest good' and the concept of happiness[9] remains a vital component of modern day philosophical debate. When Plato wrote his *Republic* the discourse on morality and happiness was based on establishing a principle rather than who would implement it. Happiness was and remains a central concept in philosophy concerning the way humans can live their lives and in the *Republic* Plato spoke of the value of what he termed 'goods' which has become established in the modern public policy vernacular demonstrated in Goodin's use of 'public goods' (1982: 39).

In Book II of the *Republic* there is a dialogue between Socrates and Glaucon and one of the most influential questions within philosophy is raised by both Glaucon and his brother Adeimantus in their exchange and challenge to Socrates, namely, why should I be moral? This eternal question remains as powerful today in relation to creating public policies that bring social benefits to society, but morality's modern day nemeses and polar opposites, namely free market ideology and free market economic rationality, place severe restrictions on acting morally towards others more deserving with less finances to attain happiness and pleasure that Plato once spoke of. To a certain extent theorizing public policy is an attempt to resolve and overcome such restrictions. In the dialogue, Glaucon asks Socrates if there are such goods as 'knowledge, sight, health, which are desirable not only in themselves, but also for their results?' with Socrates replying 'Certainly'. Glaucon then asks: 'And would you not recognise a third class such as ... the care of the sick, and the physician's art' including 'money-making' as a good. The dialogue demonstrates Plato's concern with modern day issues in public policy such as education and health, but despite his belief that money-making was in principle a 'good', Plato also argued that economic self-interest of rulers was detrimental

---

8   See 'The Common Good and the Body of Christ: St. Thomas Aquinas and the Catholic Worker Movement', http://www.cjd.org/paper/roots/rbody.html, accessed 21 October 2010.

9   The Greek word for happiness is *eudaimonia*.

to the political power they yielded in terms of recognizing social interests and implementing policies that would bring substantial benefits to the ruled. The active state, which Plato advocated, was therefore diminished in terms of its effectiveness to govern efficiently and morally. In this Platonic light, Goodin (1982: 39) defends 'state action' based on liberal thinkers exaggerating the 'competence of the individual' to exact perfection for her/his own needs and for Plato, state interests always held priority over self or individual interests.

Written around 385BC in his work titled *Crito*, Plato presents Socrates defending the benefits the state brings to citizens such as law, education, good health and others. Here Plato's work represents the original establishment of the principle of public policy that permeates through to today where governments seek to provide 'goods' that may bring social benefits to citizens, which for some constitute the good life, because it is based in the narrative of the welfare state. More contemporary research into the philosophical conception of the good life, particularly relating to happiness and well-being discussed in more detail below, has become an academic industry, particularly in psychology, a branch of philosophy. For instance, Brülde's (2007) study addresses the philosophical tradition of pondering on the meaning of the good life, as well as happiness and well-being, stating that it 'is one of the classical questions in philosophy' (ibid: 1) to which we can safely add the word 'persistent'. Brülde's statement on how the good life is both achieved and defined simply highlights what is problematic with the term: 'philosophers have formally defined the notion of the good life (well-being, or quality of life) in terms of what has a *final value for a person*' (ibid: 2).

Aristotle's *Politics*, written around 350BC, from the beginning in Book I, clearly explains the role of the state in and for society in relation to attaining the good life:

> Every state is a community of some kind, and every community is established with a view to some good; for mankind always act in order to obtain that which they think good. But, if all communities aim at some good, the state or political community, which is the highest of all, and which embraces all the rest, aims at good in a greater degree than any other, and at the highest good.

Then in Book IV 'every office should have a special function' and in Book VII Aristotle refers to the 'functions of a state' further stating: 'A state, then, only begins to exist when it has attained a population sufficient for a good life in the political community'. More specifically in relation to modern day notions of public policy – and in a similar mode of thinking to Plato – Aristotle states: 'For law is order, and good law is good order' and 'Special care should be taken of the health of the inhabitants', and in Book VIII there are references to education such as 'the neglect of education does harm to the constitution', a point I shall return into the section on the English Riots of 2011 in Chapter 2. But there are concerns with the notion of the good life particularly whether its constituent parts (mostly well-being and happiness) are universal in their application. Tiberius (2004) addresses this issue, assessing philosophical accounts concerning well-being and asking whether there are cultural differences with respect to how the good life is achieved as a social reality. Interestingly, there's not one reference to the opposite theory of universalism, namely relativism, but in essence Tiberius's work addresses this latter concept as described in the first two sentences of her work: 'In cross-cultural studies of well-being psychologists have shown ways in which well-being or its constituents are tailored by culture' (ibid: 293). In terms of how public policy is developed and administered within any given country, such relativist inflections are to be expected, thus each cultural context isn't effectively a threat to notions of the good life. But, in the larger scheme of things, i.e., assessing the economic and political system best suited to serve the needs of all people, such issues of good life presented in relativist terms, undermines the profound philosophy of the universal conception of the good life. I'd like to place a caveat here, because undoubtedly what constitutes the good life requires further explanation by those who effectively promote it, so one can remain sceptical. However, its profound nature remains when we consider the good life in universal terms for creating a system that seriously addresses issues of wealth disparities, poverty, and the unequal distribution of power and replace it with public policies that mostly dress-over the reasons why such disparities exist in the first instance. That said, Tiberius states: 'the implications of cultural differences for the philosophical project are limited' and that the aim of her work is 'to clear the ground for a universal notion of well-being', (ibid.) and thus the good life or to use Tiberius' term 'human flourishing' (ibid: 294).

A constituent part of the good life, namely happiness, was an important principle for Aquinas, demonstrated in his work the *Summa Theologica* under section titled 'Treatise On The Last End' particularly questions 2–5. Aquinas argued that there were two goods to be pursued as 'ends'; the first was 'uncreated', i.e., God, and the second was 'created' in man (sic) himself 'man's last end is something created, existing in him, and this is nothing else than the attainment or enjoyment of the last end. Now the last end is called happiness' (Article 1). This indicates that there were two types of happiness to be achieved: one is what we can safely refer to as 'heavenly happiness' ('other-worldly') considering the reference to God, which for Aquinas was the most important end. Aquinas actually called this first type 'perfect happiness'. The second type was 'temporal happiness' ('this-worldly'), in other words, a category for achieving social well-being on earth, and this, I argue, can be linked to his theory of the common good and also to Aquinas' belief in a Just Ruler to attain the good life, well-being and happiness which constituted the common good for all.

Happiness and the idea of well-being for that matter are at the heart of a key documentation on public policy produced in 2010 by the Young Foundation in conjunction with the Local Government Improvement and Development Agency (IdeA).[10] In the document titled 'The State of Happiness: Can public policy shape

---

10   Formerly the Improvement and Development Agency (IdeA).

people's well-being and resilience?' we can see how ancient ideas are integral to thinking about public policy today. For instance in the introduction the document begins with a quotation from Aristotle: 'Happiness is the meaning and the purpose of life, the whole aim and end of human existence', which is immediately followed by this:

> Democratic governments naturally try to promote a better life for their citizens. It is hard to imagine political parties being elected if they did not offer at least some prospect of improved wellbeing. And while government – central or local – cannot directly make us happier or more engaged, it does shape the economy, culture and society in which we live through policies and decisions on where to spend finite resources, and laws that regulate what can and cannot be done.[11]

The argument that economics is a key indicator of wellbeing is an established tradition and Stutzer and Frey's (2010) work is an analysis of the relationship between economics and well-being with emphasis on individual well-being. The authors begin their work acknowledging that 'Questions about the good life and individual happiness have a long tradition in philosophy' (ibid: 679), which is true, but philosophy also has a tradition of well-being and happiness within a grander social project, i.e., society. Nevertheless, they continue to state that their study is 'based on a subjective view of utility recognizing that everyone has his or her own ideas about happiness and the good life' (ibid: 679–670) and then stating the following:

> It is a sensible tradition in economics to rely on the judgment of the persons directly involved. People are considered to be good judges of the overall quantity of their lives, and it is a straightforward strategy to ask them about their well-being (ibid: 680).

The term 'subjective well-being' is, they argue, the preferred terminology of psychology and that it is 'scientific' (ibid.), giving it the air of respectability and authenticity. Stutzer and Frey maintain that their findings shine light concerning how 'individual happiness in economics affect public policy' (ibid: 681). Under the sub-heading 'The use of happiness research for public policy' (ibid: 701) it is clear that measuring happiness in relation to economic indicators is insufficient,[12] preferring what they term, 'Aggregate happiness indicators' that include 'non-material aspects of well being' (ibid: 704) and under the concluding remarks

---

11   The document can be downloaded at: http://www.youngfoundation.org/files/images/wellbeing_happiness_Final__2_.pdf.

12   See also Smith, D. M., Langa, K. M., Kabeto, M. U., and P. A. Ubel (2005) study titled 'Wealth, Health and Happiness' and also Ouweneel's (2002) study which claims that high levels of social security doesn't guarantee increased happiness.

that 'economic happiness research can make substantial contributions to a public policy designed to raise individual welfare' (ibid: 705).

This view on measuring well-being and happiness is also addressed by Diener and Ryan (2009) where they state: 'We suggest that complementing national measures of well-being should be used alongside economic and social indicators in order to guide public policy' (ibid: 400), further stating: 'Individuals now rank "happiness" as their most important life goal' (ibid,).

Rothstein (2010) also perceives 'happiness' or 'life satisfaction' as useful 'subjective indicators' and as 'the ultimate goal of democratic politics' (ibid: 442). Such indicators are preferred because according to Rothstein they are 'non-elitist' (ibid.). Rothstein explains the relationship between 'subjective well being' and the welfare state posing the question: 'does a more generous and encompassing welfare state make people happier and increase their life satisfaction?' (ibid: 444) answering with an emphatic yes, but with a proviso:

> It is clear that the welfare state is positively related to happiness. But it is not all welfare states but a particular kind of welfare state that is most conducive to the subjective well-being of citizens: the universal welfare state (ibid: 462).[13]

In 2010/11 both the British coalition government and the Sarkozy-led French government begun initiating studies into measuring both happiness and well-being. In both governments there were doubts that wealth and prosperity are essential to both producing happiness and promoting and sustaining well-being. There is however, an important point to bear in mind in order to understand how theorizing public policy in these contexts come to fruition. The context, I would argue, is not presented in the spirit of Aristotle, i.e., one of absolute principle, but rather is shaped by the current depressed economic climate of both the UK and France. In 2010 the British coalition government announced deep cuts to public services and also introduced its idea of the 'Big Society', which is largely based on the realization of cuts to services and to encourage a new vision of society, based partly on voluntary groups helping and managing services minus the financial support from central government. Perhaps a cynic may argue that to state that wealth and prosperity doesn't guarantee happiness and well-being is simply a ruse to justify low wages and the withdrawal of finances necessary to sustain public policy initiatives.

Ott (2010) suggests a three-point proposal for governments to understand and promote happiness and well-being:

> (1) They can analyse the behaviour and the decisions of citizens to find out what they want, in other words: they can try to identify their 'revealed preferences'.

---

13 'By this is meant that there is a broad range of social services and benefits that are intended to cover the *entire* population throughout the different stages of life, and that the benefits are delivered on the basis of *uniform* rules for eligibility' (ibid: 445–446).

This is common practice in economics. (2) They can analyse the 'stated preferences' of people as they express them explicitly in inquiries, referenda, polls and elections. (3) They can analyse the conditions that make people happy by comparing the conditions of people at different levels of *happiness* (ibid: 125),

Similarly Diener (2006) states,

policy makers should be interested in subjective well-being not only because of its inherent value to citizens, but also because individuals' subjective well-being can have positive spillover benefits for the society as a whole. Similarly, policy makers should be keenly interested in alleviating misery as a goal in itself, because extremely unhappy people often function poorly (ibid: 398).

Diener argues that the use of indicators relating to well-being is increasing by various governments in relation to decision-making on public policy issues, citing the European Union and Australia as examples. Under the sub-heading 'Guidelines and Recommendations' Diener proposes a five-point model where point five is as follows in relating specifically to public policy initiatives:

Well-being and ill-being measures should be seen as part of the democratic process in which citizens and their leaders are given information that can be useful in policy debates. Measures of subjective well-being and ill-being do not override other sources of information, but serve as one potentially useful type of knowledge that can be used to create better policies (ibid: 399).

But how are governments to fully understand how happiness and well-being can be assessed and duly rationalized by often disparate and atomized social contexts? Ryan's (2010) work titled 'Happiness and Political Theory' demonstrates clearly the problems associated with happiness as a concept, thus right at the beginning in sentence two Ryan speaks of being 'uneasy about the topic' (ibid: 421). The reason (partly) of Ryan's angst is the problem in determining between what is termed 'ordinary happiness' and 'all-in' happiness.[14]

In a similar vein, Schimmel's (2007) study also discusses the problems associated with the idea of happiness but unlike Ryan doesn't feel uneasy about its meaning but rather simplistically, in my view, refers to the 'confusion' over understanding happiness: 'throughout history confusion exists around the terms happiness, subjective well-being, life satisfaction, and quality of life' (ibid: 98). This apparent 'confusion' Schimmel argues is the reason why the academic fraternity have failed to agree on a consensus. With reference to Veenhoven

---

14   'There is frequent, but intermittent reference to the ordinary pleasures of existence that constitute what I call "ordinary happiness" as distinct from the "all-in" happiness that philosophers invoke as the ultimate goal of all action' (ibid: 3).

(1984), Schimmel proposes the following definition: 'Happiness is … defined as a "degree to which an individual judges the overall quality of his life-as-a-whole favorably"' (ibid.). This convenient model is used to complement the United Nations Development Programme (UNDP) in relation to assessing issues associated with wealth, poverty and development.

Since the Conservative Party introduced the idea of the Big Society, it has attracted criticism because of its apparent failure to offer concrete substance and explanation of its meaning vis-à-vis conceptual frameworks such as common good, the good life, happiness and well-being, and quite often is ridiculed for appearing to be vague and abstract and therefore far removed from the realities of everyday life. Such criticisms are entirely reasonable, but not because the *idea* of the Big Society is far removed from realities, but because the Conservative-led Government, like most governments existing within capitalist dominated economies, fail to offer a vision of society that resolves the contradiction between morality and privatized market dominated economies. The Big Society therefore allows for debates about ethical conduct that places the interest of citizens at the centre, once happiness and well-being are posited as important indicators for evaluating how best life can be lived and such debates are located in the history of ideas which come into conflict with modern life. Resolving such conflicts may well prove difficult and perhaps impossible when free market ideology dominates economic rationality, however, it does allow for a debate on public policy issues that is placed in such conflicted contexts which for the government begins to shift the emphasis from state to individual responsibility for conduct; this perspective, however agreeable or disagreeable shifts the onus from state to the virtue of individuals and here we can locate the historical debates to the work of Aristotle, particularly the *Nicomachean Ethics*. The Big Society in essence is merely a continuation of other policy debates that entails a vision of society and is of itself a vehicle for theorizing public policy.

For Aristotle virtue or becoming a virtuous person would be the door that opened one's being to attaining happiness or to use the popular ancient term, *eudaimonia*. Virtue is never biologically innate; it is always derived from learnt experience, as an inclusive act of socialization that promotes certain types of behaviour, which leans towards benevolence rather than selfishness. Thinking about behaviour and thinking about how society develops is akin to thinking about human nature itself. It is in this latter context that Aristotle posed a deep question pertaining to human nature and humanity:

> To say that happiness is the supreme good perhaps seems something that is generally agreed, and we need a clearer account of what it is. This might be available if we find the function of a human being … What might this be? (*from* Cottingham 1996: 367).

For Aristotle the underlying principles of human existence in accordance to attaining the good life are 'reason' and 'virtue' with virtue being based on two kinds, namely intellectual and ethical. The former according to Aristotle is taught and the latter accumulates through habit. Whilst Aristotle's theory is thought-provoking it's nevertheless at the same time, patently idealistic and in today's world unrealistic. The reason it is thought-provoking is due to the fact that Aristotle was writing about human nature, which is perhaps one of the most contentious and difficult issues to discuss in philosophy, for what is human nature? There isn't enough space here to address this issue thoroughly, but perhaps a clear empirical example would be the belief that human nature is based on the human desire to accumulate wealth. Capitalism is based on this very notion of human nature, particularly in respect of the liberal notion of *individualism* and the 'rights' of individuals to acquire wealth without external (mostly government) interference. It's a very dubious argument of course and one which Marxists would firmly oppose; in fact Marx's theory of *alienation* is a critique of capitalism and how it estranges human beings from each other with exploitation of one human over others necessary in order to secure surplus value or profit. These arguments are a vital part of the deliberation of public policy particularly in relation to the justification of the welfare state or the justification of repealing or rolling back the welfare state.

What Aristotle achieved was no less than begin a discussion on what society best suits human nature, which has evolved into a discussion on what actually constitutes human nature. Aristotle's emphasis on 'reason' and 'virtue' is idealistic and unrealistic today in the sense that it assumes equality amongst people in order to enact both. Undoubtedly, what may be described as reason and virtue can operate on many social levels, but there is no doubt that both are particularly acute at government level when thinking about public policy; healthcare and education for instance operate at this philosophical level. Issues such as poverty, housing benefits and unemployment benefits are consequences of an economic and political system that fails in achieving the universality of the good life where people suffer during their lives. In these contexts, public policy works on two interrelated levels; one it acts as a social cushion to ease suffering and two public policy is a means or instrument for protecting capitalism and it is more than possible to discuss the meaning of human nature in this latter context; for what is the purpose of human life?

The ancient Greek philosopher Epicurus deliberated on how to achieve happiness and if the Epicurean notion of happiness is to be useful, it could be useful in the sense that under capitalism happiness is not universally possible because of wealth inequalities. The need for public policy in some areas is evidence of the flaws within capitalism, thus the need to produce a welfare state to protect the vulnerable. Epicurus argued that wealth is not a guarantee towards achieving happiness and this may well be true, but it could be equally true that neither does poverty. Both the idea of happiness and well-being are prone to criticisms particularly the criticism that both concepts are purely academic and atomized concepts in that both are purely subjective. Indeed, one could argue that an Epicurean notion of happiness is in line with the hippies of the 1960s because Epicurus sought to remove himself from society to seek freedom and happiness; hippies called that 'dropping out' and it's not only selfish, because it turns away from others suffering, but also deeply unrealistic and at the extreme limits of this view, one becomes a hermit.

But there are other criticisms of the Epicurean view of happiness that further develops rather than abandons happiness as a principle for achieving well-being and the good life. The 19th-century English philosopher John Stuart Mill, for example, argued, like his predecessor Jeremy Bentham, that the principle of happiness could be promoted and acquired in relation to differences between 'pleasure' and 'pain'. Mill was critical of the Epicurean view of pleasure arguing in his work *Utilitarianism* that such a view was limited and vulgar: 'When ... attacked, the Epicureans have always answered that it is not they, but their accusers, who represent human nature in a degrading light' (*from* Cottingham 1996: 388). Mill's answer was to develop two notions of pleasure that was not confined 'to that of beasts' but would rather reflect human beings: 'a beasts pleasures do not satisfy a human being's conception of happiness. Human beings have faculties more elevated than animal appetites' (ibid.). Mill, like Aristotle before him, is positing a theory of human nature and for Mill morality is a means to reach the achieved end of the pursuit of happiness. Whatever we may feel about the validity of such positions there's no doubt that the 'rule' utilitarianism posited by Mill is one of the most influential theories about how to achieve a just society:

> According to the Greatest Happiness Principle ... the ultimate end, with reference to and for the sake of which all other things are desirable ... is an existence exempt as far as possible from pain, and as rich as possible in enjoyments, both in point of quantity and quality (ibid: 389–390).

The Public Interest

What is the relationship between the common good, the good life, happiness, well-being and the public interest? In Book VII of *Politics* Aristotle argues the state is awarded political rights to govern demonstrated by the following: 'and most necessary of all there must be a power of deciding what is for the public interest', which is based on an ethical criteria to govern. The theory of the common good is closely associated with the concept of public interest, and in theory one could argue that it is in the public interest to develop a theory of the common good. There are a number of problems however with this, one being that in some circles the common good is contrasted with the notion of the public interest such as the following Catholic interpretation:

> The contemporary contrast to the Catholic doctrine of the common good is the idea of the public interest. The rhetoric of the public interest

suggests that everyone has his or her own private interest and that the public interest is the sum total of these private interests.[15]

And reflecting the comments in Pope Benedict XVI's encyclical *Caritas in Veritate* discussed earlier, it continues:

> Against this idea of the public interest, which so quickly is reduced to economic interest, the Catholic doctrine of the common good rejects economics as the axis around which society must revolve. Ironically, the culture of individualism cannot keep the human person at the center of society.[16]

However, this perception of the principle of the public interest today is extremely misleading and oversimplifies what is in fact at one end of the spectrum a very complex concept whilst at the other an empty piece of rhetoric. Whilst it is true that 'public interest theory' developed originally as an economic concept, it has like the concept of culture for example, changed over time. For instance, we'll see in Chapter 3 that the principle of the public interest is central to news production, which may often differ and clash with political perceptions of the public interest. For the present, we need to discuss the principle of the public interest for three clear reasons. Firstly, to assess it in relation to the common good, secondly because the public interest principle is central to government legislation for legitimizing and justifying public policy initiatives and thirdly because the media also use the public interest principle or a variation of it in defence of news production.

As we have already seen the principle of the common good is rooted in history and that it has informed the way in which society should, can and have developed. We've also seen that when we analyse further the notion of the common good it is mostly governed and determined by elites in positions of power and influence, and is shaped by particular sets of moral values. Individualism is an anathema to the common good and economic rationality should serve, not dominate, or be the guiding principle to live the good life. The justification of public policy is located here particularly in relation to welfare, universal education and universal health systems that bring substantive benefits to all in society. However, the common good is morally driven and guided in the sense that goods are unequally distributed in class systems where wealth inequalities prevail; education includes private schooling, healthcare includes private paying customers and it's the poor who normally require extensive use of social services. In any society that is dominated by free market capitalism the common good at best is justification for a partial redistribution of wealth in a deeply divided system.

The concerns of the public interest principle outlined above by the Catholic Worker have some merit because it is historically linked to economics, but not for the reason they outline. As McQuail (1993: 21) states, its beginnings were

---

15   http://www.cjd.org/paper/roots/rbody.html, accessed 14 February 2011.
16   Ibid.

rooted in another philosophy: 'The origin of the public interest concept lies in economic regulation, where it is still widely applied.' Perhaps more importantly as McQuail further notes with reference to Mitnick (1980) the concept of public interest is rooted in 'medieval social theory, which gave normative support to ideas of economic justice.' The 'normative support' referred to here is the essential moral obligation of Office towards the community particularly the needs of community, and constitutes a policy towards the public that de-emphasizes the economic criteria, which the Catholic Worker rejects. So rather than the public interest principle being a tool for 'private interest' as they assert, here it is the opposite. Further, McQuail writes about 'numerous modern examples of public utilities which are similarly regulated for the common good' (ibid.), which appears to demonstrate that separating the public interest principle from the common good principle is more difficult than it may seem. We may be dealing with mere semantics here, but it is possible to assert at this point that achieving the common good is prior or equal to achieving the public interest; in other words the common good is in the public interest. However, the important point to bear in mind is that theorizing public policy is rooted in both concepts, which is intrinsically linked to governing bodies that either seek to bring benefits to society or are a vehicle in which to initiate policy shaped by independent bodies.

For example, the Public Interest Research Centre (PIRC) is a charity that assesses the relationship between global climate issues and economics and claims to be 'championing the public interest and informing government policy.'[17] PIRC also refer to contributing towards 'the long-term well being of society' a clear reference perhaps towards the history of liberal philosophy equally concerned with well-being and happiness as discussed above. However, the concerns of PIRC – although citing the public interest – advances that notion to more extreme heights when you consider the following:

> There are current **global trends** which present clear and **immediate risks**, and which threaten the future survival of our species. We are at a critical point in determining our relationship with the environment. As climate-related damages continue to increase, choices that we all make now will determine our freedom to act in the future (PIRC's emphasis in bold).[18]

To speak of a public interest in this context would almost seem superficial with the type of impending danger towards 'our species' but what it represents is a battle over ideas of what is contained within the public interest principle in pragmatic terms. For instance, and I'll be returning to this point in more detail later in Chapters 2 and 3, it represents a battle over what forms public policy between news media concerning influencing both public and government thinking on public policy

---

17 Public Interest Research Centre (PIRC), http://www.pirc.info/about/mission/, accessed 12 March 2011.

18 Ibid.

in relation to thinking about policy in the aftermath of the riots in 2011. Another organization, The Public Interest Research Network (PIRN),[19] operate on similar terms to PIRC and go further by attempting to define what the public interest is:

> We define public interest research as that which seeks to put wider public interests ahead of vested and sectional interests. We recognise the importance of defending the 'public interest' and helping to build an alternative to the market friendly dogma of much public, policy and media debate. This means that our work is guided by a fundamental commitment to the wider public interest as opposed to sectional and vested interests. Crucially, however, we are guided in our research by the drive to uncover the facts about the issues we research and to use these to explain how economic, social and political relationships operate.

This conception of the public interest contrasts sharply with the Catholic Worker's view by stating the desire to 'build an alternative to the market friendly dogma' (my emphasis), despite the fact that the Catholic position towards the free-market is as hostile as PIRC and PIRN. Are the differences over the meaning of the public interest merely semantic differences or are we witnessing a relative (relativism) interpretation of the meaning of the public interest according to different cultural norms? In terms of the Catholic position advocated here by the US-based group the Catholic Worker it certainly contrasts with the UK based positions advocated by both PIRC and PIRN. However, with respect to the Catholic position it cannot simply be reduced to geography in terms of its 'relative' interpretation of the public interest principle because of the trans-national religious aspect of the Catholic Church. However, despite national and/or regional variations over the use of the public interest principle in defining policy, the common good principle remains central to Catholic political principles. The view expressed by the Catholic Worker in fact reflects economic views of public interest where it is deemed to mean economic efficiency within Capitalism with emphasis on the free market and the type of individualism that many Catholics so distrust. But the truth is, the public interest principle is open to a variety of interpretations, which on the one hand appears to make it a nebulous concept but on the other hand, can make it the most complex of concepts in terms of rationalizing, justifying and legitimizing public policy in the name of the public interest.

Defining the public interest in the USA for example, in terms of providing universal healthcare, turns into one of the most divisive public policy debates known, resisted by Republicans, whereas in the UK no political party would risk removing or greatly reducing the budget of the National Health Service. In sum, the public interest principle is a battleground over where ideas of public policy are fought and in the UK the Conservative's 'Big Society' idea is an attempt at reducing the size of the state preferring voluntary involvement, and in principle,

---

19   The Public Interest Research Network (PIRN), http://www.publicinterest.ac.uk, accessed 14 March 2011.

and rationale, is an ideological attack upon public policy initiatives budgeted from central office. More importantly underpinning the idea of the 'Big Society' is a Libertarian agenda not far removed from the works of Robert Nozick and his idea of the minimal or 'night-watchman' state, preferring private-commercial companies taking over from state governed public policy offices.

Nozick's politics are rooted in Adam Smith's idea of the 'invisible hand' of the free-market whereby the market would provide for the greatest number in the name of the greatest good. The fact that the market has consistently failed to adequately provide welfare is the reason that regulation arose particularly in the 19th century. Nozick argued however that an extensive state that sought to legislate on behalf of people in wider society would ultimately be a violation of an individual's rights. Here we see a moral dimension, for any such intrusion is for Nozick an unjustified act and quite clearly any acts of charity to help other citizens is outweighed by an individual's rights to secure self-interest over and above any notion of public interest that may attempt to legitimize public policy as a central principle for creating happiness, the common good and the notion of a just society based on welfare principles. Nozick, ironically like Max Weber, recognized that the state is mostly a coercive force which attempts to assert its will over citizens which in many cases bring substantial welfare benefits to receivers of goods, but such coercion, it can be argued, is perceived as an act of violence because it entails compulsion, and as Nozick argues forcing citizens by using state coercive practices and compulsion tactics is morally corrupt (1974: xi).

On the academic scene in the USA, Nozick, who was highly critical of the welfare system, came into dispute with John Rawls who proposed a theory of the 'just society'. The right-leaning Republican Tea Party movement would today hail Nozick as their hero for he expounded the idea that individuals be free to do as they choose and that the state's attempt to reduce such freedom was an injustice and the Tea Party's attack on taxes is an attack on funding public policy on all fronts for without taxes, police, healthcare, education, rubbish collection and other initiatives that bring substantive benefits to the wider community conceptualized as public interest would effectively end. For Nozick taxing someone to bring benefits to others is akin to theft and a form or modern-day enslavement because it forcibly compels the extraction of money without consent. As Grey (1976: 877) states:

> Perhaps the most of all public issues are those concerning the proper distribution of wealth and income. Risking oversimplification, let me suggest that the standard positions taken in the unending debate over these issues can usefully be classified as either egalitarian or libertarian. Egalitarians hold that economic assets should be distributed equally – allowing various exceptions. Libertarians hold that economic assets should be left in whatever hands they reach through free and fair individual transactions – again, allowing various exceptions.

Rawls's complex work *A Theory of Justice* forwards the argument that a distribution of goods and services are in the public interest in a capitalist system that engenders wealth difference, thus the distribution of goods and services benefit the poorest. The retort of Nozick is to question the very meaning of 'justice' and criticizes the idea that justice is akin to a socialist defined state project based on redistribution of wealth, preferring that justice be akin to procedures and rights that are rooted in the idea of individualism and designed to protect the individual from state intrusion. Nozick argued that individuals have an invisible moral space round them whereby intrusion into was premised on consent which serves as a basis of critique against Rawls' theory of justice:

> Against the claim that [a more extensive state] is justified in order to achieve or produce distributive justice among its citizens I develop a theory of justice (the entitlement theory) which does not require any more extensive state.. and criticize other theories of distributive justice which do envisage a more extensive state, focusing especially on the recent powerful theory of John Rawls (Nozick 1974: xi).

Rawls published *A Theory of Justice* in 1971 and Nozick's arguments against the distributive justice forwarded by John Rawls can be partially conceptualized by understanding Nozick's support of Kant's 'categorical imperative'; humans are not a means to an end, but rather humans are an end in themselves and this effectively serves the purposes of Nozick to augment a critique of state coercion and distributive justice. Rawls is seen by many to be one of the most influential political philosophers in the USA and the egalitarian liberalism Rawls espoused therefore is seen to be central to both conceptual notions of the common good and the public interest principle and as Lehning (2009) argues:

> His ideas on 'what justice requires' have influenced the theory of government and play a role in public political debates between, and within, political parties on policies to be pursued in so-called welfare states (ibid: ix).

Both Rawls and Nozick were clearly attempting to influence government thinking on public policy and therefore were contributing towards defining the public interest. Whilst it is tempting to dismiss the public interest principle as meaningless because it is open to varied interpretations according to political viewpoints, we must not lose sight of the fact that in reality the public interest principle and the theory of the common good are in fact 'contested sites' or a 'battle ground of ideas' on which to justify, or otherwise, a public policy strategy for society of which happiness and well-being rest.

Chapter 2
Public Policy

The Social Construction of Public Policy

It's largely taken for granted that political parties elected to govern by popular consent via the ballot box are awarded the mandate to govern on behalf of citizens irrespective of voting preferences, and, therefore, public policy-making is by and large universal in its application towards citizens, if not entirely universal in its uses – educational establishment differences concerning state and privately funded schooling serve as an example. Moreover, although public policy is broadly seen to bring benefits to citizens either directly as in actual use of the National Health Service (NHS), the very notion of public policy is also central to the *idea* of political citizenship, because it is seen as essentially democratic and the end-product of citizens who exercise their democratic right to vote. Public policy is deeply rooted in political philosophy as discussed in the previous chapter, and is central to the idea of social democracy, with or without neo-liberalist economic rationality.

Public policy is first and foremost an abstract concept that can be used in any given society to denote policy made on behalf of the public by government. This broad term can therefore be effectively used and applied in practice in many different political systems, such as social democratic, socialist, communist, even right-wing fascist dictatorships. In other words it can, theoretically, be applied according to the values of each system and is not simply to be defined in terms of a system that is governed by social democratic rationale. That said, this book is essentially concerned with public policy-making in the United Kingdom and therefore is concerned to assess the relationship with public policy-making decisions governed by the values of representative democracy and the British Parliament. However, when we assess in this political context it is always useful to draw comparisons with other unrelated systems and when we do so we can assert that values – social, political and moral – differ widely, which may determine the trajectory of the aims and objectives of which public policy is meant to achieve. For example, when we assess education and health policy in Cuba we discover that its *raisen d'etre* is significantly different from the United Kingdom. There is no private educational system in Cuba and there are no private companies bidding for contracts in the health system unlike the UK. We can even take this one further step forward – and many more steps for that matter – and compare the UK to societies with very similar political systems such as the USA. The clear difference between both is the attitude towards health with the US governed by private health insurance, with almost 50 million people without. The USA can be compared to Cuba as the US documentary filmmaker Michael Moore did in his film *Sicko* which highlighted the social benefits of the Cuban system by taking US citizens who had no or insufficient insurance policy to Cuba to be cared for. Moore argued that the US system had failed its citizens unable to offer free health care for all. Moore also compared the US health system to the National Health System in the UK, spending most of his time 'wide-eyed' as he discovered that citizens could also freely access health care.

In Moore's film it was uncomfortable to watch that one American man who had lost two fingers in an accident had only the insurance to cover one finger to be reconnected to his hand. This is the immoral and extreme end of a free market capitalist system that governs the attitude towards public health policy in the US. Even though the UK has a similar political system to the US as opposed to the socialist system in Cuba, it is, nevertheless, equal by a moral conviction towards a universal health system; free at the point of need. One could argue, therefore, that even though the political systems between the US and the UK are similar and identical in many ways, the UK's health system is however much closer to Cuba, which on first glance appears to be ironic or even a contradiction in terms, vis-à-vis capitalism, which after all is governed by profit.

Of course, it would be crude of me to suggest that the excesses of capitalism cannot be curtailed, but these differences inform us that public policy is deeply complex and always relative to each system. In other words, morality – or amorality, immorality – inform decision-making, but morality is always restricted by economics thus always creating conflicts of interest such as the pursuit of happiness over fiscal realities.

Three questions that I wish pose here are: What is public policy? How is thinking on public policy defined? What are its uses? I will endeavour to address each separately in turn and beginning with the first question let's begin with Gerston (2008) in relation to public policy-making:

> Public policy-making has many definitions. At one end of the continuum, some people view public policy-making as simply whatever governments decide to do. At the opposite end, others think of public policy-making as intertwined relationships of offices, public leaders, and issues, all of which constantly change in a kaleidoscope-like fashion. Given such disagreement, it is easy for someone to scratch his or her head and wonder, just what is public policy-making? (ibid: 3).

In Gerston's later work, under the sub-heading 'In Search of a Framework', the author once again discusses the issue of definition: 'As an approach to understanding political change, public policy has almost as many definitions as there are policy issues' (2010: 5), further stating:

> The debate over parameters is more than an academic exercise or game, for it is the word *process* that differentiates public policy from other approaches to government and politics. A process is dynamic and ongoing and, as such,

is constantly subject to re-evaluation, cessation, expedition, or even erratic movement. Conceptually speaking, then, policy making exists in an open environment with neither a beginning nor an end, and virtually no boundaries (ibid.).

Gerston poses this 'erratic movement' as a 'nomadic context' (ibid.) but the word 'conceptually' – a consequence of philosophical thinking and theoretical at its base – differs significantly from applied practice. Gerston seeks to offer a 'working definition of public policy' (ibid: 6). '*Public policy* is defined here *as the combination of basic decisions, commitments and actions made by those who hold or influence government positions of authority*' (ibid: 7), which isn't entirely unreasonable but only when grounded in the context of founding philosophical concepts and principles.

Gerston's use of the term 'nomadic context' signifies the fluid-changing character of public policy according to interpretations of both the founding principles within political philosophy and the ideological bent of respective governments, such as the Big Society idea. Gerston lists five constant components believed to exist in relation to determining public policy:

- Issues that appear on the public agenda
- Actors who present, interpret, and respond to those issues
- Resources affected by those issues
- Institutions that deal with issues
- The levels of government that address issues (ibid: 8).

However abstract this may seem, Gerston does however alert us to what is principally at the heart of this book, i.e., by what means, practices and processes does public policy arise and how is it put into practice and applied to society. This is important, because government, as an elected body, constitutive of social democracy, is held accountable on matters concerning the implementation of public policy issues based on a legitimate mandate initiated by voters at the ballot box. This in the United Kingdom is Parliament and the elected government asserting its authority and constitutional right to govern.

Under the sub-heading 'A Working Definition of Public Policy' Gerston (2010: 7) states that 'The linkage between policy makers and policy receivers is vital to understanding the meaning and power of public policy' and then states that 'Public policies result from the blend of politics and government', and further quoting David Easton states that politics is the 'authoritative allocation of values'. Gerston thus concludes that public policy is 'important in defining prevailing values (politics) as it is in defining solutions to prevailing problems (through government)' (ibid.). Gerston also argues that 'Whatever the issue in question, scholars agree that public policy making has a perpetual, dynamic, and evolutionary quality' (ibid: 6), which is true but only in terms of applied practice and not so in terms of the Western philosophical context that frames the political, social, cultural context, meaning and application of public policy in modern societies, and it is the latter which I seek to address in terms of what has become known as the 'Big Society' in British political discourse.

In Lascoumes and Le Gales' (2007) work they argue that public policy thinking and subsequently its implementation – Lascoumes and Le Gales prefer to use 'modes of operation' – is a form of political and social instrumentation. Policy instruments are tools and the means to achieve strategic political objectives to varying degrees based on political philosophy and ideology. The aim of Lascoumes and Le Gales' work is 'to explain the significance of a political sociological approach to public policy instruments in accounting for processes of public policy change' (ibid: 3) in light of the fact that policy instruments have traditionally been, 'often analyzed as peripheral in the understanding of public policy' (ibid: 1). Lascoumes and Le Gales are critical of 'technical and functionalist' approaches to the study of public policy instrumentation, preferring a 'political sociology of policy instruments' in order to 'stress power relations associated to instruments and issues of legitimacy, politicization, or depoliticization dynamics associated with different policy instruments' (ibid: 4).

Using public policy instruments is essential for Lascoumes and Le Gales not only because it sweeps aside functionalist approaches, but perhaps more importantly – and this is related to the sweeping aside of functionalism – because they reject the idea of public policy production as an 'axiological neutrality' preferring to highlight public policy instruments as tools, or if one prefers, means to impose 'values' and as a 'mode of regulation' (ibid.) and in this context Lascoumes and Le Gales are interested in how power is realized and effective – via public policy schemes – as a power relationship between government and citizens:

> ***Public policy instrumentation*** *– in our understanding – means the set of problems posed by the choice and use of instruments (techniques, methods of operation, devices) that allow government policy to be made material and operational. Another way of formulating the issue is to say that it involves not only understanding the reasons that drive towards retaining one instrument rather than another, but also envisaging the effects produced by these choices* (ibid: 4) (bold and italic text in the original).

Making public policy 'operational' as Lascoumes and Le Gales clearly state is what in political circles we refer to as social and political reform. Reform can take many forms, radical, moderate as examples; based on conservatism (sometimes radical), based on social democracy (sometimes moderate) as examples of political philosophies and ideological perspectives. The relationship Lascoumes and Le Gales are interested in – namely between governing and governed as they put it – is related directly to ideology and persuasion that merely seeks to maintain a system governed by capitalist, mostly free market-based economics and this relationship is essential to the reforming process. Reforming can revert to the past as well as seeking new futures – some conservatives may seek to change or reform existing policies with a view to past traditions; to conserve – is one example; in other words reforming doesn't always adhere to a bright socialist future. Public policy thinking and implementation then becomes of interest because it is a means of securing a capitalist-based economy; it softens the blow; it makes up for the inadequacies of the deregulated free market system which puts profit above welfare; in other words public policy – reluctantly pursued by many politicians on the right for instance because it costs money, hence taxation – is a social cushion to protect citizens. Whether this is acceptable is neither here-nor-there for the moment; the fact that its purpose or *raisen d'etre* is just that; is fact.

The first question – what is public policy? – has a related question: what does public policy mean according to the prevailing dominant political philosophies that govern the United Kingdom? This attempts to unite abstract theorizing with an empirical/applied social context. Disagreements over definitions and theoretical underpinnings are further complicated by distinct procedures or what is standard language in public policy discourse and the social sciences, namely 'implementation'. For our purposes when I address issues of implementation it's worth adding both 'authority' and 'legitimacy', which refers specifically to the legitimate bodies democratically responsible for the implementation of public policy and accountable to the public, of which policy is made in the first instance.

Under the subtitle 'Implementation' Hill and Hupe (2006) state: 'What can be called "public policy", and thus has to be implemented, is a product of what has happened in the earlier stages of the policy process' (ibid: 6), but perhaps more importantly further states: 'Nevertheless, the content of that policy, and its impact on those affected, may be substantially modified, elaborated or even negated during the implementation stage', and that 'implementation is something separated from policy formation' (ibid: 7). Lascoumes and Le Gales (2007) state:

> Public policy is a sociopolitical space constructed as much through techniques and instruments as through aims or content. A public policy instrument *constitutes a device that is both technical and social, that organizes specific social relations between the state and those it is addressed to, according to the representations and meanings it carries. It is a particular type of institution, a technical device with the generic purpose of carrying a concrete concept of the politics/society relationship and sustained by a concept of regulation* (ibid: 4) (italics in the original text).

The 'Big Society', Bureaucratic Authority and Civil Society

'How does the political system really work, and why should we care?' Thus begins the preface to Gerston's (2010) book concerning public policy. The principles discussed in Chapter 1 – 'the caring' perhaps – play an important role in manufacturing and defining the political system of which public policy in this context at least, is but an extension of. The principles are propositions, where we purely abstract their inherent meaning in order to place in particular contexts: public policy is the means for attempting to achieve this process. It is easy to mock such notions as happiness, good life, common good, well-being and public interest for lacking convincing empirical substance and meaning, particularly when we ask: for what exactly is the empirical reality of abstracted propositions?

In this vein it is quite reasonable to postulate that they fail as abstract principles because of their detachment from reality and from their inherent meaninglessness in the everyday lives of every person. Happiness can for instance be viewed as purely subjective, whilst what constitutes the common good is very much a matter for debate and include abject differences on value: public policy which either is rooted or loosely connected to the principles is equally suspect, not perhaps in terms of implementation as purely functional, but rather in its effectiveness for achieving objective goals, because after all, public policy is defined as making a contribution as a 'public good'.

On the other hand, human ability to care or to think about caring is to think about what society we wish to live in, and despite the criticisms levelled at the above principles, they can nevertheless set the intellectual framework for thinking and placing public policy-making in context. Therefore, whatever the validity of the critique, the abstract value of the principles and purpose herein, is to evaluate their essential relationship to enacting policies within society in order for society to function. To offer critique is good: to over-critique is to miss the point; the point to advance is that they serve as a *functioning element for public policy rationale.*

The second question – how is thinking on public policy defined? – can now be addressed and the subsidiary question to pose at this juncture is the following: what exactly is the 'Big Society' in terms of *how is thinking on public policy defined*? On 19 July 2010, David Cameron launched the Big Society at a speech in Liverpool. Cameron referred to the Big Society as the 'great agenda' for change beginning with pilot schemes in four areas: Liverpool; Eden Valley, Cumbria; Windsor and Maidenhead and the London borough of Sutton: 'If you've got an idea to make life better, if you want to improve your local area, don't just think about it, tell us what you want to do and we will try and give you the tools to make this happen.' Cameron also spoke of 'civic action' where citizens would be empowered to enact change. There are echoes of Nozick here, if not entirely identical, but the idea of a smaller or minimal state coupled with the empowerment of individuals, volunteers etc., advocated by Cameron is very much within Nozick's philosophy. More specifically: 'The Big Society is about helping people to come together to improve their own lives. It's about putting more power in people's hands – a massive transfer of power from Whitehall to local communities.'[1]

Three key parts of the Big Society are:

---

1   The Cabinet Office, http://www.cabinetoffice.gov.uk/content/big-society-overview, accessed 25 January 2012.

- **'Community empowerment**: giving local councils and neighbourhoods more power to take decisions and shape their area. Our planning reforms lead by DCLG, will replace the old top-down planning system with real power for neighbourhoods to decide the future of their area.
- **Opening up public services**: our public service reforms will enable charities, social enterprises, private companies and employee-owned cooperatives to compete to offer people high-quality services. The welfare to work programme lead by the Department for Work and Pensions will enable a wide range of organisations to help get Britain off welfare and into work.
- **Social action**: encouraging and enabling people to play a more active part in society. National Citizen Service, Community Organisers and Community First will encourage people to get involved in their communities.'[2]

In May 2010 the Cabinet Office created the Office for Civil Society (OSC) to work 'across government departments to translate the Big Society agenda into practical policies' and to provide 'support to voluntary and community organisations and is responsible for delivering a number of key Big Society programmes' which are:

- The Big Society Bank
- National Citizen Service Pilots
- Community Organisers
- Community First

Connected to this is the Big Society Network:

> The Big Society Network exists to support and to develop talent, innovation and enterprise to deliver social impact. By working with business, philanthropists, charities and social ventures we believe we can unleash the social energy that exists in the UK to help build a better, healthier society.[3]

We can observe that the concepts underpinning public policy thinking discussed in Chapter 1 concerning political philosophy, such as happiness, common good, good life, well-being and the public interest principle are invoked in these statements. The OSC however raises interesting issues and concerns over the notion of civil society concerning 'implementation' of policy, and what role civil society has in social democratic systems and the points also made in the above quotation by Lascoumes and Le Gales (2007: 4) additionally raise interesting issues concerning public policy as a means to shaping and conditioning civil society.

---

2   Ibid.
3   The Big Society Network, http://www.thebigsociety.co.uk/, accessed 25 January 2012.

Implementation is a process containing political objectives which is based on the Weberian notion of bureaucratic authority within a social democratic logic. The Big Society idea is therefore a form of bureaucratic-state coercion specifically aimed at intervening in civil society – a space that theoretically is normally free from state bureaucratic interference. This debate regarding civil society and bureaucratic authority as state coercion is important because it highlights the contradiction between the idea of a civil society remaining independent from state authority as *interventionist* and social democracy as the ideal political system that best suits and accommodates for an independent social space (civil society). The Italian Marxist writer Antonio Gramsci argued that the concept of civil society – theoretically perhaps – in democratic systems is a space primarily defined by its autonomy and free from direct political interference; it's worth noting how the idea of civil society is viewed as anti-state as Sparks (1998: 113) states in relation to communism,

> the problem with communist societies is that the state has swallowed the family and civil society. The programme that follows from this is simple: the sphere of the state must be reduced and the family and civil society must be resurrected in opposition to the state.

It is the resurrection of civil society and the family which is so central to Conservatism vis-à-vis the Big Society idea. However, and ironically, it is the state which is constructing what in theory should be an area free from state interference; if civil society is to mean anything it is the construct of the people. By using another Weberian concept we can construct or imagine civil society as an 'ideal-type' (a model or paradigm) that is essentially measured against concrete reality in order to assess the validity and legitimacy of the 'ideal-type'. The point made by Gramsci was that it is civil society that effectively separates democratic systems from non-democratic state oriented dictatorships where civil societies are absent.

The theory of civil society has a long history in liberal thought and featured particularly in part two of John Locke's *Two Treatises of Government*. Locke developed a theory of political philosophy and referred to the 'state of nature' where man (sic) was free and equal and God through the laws of nature would regulate the activity of men. However, Locke argued that the state of nature was inherently unstable because men would infringe the *natural rights* of others. So Locke proposed his 'social contract' theory that would force men to recognize the rights of all. The overall purpose of the social contract was to form a civil society where government would enforce the rule of law to ensure the rights of men; one of which was the *right* to private property.

Locke's theory of civil society or political society, as he also referred to it *was not* the space detached from government as it was viewed by Gramsci; it was not an autonomous space but rather included government intervention; as Locke claimed 'men ... enter into society to make one people one body politic under one supreme government' (1990: 160). However, government were the servants of the people and the function of civil society was for government to protect the natural rights of men by the establishment of the social contract: 'For hereby he authorises the society ... which is all one, the legislative thereof, to make laws for him as the *public good* of society shall require,' (ibid.) (my italics for emphasis in direct relation to the 'common good').

Georg Wilhelm Friedrich Hegel's theory of civil society or as Hegel referred to it in *The Philosophy of Right*, the 'external state', contrasts with Locke's view of civil society. Hegel perceived the degree of autonomy held within civil society as detrimental to the overall objectives of the liberal state of which civil society should be united with. Accordingly, civil society cannot guarantee the moral virtue of the individual as long as it remains divorced from the state and in this context the state must contain civil society. Perceived as such the attachment of one form to another becomes a transcending force of movement from society to state, which in essence is a rightful product of mind, based on the rationalization of man. As Bobbio argued: 'the state is conceived as a positive moment in contrast to a pre-state or anti-state society, which is relegated to a negative moment' (1987: 140).

Hegel built on previous theories of the development of the state and its relationship to the state of nature, which preceded the state. Although there are variations on this theme the common denominator was 'rationalization' and by definition an argument for both naturalizing and making legitimate the state as a moral and political authority over other aspects of society. Attaining the rational state is central to Hegel's theory of the dialectic and civil society is but one stage in the logical process in achieving this higher and more profound goal that reflects the true nature of humans. For Hegel, civil society is a site of struggle in terms of education (*bildung*) which is a force for liberation, claiming that 'subjective will ... attains objectivity within' and through 'education struggle' (1967: 124–125). This for Hegel is a vital aspect of movement because civil society is *the* site where the relationship between master and slave are reproduced.

One such struggle within civil society is the fight for attaining 'personality' which for Hegel formed the framework of recognition, the basis of Fukuyama's *End of History* thesis and the celebration of the universal liberal 'idea'. The ownership of property was the means to fulfilling 'personality' claims, an essential characteristic of the capitalist, but not of the worker. Both of course formed the business class who although at one moment stood opposite to each other nevertheless shared a commonality of feeling based on a common interest.

Ultimately, resolution of conflict within civil society would be instigated by the state who after all held a greater political and moral authority to rule and control agents within civil society. Hegel argued that both workers and capitalists, the two groups that constituted the business class, had limitations and were essentially concerned with their own material interests and this constituted an obstacle to the overall interests of society. Hegel resolves this conflict by arguing that it is the universal class (civil servants) who are ultimately tied to the government and therefore the overall interests of society. To a certain degree their role is to arbitrate between the competing interests but ultimately they represent the interests of the state, a political space in which the universal class are its natural representatives; there to monitor and control other sections of society to the will of the state which acts in the interest of others.

As Splichal states, the concept of civil society has undergone substantial changes throughout history: 'From Hegel onward, civil society by and large came to mean the domain in which civil rights and freedoms protected from state interference and legally guaranteed by the same state were executed' (1994: 11). In this context, Gramsci's theory of civil society reflected this shift, which was based on, 'a set of social relations "mediating" between the economy and the state and linked to, rather than separated from, both of them' (ibid.).

Habermas' theory of *Lebenswelt* or *lifeworld* is a notion of civil society that is similar to Gramsci's theory, albeit expressed in more explicit normative terms. Habermas argues that society is posed in terms of a dichotomy between 'system' and 'life-world'. Borrowing from Max Weber and Talcott Parsons, Habermas (1995: 209–213) argues that the former – 'system' – is constitutive of 'purposive-rational action'. The category 'system' therefore contains the state and the economy and is concerned with the material production of society. Whilst both system and life-world are two distinct forms of rationalization, the latter is distinguished from the former in that it is constitutive of 'communicative action', of attaining understanding between people in a space normatively separate from system. The rationality of 'system' is defined by bureaucratic authority that characterizes its essential form, whilst life-world includes the production of cultural forms and the wider category of socialization.

Although Habermas claimed that civil society is a third realm or domain 'uncoupled' from the state and economy in terms of its logical performance, civil society is equally connected to state and economy; tied interdependently and coexisting between each other. The normative aspect of Habermas' argument is based on the recognition of the increasing intervention and bureaucratization of civil society and consequently 'purposive-rational action' begins to dominate the realm of life-world corrupting its moral practice. The way to combat this process is through the mobilization of movements in civil society to retrieve lost ground by addressing the balance of power through the re-emergence of communicative action as a counter-balance to increasing bureaucratic authoritative intrusion. Interestingly, this latter perspective reflects Locke's theory that civil society must tame the excesses of government, although the vital difference is that Habermas awards a greater degree of autonomy from government and state apparatuses in which forces within civil society can activate resistance to the state. In this context, Habermas claims that 'purposive-rational action', whilst not destructive to civil society nevertheless needs to be kept in check by a space with relative autonomy and what is more the rights associated with democratic civil society must be guaranteed by government.

Under present structures governed by liberal-social democratic ideology, the most one can envisage as a liberal civil society is a realm in which the state formally protects the rights of citizens to perform their duties democratically, one of which is the right to stand in opposition to state structures, such as the right to form non-state organizations. This realm is not totally separate from the state because it is governed and monitored by governmental legislation. Therefore, in broad terms, under liberalized-social democracy the key issue is the *degree* of state involvement in the realm of civil society, whether it's positive (protecting rights of citizens) or negative (protecting state interests) and whilst it is widely acknowledged that under such circumstances the state exists, the logical conclusion is how best to keep its excesses in check.

So what can we deduce from this discussion in relation to the idea of the Big Society and bureaucratic authority, particularly its normative insertion for regulating civil society by public policy initiatives? It's perhaps worth noting that another Marxist writer, Perry Anderson wrote in his 'Antinomies of Antonio Gramsci' in the *New Left Review* that Gramsci had got the idea of civil society wrong and argued that no such autonomous space existed, not at least within a capitalist economy and one conditioned by social democracy. Anderson argued that – and gave examples of how the political sphere constantly invaded civil society; what Habermas described as the increasing bureaucratization of civil society by legal means.

Why is this important? One reason it is important is because if civil society characterizes social democratic systems it only does so on normative and political terms. Civil society it is argued is constituted of organizations free from direct state control such as the Women's Institute, Boy Scout Movement, the Church, the media, Non-Governmental Organizations (NGOs) etc., and thus defines a democratic life (Locke etc.), and yet for all the 'autonomy' of such groups, i.e., in making independent decisions without being dictated to by government, Anderson was right to argue that it isn't a totally independent space, but rather one that has relative autonomy because of the fact that government politically intrudes into this space at strategic times.

In my view, public policy is perhaps one of the greatest examples of how government seek to intervene into civil society – Cameron calls this the 'Big Society' – and thus is instrumental in setting the framework for public debate. This becomes of interest because public policy is also seen as inherently democratic – working on behalf of the people – and so too is civil society – if it is seen in Gramscian terms – but it seems that public policy contradicts the independent ideal of civil society because it is decision-making by government, and is reflective of liberal-social democracy. Ministers can always argue therefore that it is perfectly proper because public policy is seen as intrinsic to social democracy based principally on representative government. What develops from this is that civil society becomes a space for competing interests and a battleground where ideas are fought out between government initiatives and contrasting, alternative ideas to government-led public policy and these can take many forms including news media discourse, use of new media as a means of opposition and social organization, peaceful demonstrations, political protest and rioting.

Public Policy and Social Democracy

Public policy is perceived as a device that shapes and conditions social and political systems, regardless of the respective political philosophies that govern each society. Furthermore, particularly from a sociological viewpoint, public policy is a tool and means to effectively coordinate society, and if I were to use a value-judgement, one could argue that public policy is either a devious way for maintaining governmental power, and/or to selflessly bring substantive benefits to citizens of any given community. In this context public policy thinking and implementation is a process of bureaucratic authority and rational calculation, but is equally the legitimate expression of government elected democratically to power in order to act upon public policy projects set out in the political manifestos that seek to persuade citizens of such legitimacy. Public policies to varying degrees reflect social norms and values and are inherently moral and political, and further conditioned or restrained by the economy. Moral perspectives on public policy – healthcare and education as examples – create conflicts of interest when economic realities are realized that may impinge upon the moral imperatives that underpin public policy rationale.

One of the founder thinkers of sociology, Emile Durkheim and a socialist of sorts argued against revolutionary tactics to change society and preferred the slow and steady pace of reform. Restructuring society was for Durkheim more of an evolutionary passage rather than impulsive or planned revolutionary practice. Durkheim based his ideas on fellow Frenchman Auguste Marie Joseph Jean Léon Jaurès (1859–1914), a leading social democrat of the time. Social democracy differs from socialism, occupying the 'centre-left' of politics, sometimes referred to as 'evolutionary reformist socialism'. For Marxist thinkers, social democrats, such as the early founding figure, Eduard Bernstein – once a Marxist thinker – had effectively abandoned any goal of socialism superseding capitalism. Early social democrats, however, once harboured views that socialism could be achieved via reform of the free market capitalist system. However, social democracy for some time up to the present day, eventually abandoned this objective, turning instead to the welfare state as a buffer against the rampant excesses of capital and its inherent drive to profit, hence social democratic support of a vigorous public policy system that protects citizens within a given society. Public services are an important part of this thinking, as governments seek ways to work or be seen to be working on behalf of society. For Durkheim, reforming and taming capitalism, as an economic field, was vital only in so far that the individual, and the rights of the individual, were fully protected from what is often referred to as 'administrative socialism', although the term can have many uses and applications.[4]

----

4   See discussion in Chapter 18 titled 'The variety of economic systems' in Goodwin *et. al*'s *Microeconomics in Context* (2008), second edition, on the differences between market socialism and administrative socialism as an example.

Using Durkheim's insights on suicide Berger and Neuhaus (2003) argue that public policy can be perceived as a mediating structure between the state and the people. Durkheim had noted in his works on suicide how modernization had a propensity towards this dichotomy – state/public – and nothing in between has effective autonomy. Berger and Neuhaus state that 'mediating structures are defined *as those institutions standing between the individual in his private life and the large institutions of public life*' (ibid: 231). Durkheim for his part was committed to a positive approach to industrialization with the caveat that structures be embedded as social norms. In this context Durkheim had rejected many traditional political philosophies such as conservatism, liberalism with its utilitarian turn and socialism with its Marxist turn, arguing that individual liberty – removed from selfish egoism – was the ultimate goal of society, yet to be realized. It's in this context which Berger and Neuhaus with a nod to Durkheim place in context the position of public policy within civil society and echoing Durkheim they state:

> Modernization brings about an historically unprecedented dichotomy between public and private life. The most important large institution in the ordering of modern society is the modern state itself. In addition, there are the large economic conglomerates of capitalist enterprise, big labor, and the growing bureaucracies that administer wide sectors of society, such as in education and organized professions. All these institutions we call *megastructures* (ibid.).

In support of the classic and now familiar social democratic turn or compromise – depending on one's viewpoint – Berger and Neuhaus confirm a commitment to the broad framework of capitalism, rejecting, as did Durkheim, any notion of revolutionary practice to overturn it by insisting on reform via the welfare state: '[We] suggest that the modern welfare state is here to stay, indeed that it ought to expand the benefits it provides – but that *alternative mechanisms are possible to provide welfare state services*' (ibid.). Furthermore, Berger and Neuhaus argue that their proposals – alternatives to what presently exists – can, if taken seriously enough, 'become the basis of far-reaching innovations in public policy, perhaps of a new paradigm for at least sectors of the modern welfare state' (ibid.). The basis of the work by Berger and Neuhaus is the approach to society by Émile Durkheim, updating his work to the present context, whilst not losing sight of the fact that perhaps little has changed in the intervening years since Durkheim's departure from this earth.

Max Weber's study of bureaucratic authority is informative despite the fact that many believe Weber's ideas have been superseded by the apparent annihilation or partial destruction of bureaucratic authority and industrialization. Weber's writings were directed at modern society, the emergence of new forms and structures and the way society was managed and controlled. The overall industrialization process required careful monitoring and surveillance – in other words bureaucracies – that effectively managed new forms of social organization. Modern society, many have argued, has given way to a post-modern condition, where bureaucratic control has greatly diminished along with rational-coherent visions of society and industrialization has given way to a post-industrial context. In the UK for example, the prioritization of the capitalist free market adds to the notion that governments' bureaucratic authority is essentially undermined because of the freedom awarded to big business, and therefore political philosophical visions of the now and the future are greatly diminished, unlike the post-war doctrine of social house building, the universal expansion of education and the creation of the National Health Service, which had its basis in political philosophy. Corporatism and the increasing monopolization of business has effectively shifted power away from government, increased fragmentation of society, increased divisions in classes – despite capital's claim to the contrary – and further undermined community, identity and culture. For many, the issue of immigration in a contemporary context has further complicated the issue of cultural and national identity, and the 'other' has offered challenges to the host culture in terms of integration.

This is why the idea of the Conservative-led 'Big Society' is important and we should not ignore it, for it is essentially government attempting to reassert its bureaucratic authority with a political philosophical vision – once lost – and to use public policy as a means to achieving it, in a post-modern and uncertain context. It is the *modern* going head-to-head with the *post-modern*. Bogason (2000) is informative on this very issue:

> The *modern society* is characterized by *rationalization*, the systematic use of reason based on an overarching vision. Its main organizational forms are industrialization and bureaucratization where rational organizational measures are used to perfection (ibid: 2).

Despite a rigid division of labour indicative of modern systems in its infancy and middle phases and high degrees of differentiation in the production process, it nevertheless acts as 'coordination' based on 'centralize[d] powers' that seek 'to control the activities of society' (ibid: 3). As stated above the post-modern phase or if one prefers the dialectical struggle between modern and post-modern, sees the latter as essentially subversive to the former's structures and forms; central coordination is dispersed, differentiation is exacerbated resisting exogenous forces of control, thus as Bogason points out: 'There is a high degree of individualism, based on an unprecedented system of social security rooted in the modern society. The nation state becomes of less importance in politics, in the economy, and in cultural affairs' (ibid.), and in a global context with the expansion of communication networks, the influences set forth by international imperatives increase and bear down upon the national context, and this goes some way to explaining the rationale behind the Big Society, as well as the economic limits of capitalism and its essential *raisen d'etre* to commit towards maintaining public services through financial support, because in the main, public services are not productive structures that increase capital and return for shareholders.

Thus the idea of the Big Society is an attempt to convince citizens that it is firmly based in morality, economic reality and that public policy thinking is equally rooted in a commitment to a political philosophy that in this instance is rooted in conservative values. Public policy in this context is therefore a form of 'calculated rationality' in a post-modern context; of rationalization over fragmentation; of the collective – steeped in morality and neighbourliness – over the heightened sense of individuality so central to the post-modern condition. This is a turn to Ferdinand Tönnies specifically in relation to his two concepts 'gemeinschaft' (community) and 'gesellschaft' (society) with its emphasis on individual rather than communal needs of which the former is rooted in morality. Gesellschaft has all the hallmarks of the dialectic mentioned above between the modern and the post-modern, whereas gemeinschaft is traditional and certainly pre-industrial.

However, the *idea* of the Big Society is also an attempt to re-establish or more cynically re-invent and manufacture *memory* by appealing to a lost past. Memory was something Tönnies was also interested in particularly in his monumental work *Community and Society* and I would argue that not only is the *idea* of the Big Society an attempt at reaffirming memory, but it is also, and perhaps more importantly, a conviction that its essential rationale is bearing witness to human nature; a point also central to Tönnies work above. In reference to the Portuguese philosopher Spinoza, here is what Tönnies says: 'Spinoza has recognized memory as an element of human will' and quoting from Spinoza's book *Ethics*: 'There is another fact to which I particularly wish to draw attention, namely, that we cannot do anything by free decision of our own will if we do not remember it' (2002: 114). It is then remarkable, if it is accepted that the *idea* of the Big Society is nothing more than a process of re-inventing memory, that Spinoza says this: 'Those who believe that they speak or are silent or act by free decision of their own will are dreaming with their eyes wide open' (ibid.). Spinoza was specifically relating his argument to the notion that the 'mind' – the source of independent rational will, which Spinoza disputed – was not free or isolated from 'imagination' or 'memory' and that ideas come to mind in relation to existing material things in reality. Tönnies goes onto argue that 'we shall be able to formulate this truth with still greater precision' in relation to 'rational will'. Even though Spinoza used the term 'reality', what happens if I argue that the *idea* of the Big Society contains large elements of ideology turned into *a* reality, which in turn becomes 'rational will' that shapes consciousness?

The English Riots of 2011: Perceptions and Influence on Public Policy Thinking

Frank Zappa's track titled 'Hungry Freaks, Daddy' from *Freak Out* described how 'Mr America' was ignorant of the dispossessed and how consumerism governed the lives of American thinking. Swap 'America' for 'Britain' and Zappa's lyrics go some way to explaining the reason why many people took to the streets in the summer of 2011 and the rioting and looting that occurred in August 2011 across England – Marx called this 'alienation'. Use 'hungry' as a metaphor for 'consumption' and the desire to own without the finance to purchase, and perhaps we can also begin to understand some of the rationale behind the events. The fact that the sportswear shop JD Sports was predominantly targeted amongst others such as electrical goods shops, reflect the materialism that is advertised, which many will never have. This is Marx's commodity fetishism by other 'illegal' means in a society that generally worships and celebrates the product and celebrity that aims to shape identity and lifestyle. The August riots also represented a major moment in British public policy thinking towards society, impacting upon citizenship and civil society.

For many members of parliament, particularly conservative members, and right-wing news commentators – Peter Hitchens of the *Daily Mail* and former editor of the *Sun*, Kelvin McKenzie, are examples – the word 'rioting' was a misrepresentation of the events, instead arguing that the events were acts of 'criminality' against persons and property, and not driven by politics. For many other onlookers of the events they were seen as more complex and perhaps even a combination of politics and criminality. This *perception* of the events is important because such analysis becomes *a* basis on which public policy by response to social events is implemented and this is coupled by government perceptions of the reactions and thinking of the majority of the public to events, which were laid bare in public polling and public debates in the press and on television. The fact that responses which become policy were condemned by the leader of the Labour Party, Ed Miliband – and many others – as 'knee-jerk' responses, informs us of the way perceptions work; and subsequent implementation of policy to both contain such events happening again to win favour with the public. Any perception is by its very nature inadequate – and unscientific – as a way of thinking and implementing public policy because events and social happenings remain essentially unknown to many politicians, particularly within a political system based on wealth disparity, privilege differentiation and class distinction.

Interestingly both Wales and Scotland were unaffected, but riots of a similar nature occurred in Northern Ireland earlier that year where unemployment levels and public service spending remain high in comparison to the rest of the United Kingdom. The major difference between the rioting in England and Belfast was the looting of shops and stealing of products in the former. Despite government's retort that these were acts of 'criminality' the fact was however that the rioting and looting was not only deeply complex but moreover, and perhaps ironically, it forced public debates on social, cultural and economic issues in society that require political responses through public policy measures. Members of Parliament (MPs) were recalled to parliament from their holidays, the press and broadcasting media debated the horrors of looting and asked questions such as, why has this happened? The BBC's political flagship programme 'Question Time', not due to return until September 2011, aired an emergency programme on 11 August 2011 and it was clear from the questions and responses of the audience how complex this issue was, and that it clearly represented a divided British society, but placed firmly in the context of the credit crisis, banking crisis and the issues concerning the MPs' scandal, and the immorality behind the phone hacking scandal under investigation at the time. Channel 4 also aired a special programme on 13 August 2011 called 'Street Riots: The Live Debate' and the BBC's other flagship current affairs programme, *Panorama* screened 'The August Riots', 15 August 2011, all detailing what was termed the 'worst civil unrest for decades' in the United Kingdom. The issue that Britain was divided and had greater wealth differentiation between the richest and poorest since the 1930s, was not news to anyone, but the *new reality* was that social networking allowed individuals to take action.

So at this point it's perhaps wise to address the third question – what are the uses of public policy? Here at least it is intrinsically linked to the second question: how is thinking on public policy defined? It's clear from the political statements made by Cameron below that perceptions of parts of the community help shape thinking on public policy and it is correct to question perceptions as a basis for such thinking. In Chapter 1 I discussed Marsilius of Padua and claimed that his work 'has a profound impact on policy initiatives today' indicated by the 'title of the book the "defender" of the peace' with respect to how conflict can be resolved, and perhaps the riots that occurred across England in the summer of 2011, serve as a reminder of the contribution of Marsilius.

In the intervening period between July 2010 and July 2011 the idea of the Big Society had lost credibility, but the riots that occurred across England in August 2011 provided a new impetus for it. On Wednesday 25 January 2012 David Cameron gave a speech in Strasbourg on reforming the European Court of Human Rights. Responding to a question regarding the riots that occurred across England during August 2011 and the relevance of the Big Society in attempting to resolve such social conflict, Cameron outlined the key elements that underpin the idea of the Big Society, which were basically a reformulation of the original ideas. Cameron claimed in his speech to the House of Commons that the riots were not about 'poverty' but rather about 'culture' and statements concerning public policy on law and order, education and welfare were apparent:

> A culture that glorifies violence, shows disrespect to authority, and says everything about rights but nothing about responsibilities … We need more discipline in our schools. We need action to deal with the most disruptive families. And we need a criminal justice system that scores a clear, heavy line between right and wrong. In short, all the action necessary to help mend our broken society.

Cameron had emphasized and simplified the riots referring specifically to reasons pertaining to 'criminality' rather than other related social contexts. Figure 2.1 and Table 2.1 demonstrate the criminal context:

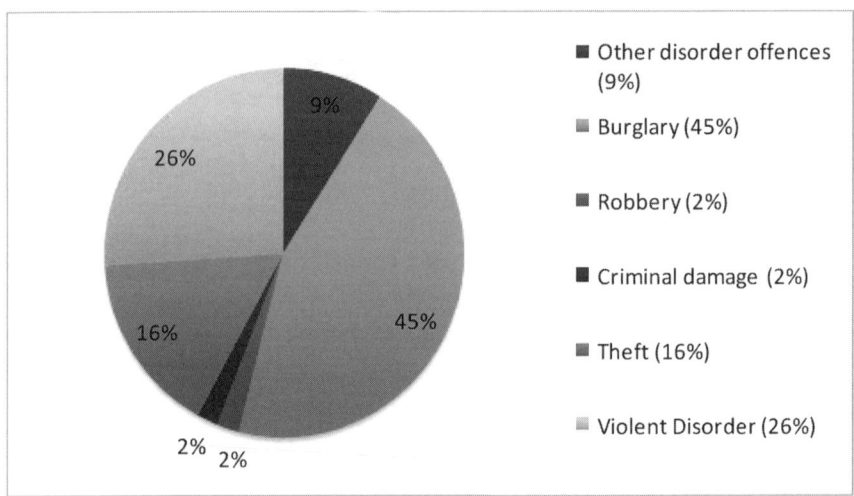

Figure 2.1[5]   **First hearings for offences relating to the public disorder between 6th and 9th August 2011 at magistrates' courts by offence category**

Table 2.1[6]   **Immediate custody rate for offences related to the disorder between 6th and 9th August (data as of midday 12th October 2011)**

Offences related to the public disorder of 6th to 9th August 2011			
Court type/Offence category	Immediate custodial sentences	Immediate custody rate for those sentenced	Immediate custody rate in England and Wales 2010 for similar offences
Magistrates'courts			
Burglary	57	50%	23%
Robbery	0	*	13%
Criminal damage	3	17%	6%
Theft	43	58%	16%
Violent disorder	27	33%	2%
Other disorder offences	9	22%	9%
Total (Magistrates')	139	42%	12%

---

5   Ministry of Justice: 'Statistical bulletin on the public disorder of 6th to 9th August 2011 – October update'. Ministry of Justice Statistics bulletin, published 24 October 2011. Reproduced with permission of the Ministry of Justice.
    6   Ibid.

Crown Court			
Burglary	124	91%	68%
Robbery	1	*	41%
Criminal damage	0	*	42%
Theft	41	75%	52%
Violent disorder	16	94%	46%
Other disorder offences	10	77%	36%
Total (Crown)	192	86%	33%

The opportunity to connect public policy strategies with the Big Society was also evident with specific reference to the volunteers within communities who sought either to protect property and livelihood and/or citizens that helped restore order:

> We saw this resolve in the people who gathered in Clapham with brooms to clean up the streets. We saw it in those who patrolled the roads in Enfield through the night to deter rioters. We saw it in the hundreds of people who stood guard outside Southall Temple, protecting it from vandalism.

Finally Cameron's narrative is couched in terms of his vision for the Big Society: 'This is a time for our country to pull together' he concluded.[7] This statement perhaps has greater resonance particularly in relation to the ethnic backgrounds of the rioters who were sentenced at court, which reflected a broad ethnic demography (see Table 2.2 below).

There are three questions I would like to pose at this juncture that can, however, be addressed collectively: Firstly, how did the riots in England 2011 further influence and broaden-out the idea of the Big Society and public policy thinking? Secondly, can the concepts such as happiness, common good, the good-life and well-being discussed in Chapter 1 be informative and decisive in shaping thinking on society in such circumstances dictated by conflict that seek to produce more harmonious social outcomes? Thirdly, what impact does economic realities, such as the debt burden and the budget deficit have upon attempts at resolving conflict through public policy and creating harmonious conditions as pursued by the Big Society idea?

---

7 'Full transcript: David Cameron Statement on public disorder House of Commons 11 August 2011', http://www.newstatesman.com/2011/08/police-streets-violence, accessed 26 January 2012.

Table 2.2[8]   Final defendant outcome at court and defendants proceeded against at magistrates' courts, found guilty and sentenced at all courts for offences relating to the public disorder of 6th to 9th August 2011, by ethnicity – data as of 12th October 2011

Final defendant outcome at court

Ethnicity	Convicted and sentenced			Not convicted	Total final outcomes
	Sentenced to immediate custody	Sentenced to non-custody	Total sentenced	Dismissed/ acquitted	
White	146	104	250	28	278
Black	112	65	177	35	212
Asian	14	8	22	3	25
Other	16	10	26	3	29
Note stated	43	33	76	2	78
Total	331	220	551	71	622

8   Ministry of Justice: 'Statistical bulletin on the public disorder of 6th to 9th August 2011 – October update'. Ministry of Justice Statistics bulletin, published 24 October 2011. Reproduced with permission of the Ministry of Justice.

Defendants proceeded against at magistrates' courts, found guilty and sentenced at all courts for offences relating to the public disorder of 6th to 9th August 2011, by ethnicity – data as of 12th October 2011

Ethnicity	First hearing	Found guilty	Sentenced	Discharge (absolute or conditional)	Fine	Community sentence	Suspended sentence	Immediate custody	Otherwise dealt with	Average custodial sentence length (Magistrates)	Average custodial sentence length (Crown)
White	726	302	250	12	11	48	19	146	14	5.4	19.1
Black	803	229	177	3	2	44	12	112	4	5.7	17.0
Asian	116	28	22	1	0	5	0	14	2	5.4	15.9
Other	84	32	26	2	1	6	1	16	0	7.8	15.6
Not stated	255	95	76	2	3	18	8	43	2	5.6	14.2
Total	1984	686	551	20	17	121	40	331	22	5.7	17.4

It's worth bearing in mind that the Big Society idea was borne out of the economic problems confronting the United Kingdom and not problematic social and cultural issues in society. Cameron's Big Society idea however now came in direct conflict with what he now referred to as the 'broken society': 'David Cameron has said tackling the "broken society" is back at the top of his agenda following last week's riots' (BBC 15 August 2011).[9] Further to this, 'David Cameron is promising a "social fightback" in response to the rioting and looting in England last week. The prime minister says he's determined to take on long-standing social problems'. Cameron, like his predecessor Prime Minister John Major, spoke of a 'moral collapse' but perhaps more importantly for the purposes of this present chapter: 'He said he would review *all policies*, speed up plans to improve parenting and education and turn around the lives of 120,000 "troubled" families' (my italics).

The criticism and cynicism towards the idea of the Big Society is that it is an excuse to implement cuts across the public sector and other aspects of the wider economy because of the debt burden and economic deficit. Whether this is entirely true or fair is no doubt a matter for serious debate. In the context of the riots and looting that occurred across England during the summer of 2011, the Big Society was used to oppose and in part resolve the conflict that occurred. The riots were also an opportunity by the government to forward the idea of community against civil disobedience and social unrest; in sum the rioters were outsiders or the 'other' pitted against perceived social norms, accepted values and tradition – this was an opportunity to reconstruct national identity by means of the idea of the Big Society and it would impact on public policy thinking related to other important social areas such as law and order, education and health, and underpinning this was an omnipotent economic imperative.

The issues addressed here become particularly pertinent in relation to the way policies are implemented, which ordinarily will be based on both political philosophy and the perceptions of the public and the organization of society which in turn arise from political philosophical differences that condition the various ideological positions of governing bodies. So perhaps we should consider the following questions: How does each political philosophy, i.e., social democratic, conservative, liberal, neo-liberal, influence the way perceptions of the public and the organization of society work? What other forces and organizations influence political philosophy, influence or change perceptions, decision-making and implementation of public policy?

In a political system which provides legitimacy to political parties to govern through the democratic electoral process, it's easy – although not always wise to do so – to take-for-granted the subsequent belief that authority to govern is fundamentally rooted in political philosophy and ideas pertaining to various political traditions and stances, i.e., conservative, labour or in some minor and occasional instances liberal democrat in contemporary society. The ideas that

---

9   'England riots: Broken society is top priority – Cameron.'

provided each party its essence, often very distinct, in any historical sense has today given way to a far more acute-mosaic structure, which incorporates perceptions of the public as a social organism (society and communities), perceptions of public thinking and perceptions of 'others' in relation to constructs of the social organism constituted of the idea of community; in other words, such perceptions – for right or for wrong – have corrupted, or to put it more mildly, radically changed the political philosophy that provided the ideological framework and character of political parties. Indeed, one of the common accusations levelled against modern political parties is the common, rather than distinct identity of each, and their respective attempt to occupy the so-called middle ground of politics of which perceptions are visualized as the so-called 'extremes' become peripheral to the substance of ideas.

The question, to what degree such perceptions influence public policy thinking and implementation is difficult to accurately assess without clear empirical data, and as such research is much needed to assess the complex character involved in public policy thinking based on the relationship of political ideas – as a basis and starting point – and the perceptions – sometimes stereotypical, sometimes rooted in or conditioned by one's belief system – that turn thinking into implementation. The reasons it is important to ascertain a better understanding by processing empirical data is due to one: The possible conflict between original statements and claims made in a party manifesto and subsequent outcomes influenced by perceptions, two: how each party attempt to out-manoeuvre each other by use of perceptions and three: how the media as a social, cultural and political force also utilizes its own types of perceptions that conflict and/or influence government thinking on public policy. With regards to the latter, such issues are addressed in Chapter 3.

However frustrating it is presently only to theorize how perceptions may work, what I can assert is that such government perceptions are a process of analysis from a distance and they become the building blocks not only of public policy thinking and implementation, but far more importantly, perceptions become the central component of British social democratic processes. This informs us either of the inherent flaws of the political system, i.e., distance between governing and governed being one, or according to supporters of liberalized conditions it becomes a positive attribute because governments despite this distance respond to events and social conditions because of their political accountability to citizens at the ballot box. Such perceptions and the separation of government from the people is largely the reason that such concepts as happiness, common good, good life, well-being and public interest are posited as the basis for thinking about policy-making because such concepts are presented as perfectly rational, legitimate and acceptable within social democratic Britain, despite their inherent flaws, and perceptions are rooted in such conceptual frameworks.

It is informative when we realize that polling – for all its flaws, limitations and inherent unpredictability – are seen by governments as useful resources for understanding the 'public pulse' of the moment, which may change – how fickle can they be and how reliable is such data that may influence public policy thinking? This is coupled with the rise of social media and its ability to communicate to many across time and space, which governments fear – Mumsnet is but one example. The qualitative and quantitative data gathered by polling systems does however demonstrate the distinct possibility that the information gathered impacts in some form, particularly if it suits the news values of a powerful newspaper and/ or broadcasting corporation which may use it in various ways.

For instance, a YouGov poll revealed, in relation to the riots across England during the summer of 2011, that the Prime Minister, David Cameron, the Home Secretary, Theresa May, and the Mayor of London, Boris Johnson, all Tories, were unpopular due to their apparent bad handling of the riots.[10] During an interview on the BBC a representative from the Institution for Public Policy Research (IPPR), stated clearly that each will have to respond positively to the damning poll. What this demonstrates is the distinct possibility that subsequent perceptions of the public are like *shifting sands*, drifting across the political landscape and influencing political thinking in the process. The fact that perceptions of the public are always produced at a distance between the governing and governed is linked to the work of Lascoumes and Le Gales detailed above, but equally brought to public attention when a teaching assistant on the same BBC news report invited the entire Cameron family to live in Peckham, London for one week to understand and fully appreciate how poorer sections in society live, thus perhaps understanding the reasons behind why people were rioting and looting consumer goods, which they can ill afford.

One more important issue to raise here is when credit cards were first introduced into the United Kingdom in the early 1960s – an imported economic reality from the USA – this represented the expansion of global capitalism, and from there-on-in offered new opportunities for the majority of citizens to seek credit and purchase consumer goods thus boosting production through consumer demand. The American Diners Club Card was first in 1962; then followed American Express a year later in 1963, and the first British-based bank to launch a credit card was Barclays in 1968. The credit card 'revolution' was expanded during the time of the Cold War between the West and the USSR and thus also represented a clear signal to the latter that capitalism was able to expand exponentially where the latter represented pure economic stagnation. The fact the latter is true cannot be disputed, having witnessed the inevitable decline and collapse of Stalinism in 1989; the point that the former is false is ironic as the old USSR and its satellites saw no alternative to capitalism. What does all this mean for public policy in capitalist United Kingdom? The limit of credit for many citizens and the withdrawal of credit for poorer sections of society clearly represents a retraction of the 'golden age' of credit and capitalist expansion in the 1960s, and the credit and banking crisis, has impacted upon the way public policy thinking is enacted in the UK, and represents a radical rethink of how public policy will cope with economic instability in the West.

---

10   *The Guardian*, 11 August 2011, titled 'UK riots: Commons debate as it happened', accessed 12 December 2011.

Education, Equality and Social Mobility

In the aftermath of the riots during the summer of 2011, the Ministry of Justice published a paper soberly titled 'Statistical bulletin on the public disorder of 6th to 9th August 2011 – October update' (24 October 2011) with the Department of Education and the Department of Works and Pensions involved. Under the section 'Socio-economic and educational factors' the report states:

- 35 per cent of adults were claiming an out of work benefit at the time of the disorder (compared to 12 per cent of the working age population in England in February 2011. 45 per cent of all offenders who were sentenced for an indictable offence in 2010 were claiming benefits).
- 42 per cent of young people were in receipt of Free School Meals (compared to 16 per cent of all pupils in maintained secondary schools).
- Young people appearing before the courts came disproportionately from areas with high levels of deprivation as defined by the Income Deprivation Affecting Children Indices 2010. 64 per cent of 10–17 year olds for whom matched data were available lived in one of the 20 per cent most deprived areas whilst only three per cent lived in one of the 20 per cent least deprived areas.

Under sub-section titled 'Educational factors' it continued:

- 66 per cent of juveniles were classified as having some form of special educational need (compared to 21 per cent of all pupils in maintained secondary schools).
- Over a third (36 per cent) of juveniles were identified as having had at least one fixed period exclusion from school during 2009/10 (compared to 6 per cent of all Year 11 pupils).

These are important findings in light of the commonly held views of leading Tory politicians that 'gang culture' was chiefly responsible, which the above undermined, but more importantly the report concluded:

> Overall, these analysis show that the individuals brought before the courts had a complex set of characteristics (age, previous criminal history, socio-economic background and education), with no one factor standing. It is clear that compared to population averages, those brought before the courts were more likely to be in receipts of Free School meals or benefits, were more likely to have had special educational needs and be absent from school, and more likely to have some form of criminal history. It is important to note that none of the factors explored imply causality with the public disorder events, but provide a deeper background understanding of the characteristics of those brought before the courts.

Data specific to absence rates and attainment of grades in English and Mathematics were also revealing, indicated in Figures 2.2 (below) and 2.3 (opposite):

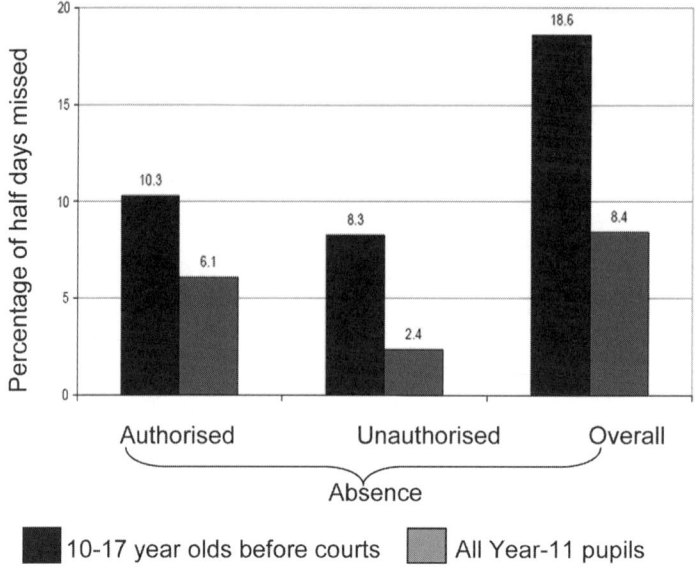

Figure 2.2[11] **Absence rates among 10–17 year olds appearing before courts. Comparison with all Year 11 pupils in maintained secondary schools in 2009/10**

In early 2011 key reforms were introduced to the educational policy by the conservative led coalition government aimed to address 'equality' and 'social mobility'. The English Baccalaureate (Ebacc) was partly introduced to address the issue that children from lower income families and poorer backgrounds were failing to study 'traditional subjects' that subsequently disadvantaged them from attaining places in the higher universities, thus linking equality to social mobility:

> In May, schools minister Nick Gibb told MPs that the Ebacc was a 'key component' in the 'overall objective of closing the attainment gap between wealthier and poorer children' (*The Guardian*, 28 July 2011, titled 'MPs, teachers and academics criticises education reform plan').

---

11   Ministry of Justice: 'Statistical bulletin on the public disorder of 6th to 9th August 2011 – October update'. Ministry of Justice Statistics bulletin, published 24 October 2011. Reproduced with permission of the Ministry of Justice.

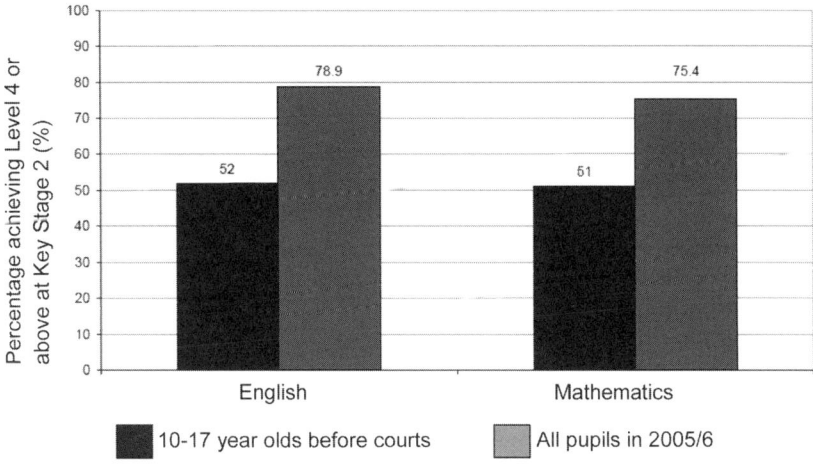

Figure 2.3[12] **Proportion of 10–17 year olds appearing before courts achieving Level 4 or above in English and Mathematics at National Curriculum Key Stage 2 tests. Comparison with all pupils in 2005/06**

The government's social mobility tsar, former Labour Party MP, Alan Milburn began reviewing equality and social mobility under the coalition government and placed education at the centre of the review. Introduced by Labour Prime Minister Gordon Brown, Milburn chaired a cross-party committee and reported that 'social mobility must be the top priority for any government, now and in the future' (*The Independent*, 21 July 2009, titled 'Alan Milburn: "End old-school-tie elitism over jobs"').

The issue concerning education and equality has been previously addressed by Wexler (1991: ix) in his analysis which begins thus:

> Over the past two decades, radical traditions in both the sociology of education and curriculum studies have drawn upon each other to build a critical analysis of education. They have focused increasingly on the complicated relationship between curriculum, teaching and evaluation in schools and the structures of *inequality* in the larger society (my emphasis).

One particular issue concerning education policy – and by definition equality and social mobility – and implementation, is the impact that economic realities have on both political and moral-philosophical thinking. In Marginson's (1993: xii)

---

12   Ibid.

study of education and public policy in Australia the author states: 'My concern was that economics (economic thinking and economic practices) had seized the role of master discourse in education policy, pushing aside other understandings of education', and that the aim was to argue the 'essential mission' of 'education' against what Marginson termed 'economic rationalism' (ibid.). It is perhaps stating the obvious that in any system the economy, monies available or what are termed 'fiscal restraints' impact upon ideas and implementation of public policies.

The economic ups and downturns associated with capitalism in general invariably impact upon public policy, and in this context, the debt crisis was used by the conservative led coalition as justification for placing restrictive measures on many areas of education, from canceling new school builds, inherited from the previous Labour government to introducing higher fees for university students. That said, in times of crisis, as in the August 2011 riots or civil unrest, perceptions of public thinking, coupled with political opportunism to make gains over the opposition, re-engages morality and political philosophy, and although fiscal realities remain *the* conditioning framework for thinking, morality however, is thrust centre-stage to justify policy initiatives. One additional combination of elements to consider, is the roles that Public Relations, Political Spin, and the news media who are sympathetic to new public policy thinking have in helping to enforce a new morality, over combating the problems associated with the riots; education, and in this present context, rates of illiteracy amongst children and adults became a central moral issue concerning the events in August 2011. Literacy is broader than simply being able to read and write as The National Literacy Trust document *Literacy: State of the Nation* reminds us:

> Literacy is the combination of reading, writing, speaking and listening skills we all need to fulfil our potential. These life skills are essential to the *happiness*, health and wealth of individuals and society (my italics).

These are indeed noble aims, but the fact that the United Kingdom under capitalist economic relations has failed to achieve this idea in a universal sense, only reinforces criticisms of the futility of public policy initiatives if the economic relations of production and at the very least, the redistribution of wealth are not confronted in any radical way. The failure to achieve universal literacy in one of the world's richest nations is telling and in 1999 The Basic Skills Agency claimed that almost one-fifth or seven million adults were illiterate in England and a year later a United Nations survey provided an identical figure across the United Kingdom. Perhaps the following quote is informative of what may lay ahead, reported by the BBC in 2000 headlined 'One in five adults "illiterate"':

> Andy Westwood, a spokesman for the Employment Policy Institute, said of the UK's illiteracy: 'It is going to get worse for people who are functionally illiterate because the types of entry requirements in low skilled jobs are going to increase.'

Further the BBC reported the following:

> The report found that the US had the highest level of 'human poverty' – relating
> to life expectancy, illiteracy and unemployment – among industrialised nations,
> followed closely by the UK and the Irish Republic.

Many of these issues were addressed by the Panel on Fair Access to the
Professions, an independent cross party panel, created from the *New Opportunities*
White Paper in 2009. Publishing a document titled 'Unleashing Aspiration:
The Final Report of the Panel on Fair Access to the Professions' in July 2009
a number of recommendations by the panel were made (see Annex B Table of
Recommendations), one of which set-out 'Social mobility as the overarching
social policy priority'. The only issue is that the Panel sat as a consequence of an
'economic upturn' – illusory or otherwise – as the then Labour government had
stated in the White Paper document.

As detailed above in the National Literacy Trust's document, literacy and
education is intrinsically linked to 'health' which in turn is intrinsically linked to
'happiness' and to add another term, 'well-being', and perhaps even, 'contentment'.
In Chapter 1, we saw how 'well-being' and 'happiness' are objectives of what is
often termed as the good society and for achieving the 'common good' and this
can be central to the relationship between education and work – as in the protestant
work ethic to do good and live a moral life.

Bills (2004) study details the relationship between education and work and
contextualizes it as a process of 'socialization' between the two social institutions.
Parsons (1959) structuralist-functionalist approach perceived education as
a mediating institution between the moral sphere of the family and society.
Amongst many other things, education served to establish 'moral norms' for
society to function properly. 'Goal attainment' – the idea of social and political
objectives under capitalist relations – was for Parsons central to education. So
too was 'pattern maintenance and tension management', which were methods
used to resolve differences, particularly aggressive conflict through the process of
reason. Overall, education as Bills alludes to above was an institution on which
'integration' of subjects – 'socialization' – would be effectively achieved. The use
of the term 'feral youth' applied to the rioters, is a pejorative term meaning *lack of
education* and predominantly 'work-shy'.

In this context the purpose of education comes to the fore to reveal the
contradictions in establishing education as a moral imperative. Educational
processes – content-based – vary, accommodating conformism and critique.
Political intentions, objectives and means as a basis for learning, particularly
whereby social integration is prioritized, do not always correlate with the end
product; this is why discipline is installed in order to enact conformity to rule. In
sum despite the best attempts at policy measures to address conflict the fact is;
education is riddled with paradoxes, intentionally or otherwise.

Jean Floud's 1960's study on the 'sociology of education' remains revealing for highlighting the complexities in education in 'industrial society' detailing the role of education in relation to labour. Floud highlights how 'opportunities in the labour market' (1968: 238) are changing and how sociological data is 'indispensable to policy-making in both education and economics' (ibid.) whilst also focusing on the role of education as a process of 'assimilation':

> Margaret Mead and Karl Mannheim, each in their different ways, have insisted on the need for sociologists to take account of the educative implications of all our social arrangements in order to gain a complete picture of the process of assimilation of each individual to a cultural tradition (ibid: 246).

Today the sociology of education is no longer rooted in an industrial context but rather a post-industrial context, with a debt burden, increasing unemployment and a global crisis in capitalism, which conditions new thinking on public policy, hence the Big Society idea and its controversial emphasis on 'volunteering' in the workplace; otherwise known as unpaid labour. It is however in this context that Floud's research remains pertinent.

Law and Order: Causes of Conflict

Understanding root causes of riots or conflict is central to thinking about public policy, if not always convincing in outcomes; what impact does rioting have on politicians that stereotype people who participate and what impact does this have on the perceptions of politicians which act as a basis for thinking about policy? Following on from this Dominic Casciani, the Home Affairs Correspondent at the BBC asked:

> So what do we know with certainty about the rioters and looters? Are they a criminal, feral underclass or victims of socio-economic blight getting their own back on the rest of society?[13]

Similarly, a study titled 'Reading the Riots' sponsored by the Joseph Rowntree Foundation and Open Society Foundation, conducted by the London School of Economics and *The Guardian* detailed more complex findings than first assumed. Head of research, Tim Newburn stated:

> It reveals the anger and frustration felt by those who were involved in the disorder, in part a product of the unfair and discourteous treatment they feel they suffer at the hands of the police, but also reflecting the disillusionment many feel

---

13   'Analysis: The riots data so far', http://www.bbc.co.uk/news/uk-14931987, accessed 18 January 2012.

at the social and economic changes which leave them increasingly disconnected from mainstream society.

Summing-up the findings, Newburn articulated two important points:

- Rioters identified a range of political grievances, but at the heart of their complaints was a pervasive sense of injustice. For some this was economic – the lack of money, jobs or opportunity. For others it was more broadly social – how they felt they were treated compared with others.
- Gangs behaved in an entirely atypical manner for the duration of the riots, temporarily suspending hostilities with their postcode rivals. However on the whole, the role of gangs in the riots has been significantly overstated by the government.[14]

The 'economic' and 'social' issues raised in the first point are the two main issues used in the Marxist theory of conflict ('conflict theory'), which broadly speaking maintains that capitalism has inherent contradictions such as economic and social inequalities that become the cause of conflict and rioting. For the Tory led coalition government the Big Society idea is an attempt to implement public policies which seek to resolve such conflict. In fact, public policy in any guise attempts to achieve this, i.e., to create a better sense of well-being, happiness and contentment that purports to the common good theory which further acts in the public interest. Conflict, is seen as not in the public interest; contravenes the common good, denotes unhappiness – unless rioting makes people happy – and is not indicative of the general and dominating view of well-being – well-being could be an outcome of rioting and looting however if the perpetrator believes one's life has been significantly enhanced by stealing a plasma television set that makes viewing more enjoyable than previous.

The point here, however, is that Marxists argue that public policy is unable to absolutely resolve conflict in a system entrenched in class division with discrepancies in wealth and opportunities in society; public policy is the cushion sometimes used to soften the blow of such reality and the point of politics is to convince by rhetoric the case for reform. Broadly Marx's emphasis on conflict is based on the following:

- Stratified societies contain divided social groups.
- The ruling class derives power from economic ownership and control of industrial forms.
- The ruling class exploit other less-powerful groups in society to extract a surplus.
- This inevitably produces social tensions and leads to conflict.

---

14 'LSE and *Guardian* study finds anger with police fuelled summer riots', http://www2.lse.ac.uk/newsAndMedia/news/archives/2011/12/riots.aspx, accessed 19 January 2012.

It is in this context that the Marxist philosopher Louis Althusser argued that educational establishments in capitalist systems are a crucial part of the 'Ideological State Apparatus' attempting to induce a system of conformity and thus attempting to reduce resistance to established norms. Indeed, the 'state of nature' premise forwarded by the English philosopher Thomas Hobbes in *Leviathan* (1651) was based on reducing conflict and planting the seeds of order by legitimizing a strong central government.

Curfews and Virtual Prisons

On 11 August 2011, the Home Secretary Theresa May gave a speech to the House of Commons on the riots:

> Mr Speaker, the last five days have been a dark time for everybody who cares about their community and their country. Violence, arson and looting in several of our towns and cities – often openly in front of television cameras – has destroyed homes, ruined livelihoods and taken lives. As long as we wish to call ourselves a civilised society, such disorder has no place in Britain.

May, like Cameron, also reduced the rioting to a limited source: 'Why does a violent gang culture exist in so many of our towns and cities?' and laid the foundation of new public policy asking: 'Why did the police find it so hard to prevent or contain the violence'? May added: 'we will also look at the use of existing dispersal powers and whether any wider power of *curfew* is necessary' (my italics).

On 13 October 2011, the Home Office produced a new paper titled 'Consultation on police powers to be launched', sub-headed: 'Proposed police powers to remove face coverings and impose curfews are being put to public consultation', stating:

> The Home Office today launched the study to consider how to give officers more tools to tackle disorder in the light of the summer riots. It comes as the Home Secretary hosts an international forum as part of the cross-government work she is leading on gangs and serious youth violence. The police, the public and campaigners will be asked for their views on the proposed new powers and the best way to introduce them. Consultation questions are also being posed on Section 5 of the Public Order Act, which makes 'insulting' behaviour a criminal offence.

On 25 August 2011 there was a '"Constructive" social media meeting':

> Facebook, Twitter and Blackberry messenger were among those discussing cooperation with law enforcement agencies in situations where networks are being used for criminal behaviour. A Home Office spokesperson explained: 'The Home Secretary, along with the Culture Secretary and Foreign Office Minister Jeremy Browne, has held a constructive meeting with ACPO, the police and representatives from the social media industry. The discussions looked at how

law enforcement and the networks can build on the existing relationships and cooperation to crack down on the networks being used for criminal behaviour.'

In an attempt to tighten-up curfew laws it was announced on 24 February 2012 that 'virtual prisons' could be introduced in an attempt to strengthen community sentencing by using electronic tags and keeping individuals in their homes for 16 hours. This measure has in fact deep roots in English philosophy regarding moral behaviour and correction. Jeremy Bentham's 'panopticon or correction house' produced late 18th century was a proposal for a new penitentiary system based on surveillance. Bentham's 'inspection principle' was based on the idea that the 'watchman' would never be seen, thus the 'watched' would in theory be subject to not ever knowing if the 'watchman' was ever there. The panoptic vision was based on a perpendicular prison, and Bentham argued that the costs would be low because staff levels would be lower than prisons at the time. Using Foucault's idea of panopticon as a metaphor for increased surveillance, it's reasonable to argue that the newly developed 'virtual prisons' are exactly that, and are certainly cost-effective in the tradition of Bentham's writings.

Blair Gibbs, Head of Policy Exchange's Crime & Justice Unit – a conservative think-tank – argued for a tougher community sentencing system.[15] This is based on the idea that the conservative party need to be seen by the public as tough on crime. The conservative Lord Ashcroft Report[16] – an opinion poll – found that four-fifths of the public polled believed that community sentencing was a soft option.[17] Nick Nye, Director of the market research group, Populus claimed that in the latest poll on public opinion three-quarters of those polled believed the coalition government to be 'no tougher on crime than the previous government' and that there was 'a desire for the government to be tougher on crime particularly since the *riots* last summer'[18] (my italics). Such polls, for all their weaknesses, particularly being a 'snapshot', nevertheless help shape perceptions of public thinking and subsequently shape thinking on policy. The virtual prisons idea therefore is a response to what 'some' citizens – presented as 'public opinion' – believe to be soft community sentencing.[19]

---

15   See BBC Newsnight, 24 February 2011.

16   Lord Ashcroft is a Tory donor.

17   Op. cit.

18   Ibid.

19   Judges and magistrates would also have the power to confiscate passports and driving licences.

Chapter 3

News Media Representations and Discourse of Public Policy

News and Public Interest

The *Sunday Times* (25 March 2012) front page detailed an investigation into the former Tory fundraiser, Peter Cruddas, who had claimed on camera that the Prime Minister, David Cameron hosted private meals at Downing Street and Chequers attended by people who had donated millions to the Conservative Party. This became known as the 'cash-for-access' scandal. In this one act, the *Sunday Times* owner Rupert Murdoch had sent a simple reminder to all British political parties post-phone-hacking scandal, which appeared to have loosened Murdoch's power and influence over British political parties that he continued to yield great power and authority over news discourse, public opinion and in this context, indirect influence over government thinking: the message was very clear.

Cameron was embarrassed by the publicity and was forced to publically provide details of those who had attended dinner with him; something he had not wished to do. Murdoch had forced his hand and on the following day (26 March 2012) wrote gleefully on Twitter: 'Great Sunday Times scoop. What was Cameron thinking? No-one, rightly or wrongly, will believe his story.'[1] Cameron and Tory grandees such as Francis Maude rebuked the accusation that private individuals making donations to the Tory party could influence public policy. However, three questions pertinent here are one, does the news media influence public policy? Two, what is the relationship between the political sphere of public policy debate and news media? Three, how are news representations on public policy produced, and what is their impact on shaping public opinion?

Chapter 1 detailed how public policy is linked to a history of ideas in Western philosophical thought dating back to Plato and that in modern societies, public policy is determined by government and mostly justified in what is termed the public interest. The public interest principle can be effectively traced back to Aristotle's *Politics* thus having a long history and in doing so is an established cultural tradition, one which forms an essential part of Western systems. The idea of the public interest principle is a problematic principle in so far as effectively established principles that satisfy the wishes, needs and requirements of any given society are constituted of a complex matrix of individuals whereby at times

---

1   http://news.sky.com/home/politics/article/16196151, accessed 28 March 2012.

such needs may conflict, depending on a number of issues such as ideological differences, moral perspectives and economic capital.

Nevertheless, despite such complexities policies develop, and *in part* they do so based on the key concepts discussed in Chapter 1. For instance in relation to happiness, well-being and policy thinking an article titled 'The miserable rich – Europe's wellbeing drops as incomes rise' (*The Guardian*, 16 November 2010) written by the social affairs editor, Randeep Ramesh, detailed how the coalition government, aim to pursue happiness and well-being as markers for policy thinking. Surveys organized by the Office of National Statistics (ONS) would include data on both happiness and well-being. In the same edition article headlined 'The greatest unhappiness for the greatest number', Polly Toynbee stated: 'The less equal a society, the more unhappy it is. For David Cameron to talk of a wellbeing index is really hard to swallow.' Attached to the article was a small item by Clare Carlisle worth repeating in full to illustrate the fluidity of the history of ideas in a contemporary context:

> In the Western philosophical tradition, reflections on what the best kind of life might be have almost always acknowledged that happiness is something we all desire. Philosophers often regard human happiness as an important criterion for deciding what is good and what is right, and sometimes as the main criterion. The most straightforward expression of this last view is found in the 'utilitarian' moral theory pioneered in England in the 19th century.

Happiness and well-being are contextualized initially by government within a political and philosophical context often justifying it in the public interest and the common good. Historically philosophers and later politicians held influence over their respective meaning; in modern times such hegemony is contested, mainly by the mainstream media, because of its ability to communicate ideas from a position of power, but also because the principle of public interest in particular, often has a different meaning in the news media; this has a profound impact on the changing character of happiness, well-being and the common good; the public interest thus becomes subversive as the following quote indicates:

> Habermas' reformulation of the public sphere idea makes its relevance to current debates about the social and political role of the media even more evident, but even the earlier formulation, as many of its critics admit, still has much to contribute to topics such as … the media and *public interest*, spin and opinion management (Petley 2012: 150) (my italics).

Political 'spin' and 'opinion management' are modern techniques employed by political parties to ensure *their* voices are heard in the press, but spin and opinion management sometimes conflict with the news medias' interests or to put it another way what *they the media* believe to be in the public interest. In relation to news media the public interest is equally problematic summed up here under the sub-heading 'The public interest: a definition?' in Morrison and Svennevig's (2002: 7) study where they state: 'Prior to the interviews, professional codes of practice and regulatory guidelines from a number of different countries were studied. None contained what could be termed a formal definition of "the public interest", although the term itself was virtually universal.'

So, the principle of the public interest as a basis to govern and justify policies becomes even more complex and complicated when we introduce the news media into the equation because the news media justifies the production of content – its own form of decision-making – on a public interest principle and they do this mostly by addressing *an audience* – amongst other audiences – or loyal readers which they claim to serve. In a sense, and this is limited to a small number of media organizations, there exists varying perceptions of how the public interest is compiled, and this is often connected to the news values that form the basis of content and representation.

One further and obvious point is to recognize that whilst government, when elected, mostly have a clear mandate to rule, the media does not, however news media reports, news discourse or news media representations of public policy sometimes conflict or even support government policy initiatives which either have the potential to disrupt legitimate government mandate to rule or help forge through policy by influencing readers and/or viewers of news representations. Such news representations in general are defended on the basis of free speech and economic rights to ownership under mostly liberal political philosophical rationale, but such freedoms are limited to a small number of news media outlets, who equally have a limited and self-determined vision of the public interest principle that relates simultaneously to free speech and powerful media interests.

In Chapter 1, the Catholic Worker's view of the public interest principle was negative, preferring to use the common good principle on which to base policy thinking and this contrasted with PIRC's and PIRN's positive view of the public interest – the latter offered a definition. The news media has used the public interest principle in a different way to all the previous, for it includes free speech and independence from state intervention in news practice; this is also seen to be in the public interest for the news media is free to expose wrongdoing. But it equally suits news media to have a broad and even vague understanding of the public interest, giving it more room to operate and ethically justify content.

In reality, the public interest principle is a tool to win the battle for hearts and minds in civil society; the battle for hearts and minds or to paraphrase Milan Kundera, 'competing for the public's ear', is one based on different elements and competing interests of media organizations as well as various non-governmental organizations within society, and is a battle on two fronts; the first is for public attention and the second is for government attention on which legislation rests. The struggle to persuade both the public and government thinking takes place primarily within civil society and principally forms a crucial part of the public communicative space, particularly in relation to how communication seeks to inform on issues and how news representation and discourse seeks to assert itself in the political sphere. This is perhaps the main departure from the historical debate discussed in Chapter 1 concerning theorizing public policy in relation to the concepts discussed therein. However, for the time-being, such historical notions such as the common good, well-being, happiness and public interest continue to play important roles in determining public policy; the essential difference is the additional role media organizations and perhaps influential and powerful individuals attached to political parties play in helping to shape such philosophical thinking on the these conceptual frameworks, which perhaps reinforces, reshapes or indeed corrupts them.

In the previous chapter it was seen that the Public Interest Research Centre (PIRC) operate within the public interest principle in relation to climate change and that such organizations operate within civil society in a struggle with media over communicating information that influences public and government thinking on public policy. This struggle for hearts and minds is demonstrated in a piece titled 'No pressure: An ill-advised piece of climate change communication' and on PIRC's website there is reference to the Daily Telegraph's 'far-right conspiracy theorist James Delingpole' as he's described in relation to the causes of climate change, and this polarity of differences over climate change doesn't take into consideration the role of misinformation and/or black propaganda deliberately placed in the public domain to discredit one side or the other. Oil companies have often been accused of doing just this and the documentary filmmaker Martin Durkin who produced The Great Climate Change Swindle was said to have been financed by business with oil connections. Here then is one example of how the public interest is entwined with news discourse that attempts to persuade both public opinion and condition government thinking on public policy.

Equally, in Chapter 2 we saw how the Public Interest Research Network (PIRN) offered a definition of the public interest but also added the following which represents the struggle over communicating messages in the public interest:

> It is clear that the neo-liberal revolution in global society has been accomplished in part by the waging of the battle of ideas for the best part of 70 years. This battle has succeeded in undermining the practice of democracy and ensuring the dominance of corporations and market friendly politicians. We recognise that the defence of the public interest requires that we engage in the battle of ideas to establish greater democratic control over political and economic decision-making.

The 'dominance of corporations' clearly include the mainstream media who are seen to have more influence over public and government thinking and that the 'battle of ideas' are played out in civil society not only in defining the public interest but over the character of public policy.

In an article titled 'This media tribe disfigures public life'[2] (*Guardian* 16 June 2005) tagged: 'Humanity, imagination and a real sense of community are what is needed to rescue journalism from its parallel universe' the then Archbishop of Canterbury, Rowan Williams based on a lecture titled 'The Media: Public Interest and Common Good' given at Lambeth Palace on 15 June 2005 wrote: 'One of the most powerful defences the media can offer for controversial actions is, of course, public interest.' Other striking comments were based on news media exposing stories: 'revelation in the public interest ought to be the same as working for the common good – the journalist in the service of active democracy.' This succinctly unites the news media usage of a 'public interest defence' and the politically and morally motivated notion of the 'common good' of which public policy can be based. In sum, the news media, for all its unaccountability – unlike democratically elected governments – are ethically justified in revealing issues that may then influence government thinking on policy by appealing to the public via news. However, news representations, of which I will be attending to next, are not always produced in 'service of active democracy' as Williams' stated. To be fair, Williams recognized this, hence his title.

The Riots as News Representation

Public policy as a defined principle or concept is the starting point for its legitimate and rational application that is central to modern day social democratic systems, but the way or manner it becomes a reality *is* the 'process', and this process can be affected by other un-elected bodies such as the news media. Whether such interference, if I may use that word, radically alters the definition of public policy is of interest, but when such involvement by an un-elected media body changes the trajectory of the process, by whatever means, then perhaps we begin to question the purpose of government, social/representative democracy and indeed the news media in relation to public policy and more importantly specifically in relation to the way in which the process is framed for public consumption and this becomes of interest and acute in systems where ownership of mainstream media organizations are limited to a small number of powerful individuals.

The riots of 2011 created a reaction by government and by media; the political and news media discourse therein turns into a communicative space to sway public opinion, but mostly it was simplified rhetoric for what was in fact a complex set of events – for rioting is conflict:

> Conflict is complex. It does not happen just because people are unhappy or greedy, because a country has resources to sustain it, or because state and social institutions are weak or perverse. It happens when causes at multiple levels come

2   http://www.guardian.co.uk/media/2005/jun/16/pressandpublishing.religion, accessed 15 March 2012.

together and reinforce one another. It is the product of deep grievances, political and economic competition, irresponsible leadership, weak and unaccountable institutions, and global and regional forces (USAID 'Mitigating and Managing Conflict').

Under the subheading 'Understanding Conflict and the Politics of Identity' USAID continue: 'In trying to understand how and when identity turns violent, research has focused on competition, inequality, and discrimination between groups.' These quotes aren't directed at 'home based' or 'national conflict' (UK included) but rather concerns 'foreign aid' and 'international conflict' and what is liberally termed 'conflict reduction', which is a set of international policies designed, but not always successfully to reduce conflict; national public policy is the twin. What is also referred to as 'conflict reporting' is equally usually a Western term for reporting war based conflicts. However, there is no reason or no doubt in my mind that the USAID quote is equally applicable to home based civil unrest – as a form of conflict – and that 'conflict reporting' is a term that can – or *should* – equally be applied to national conflict, in the sense of reporting in the context of the Marxist notion of class and conflict theory.

Therefore, taking USAID's correct analysis, 'Conflict is complex', as the starting point for a discussion on news representations of the riots, let's assess the following examples to see if such complexity is apparent.

The *Daily Mail* report (12 August 2011) headlined 'Child looters they can't lock up: Rioters aged 11 and 12 let off with slap on the wrist' stated:

> A smirking youngster who hurled stones at shop windows at the height of violence in Nottingham told police she 'wasn't bothered' when she was arrested. That contempt was displayed at Nottingham magistrates again yesterday as she refused to apologise for her actions. Even as prosecutor Sumaiya Saeedullah outlined the case, the girl, who cannot be named because of her age, took little interest in proceedings, chatting with court staff and smiling.

On 19 September 2011 the *Mail* followed this up with the following headline and tag:

> 'Tagging rioters instead of jailing them "would have saved £2.4m"'
> * Releasing a defendant on an electronic tag instead of remanding them in custody saves £110 a day
> * Average cost of curfew is just £13
> * More than 700 people have been on remand since first post-riot statistics were published last month.

The end of the text stated:

G4S, the private security firm which runs one of the UK's tagging schemes, said the average operational cost of a curfew was just £13 per day, compared with £123 per day to hold someone in custody, based on a yearly average cost per prison place of £45,000.

On 17 September 2011 the *Mail* produced the following headline with the tag below:

'11-year-old boy handed a rehab order after riots was caught shoplifting just six days later'
- 'Young rioter "should be taken away from his parents", says Tory MP.'

At the end of the report the paper stated:

yesterday Tory MP for Romford Andrew Rosindell said the youngster needed a 'short sharp shock'. 'We need harsher penalties. You've got to make people fear the punishment so they don't commit the crime,' he added. 'What are his parents doing to allow their child to behave in such a way? He needs to be taken away from his parents for six months.'

The *Daily Express* (25 October 2011) headlined 'NEARLY HALF OF RIOT THUGS ARE PAID BENEFITS' wrote:

Emma Boon, of campaign group the TaxPayers' Alliance, said: 'These troublemakers give a bad name to those who need a bit of help because they've fallen on hard times. Those who have damaged public property or cost taxpayers money in some other way should be made to pay that back or have some of their benefits withheld.'

In the *Express* (22 October 2011) headlined: 'FINALLY, A JUDGE WHO UNDERSTANDS JUSTICE' it began with a reference to the popular celebrity Richard Madeley:

RICHARD SAYS: FOUR cheers for the Lord Chief Justice, the amusingly named Lord Judge. This week he showed he absolutely 'gets it' where this summer's riots are concerned.

The article concerned two men from Cheshire, Jordan Blackshawe and Perry Sutcliffe-Keenan, both of which received four years imprisonment for 'trying to incite a riot via Facebook'.

They are paying a very high price for their greed and foolishness. But Lord Judge is right. Rarely in modern times has the principle of deterrence in sentencing been so vital to the *public good*. We cannot see a repeat of mindless rioting and looting on such an epic scale: people weak-minded enough to be tempted to join in anything similar in future will now realise there is a serious risk of them doing jail time. ('foolishness' and 'mindless' were originally in black bold text to emphasize the point) (my italics).

In response to the punishment *The Guardian* (17 August 2011) produced the following headline: 'England riots: will harsher sentences act as a deterrent?' The article stated:

> The four-year sentences are the longest passed so far relating to the riots, and the fact that no one turned up to the riots in those locations, apart from the police, has sparked fierce controversy.

The Sun (12 March 2012) produced the headline: 'WITH police clamouring to be allowed water cannons to quell civil unrest, what would it be like for the rioters on the receiving end?' It stated:

> Cops have the heavy hoses on a wish list of equipment, along with Tasers and tear gas, after the nationwide mayhem in August last year.

> The Government have suggested they will give the nod to three £1.3million water cannon vehicles.

The Sun (21 December 2011) headlined: 'Police OK to shoot rioters' stated:

> COPS could shoot rioters who start fires that threaten life, a watchdog said yesterday. Water cannon and rubber bullets could also be used to stop a repeat of the summer disturbances. Live rounds could be used by gun cops against arsonists who torch businesses and homes with people inside, reported HM Inspectorate of Constabulary. (The opening sentence was originally in black bold to emphasize the point.)

The Sun (15 March 2012) headline: 'Cops could use CS gas to stop rioters, says Met report' stating: 'A Met review into the trouble, entitled Four Days in August, admits some people felt police failed to help them or stop the destruction of property.'

Daily Mail (17 August 2011) headline: 'Curfews to clear mobs from the streets, vows Home Secretary after riots' also produced an 'analysis' and recommendations for the Home Secretary Theresa May such as:

- STRIP LOOTERS OF THEIR HOMES AND BENEFITS
- REWRITE HUMAN RIGHTS LAWS
- ORANGE BOILER SUITS (for community service) (language used was 'force yobs')

- NAME AND SHAME TEENAGE RIOTERS
- BLOCK TWITTER, BLACKBERRYS AND FACEBOOK
- RE-INTRODUCE NATIONAL SERVICE
- CRACK DOWN ON YOB FAMILIES
- GIVE POWERS TO DISPERSE GANGS.

The *Guardian* (13 October 2011) headline. 'Riot curfews for public proposed by Home Office' with tag: 'Home secretary Theresa May backs police power to clear streets for first time since Riot Act was repealed.' *The Sun* commissioned a YouGov survey (10–11 August 2011) concerning 'riot punishments'[3] to gauge public opinion of which perceptions of the public are sometimes made by government. Other YouGov surveys were strongly worded with 54 per cent agreeing:

> Thinking about the recent period of unrest, please say if you agree or disagree with each of the following statements.
>
> The root cause of this mindless selfishness is a complete lack of responsibility in parts of our society, people allowed to feel that the world owes them something, that their rights outweigh their responsibilities.[4]

A YouGov survey (15–16 August 2011)[5] asked: 'Would you support or oppose the following measures that have been suggested in recent days?'

- Stopping welfare benefits for people convicted of involvement in the riots (71 per cent agreed).
- Evicting families from council housing where a member of the family was involved in the riots (46 per cent agreed).
- Banning suspected rioters from social media sites like Twitter and Facebook (79 per cent agreed).

In the *Sun* YouGov survey (18 August 2011)[6] it asked 'Which of the following statements comes closest to your view …' with,

> 'The sentences given out for offences which took place during the riots SHOULD be harsher than if the offences were committed BEFORE the riots'

---

3   http://cdn.yougov.com/today_uk_import/yg-archives-pol-sun-riotpunishment severity-190811.pdf, accessed 16 March 2012.

4   http://cdn.yougov.com/today_uk_import/yg-archives-yougov-riotsstatements-180811.pdf, accessed 16 March 2012.

5   http://cdn.yougov.com/today_uk_import/yg-archives-yougov-brattonriots-170811.pdf, accessed 16 March 2012.

6   http://cdn.yougov.com/today_uk_import/yg-archives-pol-sun-riotpunishments-190811.pdf.

with 59% agreeing. (The adjectives 'SHOULD' and 'BEFORE' were presented in upper case capitals.)

Theorizing Representation

Gerston (2010) outlines two distinct and opposite schools of thought concerning public policy. The first are *Institutionalists* who 'view public policy as a benign component of identified rules and procedures.' The second school of thought are *Behaviourists* who 'interpret public policy as the result of the interaction of powerful forces, some of which may be far removed from the halls of government' (ibid: 5): this latter perspective places emphasis on interaction between various organizations who collectively condition public policy-making.

In Chapter 2 Lascoumes and Le Gales (2007) put forward a political sociology of public policy instrumentation that was critical of technical and functionalist approaches because the latter, unlike political sociology, negated power relations in the construction and dissemination of public policy initiatives. Like Gerston, this analysis falls short – ironically considering their critique of technical and functionalist approaches – because Lascoumes and Le Gales equally negate one important and influential institution in the 'power relations' the authors are so concerned with; the news media! In fact so scant is their analysis of power relations here is what they say in relation to public policy in respect of 'youth, violence against persons, and areas inhabited by immigrant communities' (ibid: 11) that any narrative is 'amplified by the media' (ibid.) and that's all is said.

This negation of media power to influence political thinking over public policy and its eventual implementation is of interest considering this statement by Lascoumes and Le Gales: 'Public policy instrumentation reveals a (fairly explicit) theorization of the relationship between the governing and the governed' (ibid: 11). But who exactly is doing the governing if we begin to consider the distinct possibility of news media influence over politicians to think about and even change minds on public policy? And furthermore, if Lascoumes and Le Gales are interested in the relationship between government and citizens, then what role does political spin play in news discourse? What are the levels of opinion management in news discourse? What is the relationship – mostly hidden from public view – between government and news proprietors that fix public discourse with the distinct view to influence public opinion on public policy? What are the media effects of this narrative? In sum, how is public communication based on the production and consumption of news information on public policy shaping public opinion?

The idea that media representations influences policy-making was dismissed as unacceptable and undemocratic by the former Foreign Minister Jack Straw: 'This place is the elected Parliament, and not the newspapers' said Straw in a BBC interview with Jon Sopel on 19 July 2011 in reference to the *News of the World* phone hacking scandal. This statement refers specifically to Parliament's democratic mandate to assert or perhaps in this context re-assert its legitimate authority based on the electoral process.

It's a re-assertion in the context that the press in general, but with particular focus on Rupert Murdoch's News Corporation at the time of writing, had far too much power not only over citizens but over government ministers and, therefore, the parliamentary process, which in-turn influenced the political philosophies of parties, the manifestos which each produced, the promises made to the electorate, and also influence over public policy thinking and implementation in society.

So how are we to understand the process of news representations and discourse? With respect to the latter this will be presented under the final section titled 'Method: Textual Analysis of News Discourse'.

News representations are a form or sub-category of representation, which is a generic term. They seek to officially speak on behalf of a community with an explicit form of identity and are realized in language and image. When rhetorical analysts claim that metaphors are an inescapable part of how we construct meaning, so is *representation*. The use of metaphor, allegory and metonymy in the construction of representation is a powerful way of expressing ideas. But when we add a third dimension to linguistic techniques and representation, which for our purpose is the notion, appearance or pretence of producing fact by objective means, then the mediation of representation takes on a different character altogether, mainly because of the legitimacy and authenticity of news content.

Underlying the production of representations is the question, *why*? What are the motives that lay behind representation in a specific-empirical context? And what bearing does the production of representation have on truth and factual reflection? Like politicians, newsmakers build up *perceptions* of community partly through market research and partly based on historical judgements concerning culture, identity and political traditions. This image of the *essence of community* often underpins content, news values, news discourse and representations. These types of representations are both the product of 'outsider' and 'insider'. Outsider in the sense that the organization adheres to its own rationale, codes and conventions and 'insider' in the sense that the production of news representations are to be seen to be formed in reflection of target audiences and core readership, thus giving news representation a high degree of authenticity and legitimacy.

The basis of representation then is based not only upon *a* view of the public, but also on a dialectical-discursive relationship with the public. In other words representation is also built on *empathy*. More often than not this idealization of a public is largely the product of a news media organization and it is through the process of representation that the image is transferred. The motive or the objective for the production of representing forms is to convince the audience of the accuracy of the form being represented and that the image of the community is reflected through representation. Quite evidently, representation of reality and reality itself are two very different aspects of the same entity and it is the former that news media organizations produce. This of course lends the form of representation a great deal of human intervention rather than something that has a natural form, and is a product of ideology and morality.

Representation is a generic term and when images of peoples and events such as the riots are mediated through media they become ideological constructs that attempt to connect, correspond and relate to the community. The *Dictionary of Philosophy* (1979: 305) describes representation as the following: '[Representation] ... refers to the theories of perception wherein the mind is believed not to have direct acquaintance with its objects, but to apprehend them through the medium of ideas that are supposed to represent those objects.'

In this context the process of representation produces specific forms of social engineering, a term normally associated with authoritarian systems, but here it exists within the social democratic empirical form. Essentially, representation manufactures and imposes distinct ways of *seeing the world* and is a part of a process in which cultural meanings occur. Representation is a social process and a fundamental feature of news production and is a way of reaching out to an audience with distinct characteristics.

Representation is a form of 'agency', to 'cause' or to 'represent' as in news agency or newspaper. More importantly there are two uses of representation that are suitable for our understanding of how news discourse is produced, for representation is both to 'describe' and 'act for'. In its denotative (signifier-literal) state, it means to 'stand-in' for something it seeks to represent, to make representation and not necessarily on a group's behalf (consent), but also by taking liberties with the description that the representative invokes. Acting for or on behalf of the community is a taken-for-granted assumption and procedure of the local press. In its connotative state, representation is to infer or 'suggest meaning' (Berger 2000: 40). Representation can be false, true or even a combination of both.

More specifically the term 'internal representation' is 'a presentation to the mind in the form of an idea or image.'[7] This is important to understand on many levels; internal representations are manifestations of understanding that journalists have and use in their daily activity. Representations become *internalized* based on an individual's relationship with many influencing factors; the news organization's perception of community is but one. There are two useful ways to explain this dialectical process between self and world. Firstly, we could use Bourdieu's theory of *habitus*, which is the 'holding frame' for understanding, recycling and the formation of thought; representation is held here or we could use Giddens' theory of 'structuration', which is the on-going construction of identity managed through the subject-object relationship. The other reason it is important to understand internal representation is because the press, for example, are only newspapers insofar that they have a subject (community) in mind to which they can pass comment on. What the concept of 'internal representation' denotes in the context of journalism is that the ideas of an individual concerning the view and

---

7   http://www.visualthesaurus.com, accessed 16 March 2012.

representation of public policy, is based on a *perception* and such *perceptions* are the basis of news discourse.

The representation of communities is in fact passed as reality and perhaps the Factist Perspective is useful for a critical approach to news discourse. As Alasuutari points out the Factist Perspective 'makes a clear-cut division between the world or reality "out there", on the one hand, and the claims made about it, on the other' (1995: 47). Representation 'stands in for something else' (Chambers 1994: 22); it replaces what Theobald, with reference to Karl Kraus, calls 'the pure water of information with the seductive perfume of the cliché' (Theobald 2000: 14). The result can result in distorted information of the original unadulterated form.

Durkheim (1964) argued that facts exist but only science and rigorous method can reveal them. Accordingly, representation is not a science, but rather it is perceived as ideological, and the idealization of community is one based on morality, loaded with intent. As Walter Benjamin argued: 'The newspaper is an instrument of power ... not only with regard to what it represents but regards to *how* it expresses it' (Benjamin quoted and translated by Theobald in Berry 2000: 12). Whilst these views on representation are valid in certain contexts, the production of news representation is not something that always replaces fact, but rather can be based on a genuine perception of community. In other words they aren't always lies or a form of deception and are therefore deeply complex to understand.

It is true however that representations are 'often based upon selective and dramatic cores of information' (Davis and Raynor 2000: 90) and in this context framing news is not only ideologically loaded, but also intrinsically limited because it excludes other information pertinent to events. Representations always attempt to connect with the target audience, what can be described as a *discursive bond*. The authors go on to state that a news item 'is based upon similarities between the *habitus*[8] of the journalist and that of the audience' (ibid: 96), and therefore journalists/editors always have their audience in mind when constructing a news item. However, the issue to consider is how *habitus* is constructed in relation to the objectives of the media organization.

Specific forms of representation can be articulated as news discourse via a particular mode of address, which is formed on the basis of a perception of cultural identity and socio-political values. The discursive process between production and consumption can be articulated as the dialectic of representation of cultural forms and the representing of a community *in* symbolic cultural forms; that is to say that a community must be seen to recognize itself in the form of representation.

Speaking to or addressing an audience and representing in a particular and distinctive manner can result in both the viability of the product in the market place with the intention of producing the idea of a particular form of news with the

---

8   Bourdieu (1977) in the *Outline of a Theory of Practice* developed the concept of *habitus*, which was an attempt to understand how ideology conditioned the subject and how that very same ideology corresponded to and conditioned objective structures.

view of transferring it to the audience and in the process convincing the audience to purchase the product because of its distinctiveness which somehow is seen to relate to the needs and interests of the readership. Therefore, the mode of address can be particularistic rather than universal in that it speaks to a target community perceived with certain interests that define their identity and sense of place.

These are examples of the symbiotic relationship that bind the audience to the press through an understanding and recognition in ideas through language structure. The newspaper is the arbiter of cultural relativism *par excellence* and it is this perception of community that is the guiding principle for a paper's mode of address; a targeted audience for its intended reception on which identity is formally and socially perceived and then recycled through representation.

Quite evidently audiences are crucial to news organizations, however if the symbiotic relationship between news and reader is to be effective a series of common and shared characteristics must be established so that the reception of what is being spoken can be acknowledged and understood. In this context Harre's (1981) 'taxonomic collective' is useful for understanding how individuals in a community have a set of cultural characteristics common to each other. This can range from language, religion, a common heritage, a geographical area or political beliefs; further to this, Hartley, although referring specifically to television discourse, has insisted that 'they need not only to represent audiences but to enter into relations with them' (1987: 127).

But as Hartley points out controlling audiences is difficult because they appear as the 'invisible mass', so institutions have to create 'invisible fictions' (ibid.) of the audience. Market research can inform us of who the audience are and what they may require, but it's not conclusive by any stretch of the imagination. However, the notion of a 'taxonomic collective' and its imagined constituent parts can provide some indication of what characteristics may be crucial in the production of news representation specific to set audiences. Further to this is the proposition that audiences are 'categories' produced by 'institutions' and are as a consequence 'socially conditioned' (Ang 1991: 3) affecting thinking and behaviour.

News representations presented to a community are attempts to perpetuate a sense of reality and are therefore statements about the legitimization of truth. Certainly, the fixed-communal view of an audience rests upon a cultural relativism, which is a form of representation and as Davis and Raynor have asserted, 'representations are constructed by particular historical institutions that enjoy greater influence than others. Representation is, after all, a process soaked with intent, purpose and power' (2000: 95). Indeed, central to the attempt at representation is the notion of an imagined community and the perpetuation of this idea as an unfounded scientific fact is what Durkheim (1964, 1976) referred to as 'ideological analysis'.

This is to argue that an idea of this type is speculative rather than a scientific fact. Ideas of this type are illusions that distort the real aspect of things and in this sense they create the 'imaginary world' (Durkheim 1964: 17). Ideas such as an imagined community and its perpetuation are preconceptions rather than actual structures of things; herein lay the role of ideology in the construction of representation. Interestingly, Durkheim did not dismiss ideology although he opposed it to sociology as a science of facts. Rather, ideology may be a distortion on truth but it nevertheless plays a central role in organizing people's understanding of their environment in policy terms.

What we have here is an approach similar to Barthes (1973) on ideology; particularly the idea that myth is a harmonizing process that effectively regulates human behaviour (mythologies). But the fundamental difference between these two thinkers is where Barthes perceived ideology as socially constructed, Durkheim, on the other hand, perceived ideology as a phenomenon inherent in the nature of humans; that in some sense ideology is an illusion derived from an innate predisposition of the human mind and fixed by habit.

To a certain degree, the perpetuation of community imagined and cultural identification have been fixed for some time. This is to propose that humans can condition and create new myths but that they become fixed as seemingly immutable laws. Media organizations may exploit this either knowingly or unknowingly, that the community has a fixed view of itself conditioned historically, located geographically, and centred by tradition through time and space. It's interesting to note that a journalist's *habitus* will affect the way in which representations are constructed. What we may term as *representational models* are applied to a given subject matter and what is more they are tools of reference reflecting a perception of community rather than a true reflection of the reality of things. Thus, a journalist's *habitus* may be constructed in such a way that the characterization of an audience becomes an accepted norm; this is a process of naturalization of which ideology and the power to enforce representation are central.

In relation to media organizational imperatives that dictate or condition representations, it may be useful to bear in mind Lerman's (1983) argument concerning legitimizing content. Lerman claims that ideas are effectively transferred through the process of 'distancing', where the dominant discourse is the 'institutional voice'. Discourse revolves around 'central structures' that organize language into a coherent form. Lerman had centred her analysis upon the 'distanced identity' (who is speaking) and the 'distanced topic' (content and meaning). Ideas that form the essence and provide a newspaper's house-style, for example, and thus sustain, naturalize and legitimize the paper's presence within the community are based upon ideological discourses. For the purpose of this chapter it is necessary to understand what role if any ideology has for the production of representation within mainstream news organizations. We cannot detach or abstract the role and function that the news media have from their material operational structures which legitimizes its productiveness; thus, we set its content within the framework of ideology and power, a reflection of critical discourse analysis, more of which is discussed under 'method' below. For example, the editorial meeting is the seat in which specific value-judgements are asserted and events pass through this process of deliberation and interpretation. Events are discussed, digested and selected on the basis of their relevance to the editorial's perception of the community, but always within legitimate organizational structures.

It's worth bearing in mind that ultimately there is a purpose to the production of news representation and that the very act of representation from a position of power is, conversely, an act of ideology as well as an act of morality. News organizations need to survive in the marketplace and therefore representation and ideology is discussed here in the sense that the press operate within limits of commodity production and consumption; what Marx (1967) referred to as the circuits of production, a perpetual reproductive process whereby ideas are set in motion through language.

The paper's viability is the projection of itself onto the community it seeks to serve and to be seen as representing symbolic forms in their interest. Thus, to operate effectively within the relations of commodity production it devises strategies for economic survival: for a product to be fetish-like it needs a legitimate platform and the concepts to be discussed in this section provide its stability. The ideas that substantiate and legitimize an organization's primary and dominant discourse are its true ideological essence and logic, and it operates within the greater structure of the capitalist economic logic of commodity production. The representation of public policy is the project for the newspapers discussed in this chapter; the economic criteria for their survival in the marketplace, is both the driving force, guiding its logic and the determination of its place in civil society. Ideology manifests itself as a facade; that is the creation of an idea that newspapers serve the interests of the community, and in doing so defends its status and identity.

Media organizations devise strategies to survive in the marketplace and they create news representations, which attempt to symbolize socio-political values. Thompson's concept concerning the 'Mediazation of Culture' is a useful way of understanding this process whereby the 'transmission of symbolic forms becomes increasingly mediated by the technical and institutional apparatuses of the media industries' (1990: 4). Ideology here refers to the very notion of how meaning is both produced and consumed to sustain 'relations of domination' (ibid: 7) and that ideology 'is meaning in the service of power' (ibid.) – and the means to transmit ideology is through *a* representation of events.

News Frames

How are we to understand the production of news representation as news discourse? By what *means* and *mechanisms* is representation created? In this section I assess journalistic techniques and strategies that constitute daily news practice, which are the basis for the production of news, and what academics refer to intellectually as *conceptual frameworks*. The first point to make is that information can stem from multiple sources which include linguistic inflections and perceptions concerning representations produced and managed by journalists. Information is then coordinated and structured from chaotic forms of information into a coherent form, which readers recognize as news. Eventually, the process of news production manifests as news discourse, but is only made coherent according to the structures and rationale of a 'news frame', which is governed by certain institutional rules inherent within the house-style of a newspaper. This contains the type of language used, and here we refer to the codes and conventions highlighted in Thompson's (1990) second characteristic of symbolic forms, the 'conventional', which reflects the perception of a community's cultural identity, and the mode of address that clearly reflects the house-style.

The final product is a news frame, but not any old news frame, but one that is identifiable to particular sources within a community and mediated by a particular medium. The important issue to understand is how media organizations attempt to attain legitimacy and acceptance as a representative force within a community and this is achieved by successfully mediating *signifying practices* that attempt to reflect a community's sense of socio-political identity; within a semiotic analysis the news frame becomes *signifier* and the content expressed therein becomes the *signified*.

News frames are a derivative of Erving Goffman's (1974) *Frame Analysis* and are closely related to 'media frames' (Bennett 1993; Edelman 1993; Entman 1993; Pan and Kosicki 1993). Although processes of journalism are discussed within 'media frames' the term 'media' is sometimes too broad to use in terms of news and journalistic practice. Journalism is not the same as the production of quiz shows or reality television for example and therefore news frames are more specific to journalism and its practice within media organizations.

Consider the following quote regarding media frames that is typical of a conflation and confusion set against 'news frames', whereby media frames are seen as 'a central organising idea or story that provides meaning to an unfolding strip of events' (Gamson and Modigliani 1987: 143). Tuchman is more specific referring to news frames as a form of journalistic practice; accordingly news frames organize social reality and are 'an essential feature of news' (1978: 193). Despite these obvious differences Scheufele who uses both of the above in an analysis of media frames refers to 'media or news frames' as if they are identical, and then dismissing any reference to 'news frames' altogether goes on to state that: 'Media frames also serve as working routines for journalists that allow journalists to quickly identify and classify information' (1999: 106). This failure to understand and distinguish differences between media (and even within *the media* different genres have various forms of practice) and news frames only serve to indicate not only the inadequacies of this research but clouds the issue further in respect of the notoriously ill-defined concept of frame analysis.

To return for one moment to the obscurity of frame analysis, the net result is that the debate over its meaning remains largely unresolved, although a starting point for discussion is that frames are a way of reproducing meaning. Goffman (1974) argued that 'primary frameworks' are socially created and efficient ways of naturalizing events. Fisher has claimed in this context that, 'The study of framing ... is the study of representation and meaning' (Fisher, 1997: 1.2). Goffman's original work on frame analysis was the study of cultural representations, but nevertheless his attention to developing frame analysis was indeed scant. What we know is that Goffman discussed two types of frames, 'natural' and 'social' with the latter requiring the intervention of human agency.

But what constitutes a news frame? What are the characteristics and practices that separate news from media frames? In my view, the underpinning logic of the social construction of news frames as opposed to media frames are the principles of objectivity and truth; this is its normative value, and what conditions news frames, but not limited to, are news values, news sources and typifications to be discussed in this section. In a sense it doesn't always matter whether an actual news frame is based on objective reporting or truth, because what gives news frames their unique character on occasions is the pretence that news discourse is truthful and objective. This aspect provides news frames once again as opposed to media frames with a large degree of legitimacy and authority for the provision of news.[9]

Given that there are many frames within society ranging from the collective to the individual with all the differences that would entail, I would argue that for the news frame to make any sense to the community it seeks to serve then it must contain the elements and characteristics that the community recognizes as itself; in other words the news frame becomes the Lacanian 'mirror image' if it is to succeed; we have to see ourselves in it and this is the precondition of the production of news discourse. News frames are devised of patterns of life-experience that connect with other frames in society in a dialectical process, affecting each other in the process of social interaction, mediation and consumption.

News frames induce meaning and interpretation and are an essential part of social engagement and serve to make events recognizable and perhaps the, oft quoted sentence by Goffman sums up best this dialectical process: 'a primary framework is one that is seen as rendering what would be a meaningless aspect of the scene into something that is meaningful' (1974: 21), but only if it's accepted as truly representative of a community's interests.

Earlier conceptions of frames have been stifled by the idea that there are limits placed on and within them and to elaborate further Oliver and Johnston state: 'Gregory Bateson introduced the notion of frame as a meta-communicative device that sets parameters for "what is going on"' (2000: 3). Goffman built on this and even though he allowed for interpretation there was the ominous negation of power within frame analysis. The authors then discuss an alternative way of conceptualizing frame:

> The other way to view a frame is to see it as inherently malleable and emergent mental construct, in Bartlett's terms an 'active developing structure' (1932), shaped in action ... additional elements are added and linked to existing structures based on new incoming data (ibid.).

---

9   This conception of 'news frame' is analytical rather than normative.

This opens up a very interesting can of worms and one that this study can only highlight for researchers who are interested in reception studies. Firstly, there are universal principles that constitute frames such as language, cognitive-thinking practice and actions and perhaps we could say that the body itself in this context becomes the *signifier* and is universal in relation to humanity. The *signified* is less universal and more culturally relative where codes and conventions are influenced by specific socio-cultural and political practice. For instance, a nod in the UK means 'yes', whilst a nod in Turkey means 'no'. Secondly, there are social contexts to consider that have a bearing on how frames operate, such as working practices and contractual obligations that limit freedom of speech and expression, and possibly a journalist's sense of morality in relation to news practice. Working practices, expressed as a house-style, are organizational imperatives that are imposed upon journalists to ensure commodity production.

The third point – and this is for researchers interested in reception studies – the malleable concept of frame is perhaps useful for the study of how individuals decode the encoded message. But there is something to bear in mind at this point, this perception is identical to Bourdieu's theory of *habitus* and Giddens' theory of 'structuration', where identity or biographical narratives are constantly in flux reacting between subject and object. It's only that this breaks down under certain conditions such as journalism and the construction of news frames conditioned not so much by a journalist's *habitus* but rather the media organizational imperatives they work under. Whether an individual accepts the organizational frames into their own *habitus* willingly or unwillingly is not the point. For our purposes this is important because of the potential of newspapers to set the agenda is highly significant and influential as they attempt to influence society.

Frames can take many forms according to context and perhaps a useful way of understanding this is to turn to Bourdieu (1992) and his theory of 'field'. The 'field' contains a distinct logic; the *habitus* within a 'field' will differ according to the varying degrees of cultural capital that an individual has amassed. This equally applies to a journalist in their 'field' of operation and a news frame will vary according to the level of competence, experience and perhaps the location in which they exist, thus representations within a news frame may be based on their cultural-geographical setting. The 'field' is justification for using news rather than media frame because *fields of expertise*, rationale and distinct practice are specialized areas and not generalized. What's more, we can use 'field' or reduce it within a localized sense thus highlighting the specialist knowledge a journalist requires of the community's history, traditions, culture and identity. In this context news frames can be conceptualized as formats for 'agenda setting' (McCombs, Shaw and Weaver 1997).

The necessity for the press to transform events, which are at a distance from its readership into a meaningful reality, relies heavily upon the construction of news frames whereby social events are systematically presented through language and representation. News frames contain news values, sometimes from specific sources of information, sometimes written in a routine fashion that reflect the core interests of the paper and constructed according to the essential typifications that organize productive activity. In news terms, prioritizing certain events over others that relate to the experiences of people rely upon framing life in a way that one set of frames dominate others.

Journalists reconstruct events into a language that is understandable to its readership. They process information seeking to connect with the audience in a discursive manner. The public of course have their own frames of existence and it is this context that determines how individuals engage with a news frame. But the provision of information is not an arbitrary activity, rather framing accounts of social life are highly selective and by definition exclusive. In turn, other events remain unseen and are excluded. It is in this context that Gitlin maintains that: 'What makes the world beyond direct experience look natural is a media frame' (1980: 6): except I replace the over generalized 'media' with 'news'.

Whatever the obscurity of Gitlin's reference to 'media' there are nevertheless a number of implications arising from his quote. Firstly, that frames are socially constructed, but always within the parameters of media organizations and that would inevitably entail a certain degree of conditioning. Secondly, the ability to naturalize events is built out of the scientific notion of rationalization; that the project of discovering and producing news is itself attained by rational and objective criteria, which in turn lends the notion of framing events a certain degree of legitimacy. Thirdly, framing events is not a neutral pursuit but always from a position of power and ideological domination.[10]

Framing events into news entails a preconception of structure so that the news is accessible and understandable to the public. Tuchman (1978), drawing on both Schutz (1964) and Goffman (1974) has argued that news frames are ways for the journalist to create stories and a way of organizing language into a coherent and meaningful structure both for the journalist and the reader. Thus frames are efficient tools that create symbiotic and symbolic connections through time and space. Without news frames a journalist's work would be mayhem, incoherent. Frames or news structures render the text comprehensible to the reader and meaning can be extracted as a consequence.

Given then that frames are essentially tools and systems for organizing thought that attempt to unite a multiplicity of characteristics into a set text, it is reasonable to suggest that these systems are inculcated during the early training of the journalist or the subservience towards a house-style. Consorting rather than confronting imperatives and merely towing-the-line reminds one of Herman and Chomsky's (2002) 'propaganda model', which is a tool where the press generally reflect the interests of the dominant groups in society, including the wishes of corporate media owners. Perceived as such, by and large, journalists conform to the prevailing and dominant forms of ideology and submit to the dominant values inherent within the prevailing system.

---

10   For a more in-depth account of how the concepts of 'naturalization', 'rationalization', and 'legitimization' are sustained by ideology see Eagleton (1991).

However, Golding and Elliot (1979) noted that journalists do not take kindly to the suggestion that news involves a high percentage of manufacturing. Indeed, Whale (1970) Hausman (1990) and Clayton (1992), all who have worked within the journalistic profession, argue against a structured formulae of news; they argue that it is not socially patterned. Rather, the approach to news is perceived in terms of opportunistic reactions to spontaneous occurrences, 'newspapers and news programmes could almost be called random reactions to random events' (Whale, 1970: 170). This perception would allow a larger degree of freedom for the journalist's individual frame or *habitus* to condition the structure of the news frame.

Because representation in the context of locality presupposes an already conditioned context, the deterministic model of news frame applicable to this chapter is the antithesis of the approach to news set out by the three previous writers; that is to argue that news frames are an efficient means in which to reproduce a newspaper's position and set an agenda for public discourse. Accordingly, news frames are a 'mode of discourse' (Glasgow Media Group 1980), in other words a distinct mode of addressing the readership. They are ideologically defined according to the project of a given newspaper. For example, the very notion of what defines a newsworthy event is directed by organizational demands (Tuchman 1978; Gans 1979).

It's in this context that I wish to briefly reference 'frame theory' (Oliver and Johnston 2000), which has its roots in frame analysis. Frame theory can be used for the purpose of assessing the production of news representations within news frames: 'Frame theory is rooted in linguistic studies of interaction and points to the way that shared assumptions and meanings shape the interpretations of a particular event' (2000: 1). However, the authors recognize the historical limitations and the general lack of thoroughness in conceptualizing the meaning of frame, a point also noted by Entman (1993). They note that, 'Frame theory offers a relatively shallow conception of the transmission of political ideas' (ibid.). Therefore, to make up for the limitations of 'frame theory', both writers wish to add 'ideology theory', which allows researchers to analyse ideas as expressed through the construction of various frames.

News Values

News frames are made up or based on news values, which are conditioned by news organizations and editorial approval. News values allow us to understand why it is that certain parts of stories are given prominence over others in the news media. The main driving force behind news discourse, are news values, which are defined by the news organization's interests, perception of community, cultural identity and socio-political values. The link between value and news representation is dialectical; one feeds the other. Value is partly the product of internal representation (example is from *an* image or idea of community) and partly from market research. Information is then formed into a house-style that defines the newspaper as a distinctive item in the market place or more subtly as an intrinsic part of the community and it is this process, i.e., a combination of cognitive (psychological and moral) processes and labour that finally produce a news frame.

The value a newspaper attaches to a public policy issue will play an important role in the eventual framing and representation of the text, particularly the manner in which the policy relates to the experiences of the community. The value *in* the policy issue is the justification and rationalization for transforming the issue into a credible form of representation. News values are an intrinsic part of the daily routine of journalistic activity. They are there to help the journalist organize items into news that are pertinent for audience reception and journalists will, by and large, reflect the paper's interests and values in the selection of items.

For the press then, the image or idea of who the target audience is, will determine the content and structure of news. Presentation, both linguistically and visually, i.e., the paper's mode of address, will help create the house-style that reflect the values incorporated within a paper's identity: therefore, the emphasis on the cultural distinction of a community, i.e., the essential characteristics that a paper attributes to it, and the values imbued in events, have both an economic and moral criteria. The analysis by Galtung and Ruge (1965) regarding the social categories that condition news are probably the most widely referenced. The list is quite lengthy but a few poignant ones for this study are 'meaningfulness', 'cultural proximity' and 'relevance'. The values are universal categories that are seen to be relevant to a journalist in a given setting.

Golding and Elliot (1979), McChesney (1997), Winter (1997) and Herman and Chomsky (2002) have all claimed that news is mostly manufactured within the news organization, rather than an authentic product of outside sources. Manufacturing is intentional and seeks to persuade through the use of linguistic devices and strategies, which include headlines and news in black bold type. News values are a part of the organizations strategy to persuade: a means of framing events as fact. News values are an overall part of a paper's strategy (organizational imperatives). Sigelman (1973), Roscho (1975) and Tiffen (1989) all argued that organizational imperatives contribute to a journalist's training, which are inculcated uncritically. However, organizational imperatives are strategies by which representations are formed, so they not only construct the identity of a journalist, but also construct or manufacture, news discourse.

Indeed, Sigelman claimed that during the socialization and selection process the journalist is trained to reflect the ideals and objectives of the news organization and that they are the values imposed and set by the owning group rather than the product of individuality. This has implications for the content and value of news because hierarchies are applied according to company rules and organizational norms. In this context we can see how the values (ideological) of the organization, editor or even the moral-subjective position of the journalist may impinge upon and negate objectivity, which is seen as the means to truth. Tracey (1977) has claimed that organizational demands permeate into the production of news where certain values become a routine feature of production, inculcated by news workers,[11] which is a fundamentally different perspective from the notion that journalists are bystanders who respond to random events that occur on a regular basis (Whale 1970; Clayton 1992).

The selection process of items that news media deem appropriate will be based upon the values they place upon a policy issue that are pertinent to a news organization's perception of community interests. Equally, for an item to be elevated as newsworthy it must contain the essential interests that are intrinsic for the day-to-day running of a news organization. The news values may already be conditioned by the owners of the newspaper for example, or even an editor's value-judgement but will always consider (by whatever means) the audience it seeks to serve. Judgements made about the audience are sometimes based on market research where the paper can evaluate consumer tastes and social values.

Whatever the complexities over how news values emerge or whose values dominate in the production of representation, it is clear that any assessment or consideration of the audience will ultimately be 'interpreted' and finalized by the editorial board that is ultimately fixed by an organization's mission.

News Sources

The fundamental problem that journalists face is the race against a limited time schedule; time impositions are repressive features of their daily activity. Thus, reliable sources of a continual flow of useful information is undeniably an attraction in fulfilling editorial and owner demands for productive efficiency. The time constraint may result in referencing, elevating and privileging, in certain circumstances, some groups over others. In this context journalists are one part of the production process in terms of mediating information to the public and the reliance upon powerful sources can create problems for the journalist's sense of objectivity, balance, fairness, truth and authenticity if they prioritize and trust one source over others (assuming they have a sense of objectivity etc., in the first instance). Sources of information play an important role in the production of news and are intrinsically linked to the concepts of 'news frames' and 'news values' that structures the final product. Information provided by a source helps frame an item of news and depending on the source may substantiate a value attached to a public policy issue. Selecting the right source is useful in the production of representation if it fits a news agenda, a point not lost on critical discourse analysis.

---

11 Although Tracey is specifically discussing television news, we can however appreciate, in broad terms, the point being made with regards to the production process concerning the gathering of information.

Hall *et al.* (1978) launched a critique concerning sources of information by highlighting that content is bound and ultimately conditioned by 'primary' definers of news. Hall maintained that primary sources condition the productive patterns of a journalist's work, which subsequently construct news frames. The primary definer conditions the initial interpretative framework and the crucial point here is that the press tend to play a secondary role ('secondary definer') to the dictates of the primary definers and in so doing they position themselves in 'subordination to the primary definers' (ibid: 59) and consequently act as a reproductive conduit for its 'definitions' (ibid.). Lang and Lang (1955) referred to this defining aspect as the 'inferential structure'. This type of relationship has led Ralph Negrine (1994) to declare that there exists a 'source domination'; an unequal balance between primary and secondary definers. The reliance upon institutions for information involves a restriction to events and this act, stands in an unflattering opposition to the popular notion of a free press writing in an unfettered way. Equally, the reliance and privileging of certain sources of information over others may produce a non-objective view.

However, do most of these views award far too much power to the source of information and do they fail to recognize that under certain conditions, i.e., when a newspaper has a specific agenda that journalists select sources carefully to flatter that agenda, not subvert it? Schlesinger has levelled a series of criticisms against the notion of primary definers, one of which is how journalists are able to negotiate through the problems of reliance on sources, not necessarily for manipulative purposes but rather to unveil and interpret source information in a less dominated fashion. Schlesinger claims that Hall's primary and secondary definers model is 'atemporal' and 'unidirectional' (1993: 67); in other words, it's deterministic.

Whatever the complexities over who is manipulating whom (is the dog wagging the tail or the tail wagging the dog?) we can nevertheless use Goffman's concept concerning 'connectives' to understand how the *mediation* of the finished product may work: 'It has been argued that a fundamental feature of experience is that ordinarily this connection is something that we can take for granted, something that ensures the anchoring of activity' (1974: 479). This is a poignant statement and one in which we can utilize to evaluate how information is not simply anchored or embedded in its referential reality but how news, as information, is both legitimized and drawn from reliable and accepted sources of news. Goffman's 'connectives' may allow us to perceive journalists as intermediaries between source and reader, whilst simultaneously understanding that journalists relay a distant message that may be ideologically inflected, but only implicitly defined.

Connerton (1989) has correctly observed that the majority of human experience is mediated. Added to this, Kress (1983) has argued that the act of reporting for a journalist is a process of mediation from the source to the reader. The proposition that controlled information is limited in scope from a primary source, also means that as a logical consequence it's limited in its final descriptive form, which would have further consequences on the construction of meaning. When Wittgenstein said 'the limits of my language means the limits of my world' (Lazenby 2006:

46) he was not specifically referencing journalism as an object of enquiry, but this statement reflects journalistic activity. When journalists work to a routine daily activity, sometimes bound by external and internal restraints, this statement is more than applicable and it has serious consequences for the stubborn defence of the notion of the freedom of the press, because subordination (Hall *et al.* 1978) either to the source or organizational directives is subordination to an institutionalized and legitimate form of language.

The domination of ideas through language led Wittgenstein to develop an understanding of this process through the concept of the 'language game', and observed how symbols, words, sentences, etc., are distributed as an element of social activity, which allow us to understand the production of representation. Further to this van Dijk (1991) evaluated how dominant white groups have more access to the distribution of news as social reality over ethnic groups, which quite evidently would have repercussions on how representation is formed in the initial instance. It is in this sense that sources of news can effectively frame content and organizational structures can emphasize particular aspects of events.

Gans had recognized that there is a relationship between sources of news, the journalist and the readership. Sources of news may well depend upon the type of audience the news organization seek to serve. This relationship would entail a modification of news suitable for audience reception. However, this model is less deterministic than that of Hall *et al.*'s (1978), and Gans refers to it as more of a 'tug of war' for determining the final outcome, rather 'than a functionally interrelated organism' (1979: 81). Various studies of television had noted that predictable-selected sources were incorporated into the routine daily practice (Elliot 1970) because of their efficient and trustworthy nature. Above all else these are norms, which are requirements of the media organization that are paramount in constructing news programmes (Epstein 1973) and it is these demands that produce news (Altheide 1976). The ideals, norms and objectives of the media organization are normalized during the training process of the journalist (Sigelman 1973; Roscho 1975).

Thus, the imperatives and primary concerns of the media organization are translated into daily routines (Tracey 1977; Schlesinger 1978). The whole process constitutes a ritual according to organizational logic (Tunstall 1972; van Dijk 1988). The news gathering process is both centralized (in the workplace), and efficiently organized to filter out relevant material (Tuchman 1978; Gans 1979; Fishman 1980; Lester 1980; van Dijk 1988). This activity stifles subjective articulation (Boyd-Barrett 1970). Journalists work in an environment where the information they eventually distribute is not necessarily the most significant but the most attainable by easy access (van Dijk 1988). More than this, although some journalists new to the industry can bring with them a unique style and approach to a subject matter, it is, nevertheless, the overriding structures that not only subsume the individual but also conditions the production of news (Golding and Elliot 1979).

It's reasonable to argue that news representations concerning news discourse relating to community and 'others' (rioters for example) is not solely the product of the image and idea of culture; it's not a phenomenological creation of the internalized representation and thus purely subjective, but rather a combination of selective source, organizational imperatives and internalized representation, with the latter as the basis for the former. In other words, sources in the context of creating news representations invariably conform and are useful to the image and idea (internal representation) of cultural identity and the constitution of the community as outlined by organizational requirements.

Typifications

Typifications are linked to news frames in that they indicate a specific form of practice according to the working routine of journalists and not media in general. In turn, typifications are conditioned by news values and news sources, which then play a very important role for defining a news frame of which representation and discourse are held therein. The idea of a typification suggests a degree of autonomy during the news gathering process. It also provides – wrongly some would say (myself included) – the journalist with a considerable degree of power over the production of news. Drawing on Schutz' work, Tuchman states that: 'Typification refers to classification in which the relevant characteristics are central to the solution of practical tasks of problems at hand and are constituted and grounded in everyday activity' (1978: 50).

Interestingly, typifications can be perceived in terms of Bourdieu's theory of *habitus* or an individual's frame (subjectivity) and may be more useful in reception studies. However, in terms of deterministic models of news frames, typifications may be more a product of the organization than it is of the individual. I would argue that in this context we can also perceive typifications as methodological tools or heuristic devices that are of practical and theoretical use to news workers who will apply them in their everyday activity in accordance to the broad agenda setting framework of the paper. They are functional devices that systematically arrange information into a cohesive and coherent unit; they are aids to construct news frames, using news values and news sources as the basis of structure. Underpinning typifications are the various linguistic techniques and strategies employed to produce news representation, such as metaphors, allegories and metonyms that are often used in the production of news discourse.

Fishman's study of journalists in New York revealed that typifications help journalists 'make sense of the accounts they receive' (1980: 109) and provides examples arguing that 'phase structures', types of typifications, can make sense of bureaucratic accounts; what we now refer to as 'political spin'. Phase structures are defensive tools 'for detecting irregularities in bureaucratic accounts of events' (1980: 109). Tunstall (1971) is less convinced and offers a more sobering if not negative approach to the way in which journalists work. Journalists, he claimed, had more or less taken its structures for granted during its evolutionary transition and the selection and presentation are subordinate to organizational guidelines. Golding and Elliot (1979) frequently equate journalism as having structures that act as defining rules, in the same way as the educational system works. In this context the typifications journalists employ are sanctioned by the media organization; they are not expressions of free will. It is worth considering that typifications, even if employed positively, i.e., of providing the journalist with a degree of control over their work can always be cancelled out by the vulture-like tendencies of the sub-editor who pick over the content and rearrange it according to a paper's house-style and of course the obvious way to avoid this is to submit to a greater authority in the first place.

However, for typifications to be truly effective a journalist must constantly challenge the conventions of internalized structures and not allow typifications to stagnate into routine methods of problem solving, which more often than not they do. For example, when an 'exclusive' piece of information enters the newsroom the activity is pretty frantic and to impose order upon the new information news workers routinely apply their experience to coordinate it into the house-style with a recognizable and predictable mode of address; in effect their routine typifications come to the fore and these are primarily conditioned by the media organization.

In broad terms, Schutz (1964) claims that typifications are an active element of the daily routine and in this context typifications are equally a way of understanding how journalists have developed rules and norms that allow them to function cogently and to relay the most unusual, problematic and challenging social events into a coherent text (Tuchman 1978). Typifications are a way of absorbing both the predictable and the unpredictable and unite them into units of understanding; routine practices envelop all foreseen and unforeseen events and sometimes they simply become *stereotypes*; a point worth thinking about in the news representations of rioters.

Method: Textual Analysis of News Discourse

News representations are presented in what is termed a 'news frame', which is compiled on the basis of both 'news values' ('ideology') and 'news sources'. The latter epitomises a process of selectivity or choice, which often negates objective news accounts. For example, the *Daily Mail* above (17 September 2011) used Tory MP Andrew Rosindell and in the 25 October edition the *Mail* used the Tax Payers' Alliance, the former a right-wing politician and the latter a right-wing think-tank.

The *Guardian* used a more balanced approach quoting the 'crime and security minister, James Brokenshire', and 'Isabella Sankey, the policy director of Liberty' stating that 'Civil liberties campaigners were appalled by the proposed curfew powers', demonstrating a counter-representation to the right-wing press, but the audience to which the *Guardian* is addressing is not conservative, raising the issue of which newspaper has the greatest influence over public policy thinking.

In this final section, I would like to present a discussion on methods of analysis which help us to understand how language and discourse, frame the representation of news. To be begin with, textual analysis is a form of investigation and one is always looking for 'clues' (Alasuutari 1995) to help resolve the mysteries of the production of meaning or reveal latent meanings that are not obvious to the untrained eye. There are many issues to consider when embarking on a textual analysis such as the key issues being addressed, the position of the writer, the purpose, motives or intentions for creating text, for nothing is accidental in language and news discourse.

Influenced by Paul Ricouer depth hermeneutics has been developed by John B. Thompson (1990) and is a method of research into representation as a form of social communication. Depth hermeneutics is useful because it includes an historical consideration within a contemporary context and Thompson calls the first stage of hermeneutic analysis the 'social-historical analysis' and it makes up for the non-historical context that semiotic and rhetorical analysis seem to avoid. The reason that depth hermeneutics becomes useful for analysing news discourse in the context of rioting as an example, is due to the 'traditions', 'historical values', and 'established norms' that are either implicit or explicit in news text.

The second stage is 'formal or discursive analysis' and as Thompson states: 'To undertake formal or discursive analysis is to study symbolic forms as complex symbolic constructions which display an articulated structure' (1990: 22). This is the articulated structure that Stuart Hall spoke of when he claimed that 'the word suggests some kind of joining of parts to make a unity' (Hall in Morley and Chen 1996: 115). Hall claims that text is often the result of diverse moments and elements that cannot be reduced to a single identifiable factor; this is where textual analysis becomes relevant; to search for hidden clues and reveal the sources of news discourse. Within depth hermeneutics this second phase includes semiotic and rhetorical analysis, and Critical Discourse Analysis (CDA). The third phase is 'interpretation' and/or 'reinterpretation', and this is 'concerned with the creative explication of what is said or represented by a symbolic form; it is concerned with the creative construction of possible meaning' (Thompson 1990: 22). This last phase is based on the previous two and is thus organic in structure and scope.

Depth hermeneutics attempts to understand the motives of the writer and thus seeks to *empathize* with the author of a text. In this sense, depth hermeneutics attempts to locate and identify news representation and discourse through the process of interpretation. However, depth hermeneutics assumes that we cannot know in absolute terms the reasoning behind motives and therefore the interpretation of text sometimes requires the researcher to apply *intuitive thought* that can locate the underlying rationale of a productive act.

Central to this analysis are 'symbolic forms', which are ways of communicating ideas, beliefs and values through varying modes of communication. In essence symbolic forms provide meaning and are 'a pervasive feature of social life' (ibid: 1). Symbolic forms are also ways of communicating ideology, which is 'meaning in the service of power' (ibid: 7). As we have seen in the above examples newspapers clearly express established norms – sometimes taken-for-granted as universal – through linguistic expression, which are symbolic in form; moreover symbolic forms are *representational* in form and thus are expressions of national/ cultural representation.

Semiotic analysis is useful for assessing linguistic expressions and techniques and is also a research tool that seeks to assess representation as a language of signs; representation as ideology, and, representation as symbolic form. The focus here is upon Roland Barthes' (1988) contribution to the discussion of signs, codes and meaning systems produced in the process of articulation. Barthes was interested in signs and how they were organized and how they operated within specific cultural settings. This perspective emphasizes cultural distinctions in language when expressing ideas, hence an interest in cultural and social values. This perspective ultimately recognizes that a degree of relativity is at play once value – according to which society or event (riots) is being studied – has been posited. But within the confines of any given cultural system lies a universal set of principles on which language is based, for how else would we recognize it as such?

The assumption is that through a coded system, signs provide meaning from language and in cultural expression. This is achieved by a dialectical relationship between 'signifier' and 'signified'. Semiotic analysis rests on the assumption that there are two key phases in the production of text and its cultural significance or meaning. The first is the order of signification, referred to as denotation, and at this phase of signification the sign or linguistic signal is value-free. It is only when the second order of signification, which is referred to as connotation, comes into play that the first order loses its innocence and arbitrary nature, and thus begins the process of *actual cultural meaning*. Cultural value-systems are made up of linguistic terms that people can identify with, thus language has a meaning, because it identifies objects that culture recognizes as true representations, and there are conventions, codes and gestures that add cultural inflections to statements. As Berger has claimed, 'denotative' is literal (= signifier) and 'connotative' is inferred (= signified) (2000: 40). For the purposes of this chapter, the newspaper or news frame is the signifier and news discourse (language + meaning = representation) is the signified practice producing meaning. However, the relationship between signifier and signified does not necessarily reflect objective truth, but rather how things appear as normal within a cultural system and this process of normalization is what Barthes referred to as 'myth'.

As Gunter explains semiotic analysis is useful for media analysis because it studies 'the construction of narratives and the types of information that are selected by media producers for presentation to an audience' (2000: 91). According to Deacon, Pickering, Golding and Murdock (1999) power in shaping meaning primarily lies with the producer and not with the consumer of the text. The consumer, as a consequence, has to work hard if they are to resist the ideas governing a text and then offer an alternative rather than simply accepting what is read as fact.

Considering that semiotic analysis attempts to reveal what is being articulated, so too does rhetorical analysis. Whereas semiotic analysis looks for hidden and latent meanings, rhetorical analysis places more emphasis on what is more obvious and explicit. Rhetorical analysis focuses on the use of metaphor, metonymy and allegory as a form of persuasion. Such concepts are often applied by media in relation to crime and deviancy (rioting) to separate 'them' (rioters) from 'us'; these are however false categories but they often produce moral panics.

Rhetorical analysis is the study of the *means of persuasion*, however, persuasion, as opposed to propaganda, assumes that the aim is to satisfy the needs of the readers and therefore the driving logic behind persuasion is a view of audiences' values. The question posed by rhetorical analysis is what are the means of persuasion? For semiotic analysis the means are the cultural codes and conventions used in language, but we can take this one-step further and argue that a specific form of news discourse is at play in terms of expressing representation in a cultural setting. Furthermore, and this is to return to the heart of depth hermeneutics, the means of persuasion that rhetorical analysis is interested in revealing are the symbolic forms of which representation and ideology are mediated. This in turn (or to return once again to depth hermeneutics) leads to the interpretation of the means as a medium of intentional expression and influence.

Rhetoric is of course 'intentional persuasion' (Berger 2000: 57) and despite the different contexts of the above reports, rhetoric share similar universal rules for attempting persuasion. Thus 'intentional persuasion' is coopted through news discourse and representation of symbolic forms. It's important to understand that rhetorical analysis is primarily interested in how the speaker attempts to persuade or influence the audience. The issue of 'media effects' is a concern, however the emphasis normally lies with the *intention* as an effective reflection of values and beliefs. It is also a study of what makes symbolic forms effective, otherwise referred to as 'pragmatics' (ibid.). Rhetorical analysis also seeks to understand the 'social values ... of symbolic forms found in texts' (ibid.).

Rhetorical analysis, which is used here in combination with critical discourse analysis, is useful for an assessment of representation because rhetorical analysis is specifically interested in how a text is constructed and finally framed for consumption (Hornig-Priest 1996). Therefore, rhetorical analysis is useful for understanding *modes of articulation* and the way in which a text addresses an audience. Such modes of expression are the product of linguistic techniques such as metaphor, allegory and metonymy that rhetorical and semiotic analysis are interested in. The use of metaphor as a linguistic expression is a tool of persuasion – both implicitly and explicitly in news discourse – and whether such discourse is one or the other it nevertheless impacts upon a hermeneutical approach to interpretation. What *appears* as an explicit form and what *appears* as implicit are but two means of the mediation coin. Here we are made aware of Foucault's theory on discourse, because the focus is on what is being written and in what form, which is the hermeneutic, and it is always incumbent upon the researcher to interpret accordingly.

Regarding the explicit, it may appear that there is nothing hidden or latent, but rather is blatant and obvious and that we need look no further. But in all instances the emphasis of depth hermeneutics is based on investigation, doubt and unravelling what may be hidden meaning or there really is nothing to interpret, as in phenomenology. This does not disregard intentions behind the production of representation nor does it negate an assessment of objectivity as an ethic of journalistic practice.

The use of metaphor, allegory and metonymy and the assessment of such techniques help us to understand the construction of meaning. A metaphor is a figure of speech and pervades our everyday life for creating meaning (Lakoff and Johnson 1980) and is a means to communicate through analogy. Metaphors are 'building blocks for how we code experience, the nuts and bolts of how we describe the world around us'[12] as opposed to similes, which are based on 'comparison' using the word 'like' to express a meaning.[13]

Allegory is a 'story ... or other work in which the characters or events represent particular qualities or ideas, related to morality, religion or politics'.[14] The use of allegory is particularly apt for our understanding of how representation can effectively manufacture fictionalized accounts of characters (rioters) and events (rioting). In both we can link the application of allegory to Anderson's (1990) notion of the 'imagined community' – the creation of fiction through news discourse.

In a study of melodrama and serialization Martín-Barbero argued that meaning always lay outside of the text and referred to this as the 'story genre'. He further claims that its intellectual origins lay in the 'sociology of culture' because unlike the field of literary studies and the 'authored story', the 'story genre' indicates 'the social function' (1993: 133) of a story. This function operates at a political level by explicitly highlighting the different class perspectives that operate in the levels of production and consumption, but importantly this genre is seen 'as a place outside of the "work" itself, as the place of those who produce and consume this product' (ibid.).

Interestingly, the emphasis on the political is a reference to the power of the media for maintaining class divisions and this perspective is of interest to critical discourse analysis discussed below, because the starting point for research according to critical discourse analysts is the imbalance of power between producer and consumer. The 'political' as expressed by Martín-Barbero also reflects John B. Thompson's description of ideology as 'meaning in the service of power' (1990: 7).

Metonymy is a specialized noun; 'when something is referred to by a word which describes a quality or feature of that thing'.[15] The adjective metonymic can be used in a positive form of representation such as the 'good' or 'ideal community'

---

12   http://www.metaphor.org.uk.
13   http://www.dictionary.co.uk.
14   Ibid.
15   Ibid.

(representation 'us') or negatively 'rioters' ('them'). Metonymy, therefore, is used as a way of 'communicating by association' (Berger 2000: 41).

A feature of rhetorical analysis assessment is based on the 'poetic function' (Jakobson in Berger) of language and discourse; in other words metaphor is a device used in the art of persuasion. There is also the referential function to consider and this entails the immediate environment producers of news discourse and representation inhabit. Here we can combine this element of rhetorical analysis to the 'fourth characteristic of symbolic forms' (Thompson 1990: 143) referred to as 'referential'. Accordingly, 'symbolic forms are constructions which typically represent something, refer to something, say something about something' (ibid.).

One particular branch of rhetorical analysis that is useful here is 'argumentation' and as Alasuutari states: 'in the case of argumentation the focus is on the strategies employed to persuade the listener or reader' (1995: 95–96). This is particularly useful for the study of representation because news discourse is aimed at a specific audience or locality/nationality with particular interests and identity. Emphasis is upon the style and tone of the message and 'distinctive features such as composition, form, use of metaphors' (Gunter 2000: 89). In any given study, rhetorical analysis can, by definition, comment upon what is not spoken, what is omitted, because persuasion probably entails a degree of bias.

Root, influenced by Aristotle's definition of rhetoric claims that rhetorical analysis is based on five universal principles; ethos, pathos, logos, aim and mode described as follows:

- Ethos: Character of speaker helps to convince
- Pathos: Appeal to emotions in listener (audience)
- Logos: Proof based on reason, logical argument
- Aim: Purpose of discourse
- Mode: Medium used (talk, radio, TV, film, etc.) (Root in Berger 2000: 60).

For our purposes 'ethos' is based on the newspaper as a legitimate organ of information; 'pathos' is that representation becomes the foundation of appeal to readers; 'logos' is the newspaper legitimating appeal on grounds of objectivity; 'aim' is the purpose of representation to persuade readers. This, for our purposes seeks to persuade the public of the representation of riots with a specific further aim to influence government thinking on public policy; for government are never quite sure how news discourse will impact on public opinion. 'Mode' is the newspaper – the basis of power for shaping public policy.

To sum up thus far, semiotic analysis seeks to reveal the relationship between *signifier* and *signified*. The news frame becomes the signifier and the context (representation, discourse, meaning, etc.) becomes the signified. Rhetorical analysis assesses modes (methods) of persuasion and depth hermeneutics prepares the ground for interpretation.

The final method to consider is critical discourse analysis (CDA) and this offers an additional way of analysing and interpreting representation within news frames.

CDA unifies discourse, ideology and power as a tri-partite method of analysis. CDA is strongly influenced by Foucault's concept of 'discourse' because it permits a *critical intervention* into analysis, the type of interventions and reflections that underpin critical theory. As Alvesson and Skoldberg explain:

> Discourse is ... more ... a framework and a logic of reasoning that, through its penetration of social practice, systematically forms its objects than as any use of language in a social context. Foucault's interest was more in how discourse constitutes objects and subjects than in the details of language use in social interaction (2000: 224).

This perception of discourse allows the researcher to critically evaluate how representations work; it allows for an understanding of power. Discourse is a form of social interaction that can only be set in place within a wider social framework of ideas. Foucault paid special attention to the power of institutions and organizations in society for their influence on constructing and conditioning social discourses. This way discourse and narratives interact between people and structures; they are never divorced from omnipotent power regimes. The relationship is discursive which impacts upon changing self-biographical narratives that situates an individual in society. An individual is not a remote island, and externality imposes itself as a reconstituting force, almost dictatorial in its manner. I say 'almost' because in Foucault's scheme of things there is some room for manoeuvre, albeit, limited. In this theoretically based notion of discourse we can begin to understand how media organizations frame representation within certain journalistic practices and conventions that are primarily governed or conditioned by an institution.

Foucault's contribution also widens the approach of social interactionists by including power regimes that condition the self and it is this constant interaction between people and structures that eventually produce language, ideas, identity and the imagined community and public policy thinking is often constructed of a combination of imagined community and news representation. Text or newspaper articles are in some ways the result of this social interaction rather than, the original piece emanating as an individual stream of consciousness. An individual's speech is in part constitutive of the speech of others, perhaps imposed by organizational imperatives and directives that condition the very act of representation. When journalists construct a news frame, they do so according to the house-style of the paper, which invariably is enveloped in representational forms of the community they seek to serve. Perceived as such, speech is therefore not the property of the self, but collective and shared, especially in terms of experience. However, in reality it's only collective and shared in the sense that *we* submit to the rules and ideas of other powerful-dominating players. News texts and the representational forms therein are powerful ways for mediating reality and experience, as Prior notes:

a text instructs us how to see the world, how to differentiate the parts within it, and thereby provides the means by which we can engage with the world. One might even argue that in many spheres of human practice one can only know the world through representational orders contained within text (1997: 67).

This slightly ambiguous statement has an element of truth to it. Of course in reality a text is not the only way that we know the world or become to know the world, because works of art and photography equally emit discourse that we consume and place into a narrative order. That said; texts frame instances of life that we come to know through the process of customization.

In this way, we can see why it is that Foucault's concept of discourse is useful for analysing news production. News discourse is a defined set of social practices that is conditioned by organizational imperatives or to use Foucault's language, it becomes institutionalized practice. Interestingly for Foucault power was not centralized, but rather power is dispersed and working in and through practices, and this has a bearing on how news is consumed, assuming the media is not all-powerful affecting the mind.

It's useful because Foucault considered the intimate relationship between institutional practices, knowledge and power. Practices constitute and help form the subject and here we may want to consider how news organizational imperatives that govern news practice help form the language used by journalists when constructing a text or story. This condition has a symbolic element attached to it, in that the sum total of experience is acquired knowledge over news practices and the dissemination of information is then transformed into public opinion; here then it belongs to the sphere of power.

Fairclough has argued that CDA reveals an abuse of power through language in that the press engage in misleading practices that 'purport to deal in fact' (1995: 7). Fairclough claimed that the press produce representations of events in a deceitful way, 'offering images and categories for reality, positioning and shaping social subjects, and contributing for the most part to social control and reproduction' and that 'This myth underpins the ideological work of the media' (ibid: 161–162).

Weiss and Wodak state: 'The aim of Critical Discourse Analysis is to unmask ideologically permeated and often obscured structure of power … [and] … political control … as well as discriminatory inclusion and exclusion in language use … Its aim is therefore to intervene discursively in given social and political practices' (Weiss and Wodak 2002: 8) that form and shape public policy thinking in combination with the historical conceptual frameworks discussed in Chapter 1.

Some Concluding Thoughts

Overall Part I assessed the historical philosophical concepts such as the common good, well-being, happiness, the good life and public interest detailed in Chapter 1 that continue today to underpin government thinking on public policy. Chapter 2 took this discussion one step further specifically to assess the abstract meaning of public policy. I then presented such abstractions with a discussion on the Conservative Party's idea of the 'Big Society', thus combining theory with empirical data. I then presented the riots in England 2011 as a case study on which the Big Society was reborn after a period of hibernation. The idea behind this analysis was to assess government reaction to the riots which resulted in new government thinking and initiatives on public policy. Finally, in Chapter 3 I presented a discussion on news representations and news discourse on the riots that seek to persuade government thinking on policy issues in light of the riots in 2011; news discourse after all is loaded with intent. The discussion on methodology was presented to help us try to understand language and news discourse as a source of power and persuasion, detailed by rhetorical analysis for example, and how news media interests can conflict and condition policy thinking. This wouldn't be so problematic if it wasn't for the fact that the news media is limited to a small number of powerful players, which raises the concern over democracy itself, not limited simply to government, but embraces citizens and their political rights to think and act free from the limited restraints of media. Public opinion, a type of group think, is to a very large extent the end-product of news discourse and therefore, public policy strategizing is a game played by powerful and influential players that condition *our* society. In Part II of this book many of the points raised in Part I with additional material are further explored from the perspective of psychology.

PART II
Group Processes and the Media as a Referee in Public Policy-Making

Caroline Kamau

Introduction
Why Group Processes Matter

It can be easily taken for granted that communications about public policy often take place in the media arena. I argue that public policy involves three main entities or groups: (i) the policy-makers, (ii) media organizations and (iii) the public. I argue that media organizations play the role of referee, between policy-makers and the public. This is because it is to media organizations that policy-makers often release information about proposed, revised, abandoned or alternative policies. It is from media organizations that members of the public often learn about policies. It is via facilities presented by media organizations that members of the public often voice their opinions about policies. Probabilistically, a member of the public has better access to a media discussion about a policy than to a government-commissioned opinion poll or focus group. Likewise, it is via facilities presented by media organizations that discussions between policy-makers and the public take place.

I acknowledge that each of these entities encompasses sub-entities. For example, policy-makers comprise not just the government but also non-governmental bodies. The government itself comprises not just the civil service but also elected politicians, who in turn comprise not just cabinet ministers and members of the ruling party, but also shadow cabinet ministers and other members of opposing parties. Likewise, the non-governmental entity comprises several sub-entities, such as charities, interest groups, think tanks, academics/ consultancies, and so on. However, I argue that all these sub-entities share an umbrella group identity, as policy-makers. Umbrella or superordinate categories are significant in creating a sense of a shared identity (common ingroup identity model, Gaertner, Dovidios, Anastasio, Bachman and Rust 1993). I likewise acknowledge that media organizations and other informal types of media comprise numerous sub-entities but I argue that, in particular socio-cognitive contexts, the various disparate media are bound by a common identity. I will discuss this in more detail in the next chapter. Thirdly, I acknowledge that the public comprises numerous sub-entities. For instance, the public is divisible according to whether or not people are definite end-beneficiaries of a given policy. As well, there are social groupings which can determine end-users' gain from public policy. This often depends on the political or economic climate of the society concerned. For example, nationality or residency can determine whether someone can benefit from public policies concerning employment rights, welfare, free healthcare, and so on. Another example is gender, which can determine end-users' gain from pension policy, parental rights policy, and others. Political affiliation (e.g., left-wing or right-wing) can also influence what members of the public expect from policy, in terms of whether they expect the rewards to be primarily collective or primarily individual.

Nonetheless, despite these sub-divisions, I take a group process perspective in explaining the overarching group phenomena at work. I apply social psychological theories of group behaviour (self-categorization theory, Turner *et al.* 1987, and social identity theory, Tajfel and Turner 1979). I will now explore these theories in further detail.

Why Group Processes Matter: An Introduction

Social identity theory (SIT, Tajfel and Turner 1979) argues that, in each individual, there is a constant battle in the mind between one's identity as an individual and one's identity as a group member. Whether group identity wins over personal identity depends on the circumstances of a given situation. Turner, Oakes, Haslam, and McGarty (1994) suggest that self-categorization is contingent upon the psychological accessibility of the category in question. For example, when other group members are present, group identity wins over personal identity. An MP sitting on the Opposition side in the House of Commons will think of themselves as a member of the Opposition. An hour later, sitting in the train back to his/her constituency, the MP will think of themselves as an individual, a person commuting from work. Upon arriving at his/her constituency office that afternoon, the MP will think of themselves as a political representative or as a member of a particular political party. Upon arriving home in the evening, the MP will think of themselves as an individual. The next day the MP spends the morning in his/her original profession, say, attending a medical conference. His/her group identity as a medic becomes salient, and so on. In this way, we see how individuals navigate everyday situations, with a dynamic identity process happening in their mind, according to the characteristics of each given situation. 'Context' is therefore construed as something that is subjective, varying from situation to situation, in SIT and the related self-categorization theory (Turner *et al.* 1987).

Why does group identity win over personal identity, in a given situation? Group identity wins over personal identity when the nature of the specific context matches the category's characteristic requirements – i.e., 'normative fit' (see also Oakes and Turner 1986). A person concludes to themselves that 'those' are outgroup members, whereas 'these' are ingroup members; this is called self-categorization (Turner *et al.* 1987). In actual fact, the category differences are not that simple. It is just that people exaggerate the differences between their own group and members of other groups, to make categorization easier. More technically, self-categorization happens when something known as the 'meta-contrast principle' is fulfilled (Oakes, Haslam and Turner 1994). This principle stipulates that any set of items is likely to be classified as a single unit to the extent that disparities within that set are less than differences between it and other sets. SCT stipulates that, through the seeking of only that information which confirms one's group-related beliefs (i.e., confirmatory bias) and through the belief that one's attitudes are shared by other ingroup members (i.e., false-consensus bias) individuals are predisposed to bias towards the ingroup. An implication of this is that self-categorization is a variable and dynamic process that depends on the literal context in which the social comparison is occurring. If circumstances lean in its direction, group identity prevails over personal identity.

Once self-categorization happens, the relevant social identity will be psychologically accessible and the individual will behave in accordance with that group identity. For instance, several journalists from different media organizations, standing outside a court, waiting to question someone, are likely to categorize themselves as 'journalists' or 'the press' in contrast to passersby. The cognitive assimilation of the self into the ingroup will then govern behaviour (Hogg and Abrams 1988). Abrams and Hogg (1999) further suggest that cognitions such as self-representation, perception, and emotion, will conform to the social identity in question due to the depersonalization that results from self-categorization (see also Smith and Henry 1996; Spears, Doosje and Ellemers 1997). In other words, once a given group identity is activated, people behave as group members more than as individuals. Their emotions, actions, thoughts and words are governed by the norms of that group. A paparazzi photographer chasing a famous person through the streets can be said to be acting under the governance of a paparazzi group identity. The norm among paparazzi of running after targets becomes the value that drives the behaviour of running.

To recap, individuals move from situation to situation making or accessing varying forms of self-categorization in each situation. Sometimes they think of themselves as individuals and sometimes they think of themselves as group members. The latter case produces the relevant group identity and group behaviour. Irrespective of whether self-categorization is the result of meta-contrasts or normative fit or whether it is a question of psychologically accessing a pre-existing self-categorization, the emphasis is not on *what* form of grouping is evoked, but on whether *a* form of grouping is evoked.

Simon, Hastedt and Aufderheide (1997) used the notion of normative fit to explain their findings that members of a minority group had more frequent self-categorizations (relevant to that minority group) than members of a majority group when the grouping had high meaningfulness. Applied to the question of social categories among media, the implication is that media organizations such as the *Guardian* with a smaller audience might have stronger group identities than media organizations with a larger audience share. Members of media organizations with a small audience share might actually exert more influence on public policy instigation than can be expected – because of the unrelenting group behaviour associated with more frequent self-categorizations. Another interesting application of SIT and SCT is in understanding the fluidity of the group identities of media workers. Turner (1982) argued that any social category can be internalized into the self-concept and that the subsequent group behaviour is the result of 'cognition redefinition' of the self along the lines of the group.

Applying this, for example, many journalists working in the *Guardian* previously worked for the *Sun* despite the substantial disparity and contradiction between the identities of the two newspapers. The explanation is simple, given evidence from SCT and SIT: any given person put into any given category *can* develop the group identity relevant to the new category (Tajfel, Billig, Bundy and Flament 1971). Laboratory experiments using a procedure known as the 'minimal group paradigm' demonstrate that mere categorization – however arbitrary – *can* result in group behaviour (Brown & Turner 1979; Brown, Turner, Tajfel 1980).

Self-categorization theory (Turner *et al.* 1987) also explains how people can ally themselves to one group identity in one situation, such as being a Labour MP, then ally themselves to a different group identity in another situation, such as being a politician. That will happen despite the fact that the latter category encompasses sub-categories that otherwise compete with each other. It is that people simply juggle different group identities to meet the demands of everyday social situations. Turner, Sachdev and Hogg (1983) postulated that ascription of group membership *per se* is enough to ensure 'private acceptance' of the category and subsequent manifestations of social identity. The fact that self-categorizations happen from situation to situation, or even moment to moment, explains how people are able to deal with contradictions between their various group allegiances.

Applying the Group Process Perspective: The Triad of Entities in Public Policy

I argue in this chapter that a common umbrella identity binds policy-makers, a common umbrella identity binds media organizations/workers, and a common umbrella identity binds the public. Each umbrella identity is a group identity that conforms to the principles discussed in the previous section. I do not suggest that each common or super-ordinate group identity is of greater significance than the sub-identities within it. The important point is that *a* super-ordinate category exists and a category's existence is enough to activate feelings of social identity (Turner, Sachdev and Hogg 1983). For example, I do not suggest that a politician always thinks of himself or herself as a policy-maker first and foremost. Likewise, I do not suggest that a BBC staff member thinks of himself or herself as a media professional more than as a BBC staff member. Likewise, I do not suggest that different media organizations *always* share a sense of belonging to the same category. Similarly, I do not suggest that people in the public have unified conceptions of what it means to be a member of the public. What I am arguing is important is the presence of category differences among the three entities (the public, media and policy-makers) in the context of public policy. This issue of category differences is central to the process of categorization of oneself into a group (Turner, Oakes, Haslam and McGarty 1994). Specifically, the differences are between policy-makers and media organizations, between policy-makers and the public, and between media organizations and the public. Likewise, the presence of similarities in policy concerns can unite the people within each entity. Concurrently, the lack of similarities or the presence of differences in a given socio-cognitive context can mean that sub-group identities (e.g. Channel 4 versus BBC) become activated.

Consistent with self-categorization theory (SCT; Turner *et al.* 1987, 1994) I argue that in the context of discussing something like public policy, the category differences become exaggerated in the psychological sense. In line with self-categorization theory, I argue that in such a context each entity exaggerates the differences between itself and the other entity. This is because of the meta-contrast process that precedes self-categorization (Oakes, Haslam, and Turner 1994; Salazar 1998). For instance, imagine someone who falls within the umbrella category of policy-makers. He/she will most likely, when in a media-hosted discussion, perceive category differences between policy-makers and media organizations, or between policy-makers and the public. In another setting he/she might think that policy-makers are actually quite a heterogeneous group. Another example is that, when reading about a public policy on a media platform, members of the public will most likely define themselves as just that (the public), feeling a sense of allegiance with other 'civilians' in contrast to media organizations or the policy-makers.

When, then, is each entity's umbrella group relevant? We can deduce from SCT that a group will be relevant in a situation whereby the opposite group is present or relevant. Consider a Labour MP, X, sitting in a lounge. A group of Conservative MPs walk in and sit down, and this may cause X to start thinking and acting in terms of his/her Labour group membership. This may be manifest as X perceiving vast opinion differences, given what the Conservative MPs are talking about and what the Labour party would think about it. Members of the public then walk into the lounge. X finds this brings forth into consciousness the fact that X is a Member of Parliament and, when someone asks about the issue of expense claims, X vehemently defends all MPs implicated in the expense claim scandal. After that, a group of Belgian interns walk in and sit down, and X will probably have thoughts about being British (if X is British). When a group of Japanese tourists walk in, X may think about being European. A parliamentary guide walks in and asks women in the lounge to please go to the room next door for a debate on feminism. As X walks with the women, she may find herself conscious of her gender, and so on. These basic examples illustrate the continuously dynamic process of self-categorization and group identity. Additionally, for each example (and this applies to any given social context) there is the option of eschewing social memberships in one's construal of that particular context, and instead acting as an individual (Tajfel and Turner 1979).

In public policy-making, as Chapter 4 will explore, this altogether means that the question of which group membership is influencing a given policy-maker's decision depends on the situation: who is around him/her; how does the policy issue relate to group interests? A given public policy-maker's decision may depend on the relationship between his/her group memberships and the benefits or losses in group(s) as a result of the policy. Another qualifier is the fact that the 'situation' can be psychological as much as it can be physical, such as in the examples above. For example, the situation of being a vegetarian in a society predominated by meat-eaters may lie salient within an MP's mind in parliament, irrespective of whether he/she knows who is or is not a meat-eater in the parliamentary chamber itself. Chapter 4 will explore this.

When the discussions between policy-makers and the public take place, media organizations are seldom impartial when relaying information from one entity (the policy-makers) to the other (the public), or vice versa. In fact, media organizations often strategize their affiliation with either category in the process. Sometimes media organizations present themselves as the voice of the public; other times media organizations presents themselves as the mouthpiece for public policy-makers. In addition, media organizations often give a 'voice' to the public in a manner that is not impartial. The incidence and nature of this impartiality depends on a number of factors. In Chapter 5, I will discuss the organizational factors, such as media working practices and the 'serious' nature of the media organizations, that can explain when/which media organizations will referee public policy and how. In Chapter 5, I will also discuss the characteristics of policy decisions that make policy-makers susceptible to influence from media organizations.

Media organizations are also seldom impartial in their representations of public policy issues. Public policy-makers often find out about the public popularity of policy proposals or revisions from media representations of public opinion. As I discuss in Chapter 5 and 6, media representations of public opinion about policy issues depend on whether the media organizations are playing a refereeing role in the process. As well, it depends on the nature of that refereeing role. Furthermore, as I will discuss in Chapter 6, media representations of public opinion about policy issues are the consequences of a variety of group processes among media professionals. In Chapter 6, I will discuss how media workers' professional identities can explain their susceptibility to faulty group decision-making processes. I will also discuss how the public's consumption of media changes from passive consumption to active interaction, in the process of forming opinions about policy issues.

Summary

To recap, I have conceptualized 'policy-makers', 'media' and 'the public' as three separate groups. The nature of the relationship between these three groups is illustrated in Figure 4.1 below.

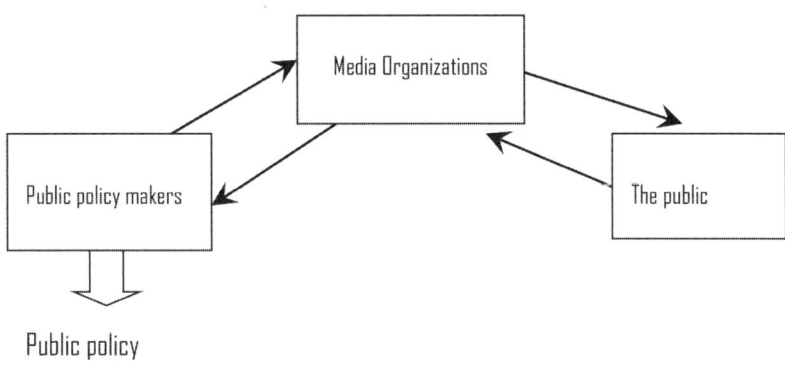

Figure 4.1   The triad of entities in public policy

I have acknowledged the fact that these group divisions are dynamic, meaning that their psychological relevance varies from situation to situation. I have also acknowledged the fact that each of these groups encompasses a number of sub-groups, some of which are in competition with each other. For example, I acknowledge that the psychological relevance of the label 'policy-makers' depends on the psychological situation in question. Likewise, the labels 'media' and 'public' are useful, psychologically, when we bear in mind the psychological circumstances under which these labels are relevant to policy-making, refereeing policy and forming opinions about policies. As I will explore in Chapter 4, group processes can predict policy-makers' agenda. Applying a group process perspective can help evaluate the extent to which public policy really is about the common good. Secondly, as I will explore in Chapter 5 and 6, group processes can explain media organizations' and media workers' part in policy-making. Thirdly, as I will discuss in Chapter 6, group decision-making processes among media workers can explain the media's powerful effects on public opinion about policies and, ultimately, the policies themselves.

Chapter 4

When the Common Good is not so Common: Group Identity Motives in Public Policy-Making

In Chapter 1, the notion of the 'common good' in relation to public policy thinking was assessed and this was explored from the perspective of political philosophy, which suggests that people feel a sense of moral duty towards others. On that basis, public policy *could* be driven by the moral philosophical notion of the common good. Policy-makers *could* be operating on the basis of a sense of moral obligation to create policies which benefit all in society. We *could* therefore conclude that satisfying the common good is the predominant motive among public policy-makers, but is this the case? I will explore evidence that policy-makers are susceptible to the socio-cognitive group processes introduced earlier on in Part II. For instance, can self-categorization or group identity predict what is on the policy agenda and how important is subjective context? I and a research assistant, Abigail Spong, conducted a study using data from UK Parliamentary records and data in the public domain. We wanted to find out whether there is a systematic effect of any given MP's group membership on what is on his/her policy agenda. In the first part of this chapter, I will discuss the results of this research and the implications for different policy contexts. I will then discuss reward motives as a key explanation for policy-makers' susceptibility to group processes when setting their own policy agenda.

Why Group Memberships Matter in Public Policy: An Archival Study

Earlier in this book, the political and moral philosophical notion of the 'common good' was discussed. Such a moral ideal has been a key theme in public policy but it is important for us to ask: to what extent is public policy driven by the inclusive notion of the *common* good? Could it be that the group identities involved in public policy-making are more exclusive than the ideal implies? To answer this question, I conducted some empirical research with a research assistant (Spong and Kamau 2009). I wanted to find out: do policy-makers who belong to group X propose more policies pertinent to group X than policy-makers who do not belong to group X? I took UK Members of Parliament as an example.

As discussed earlier, the theoretical basis of this exploration was social identity theory (Tajfel and Turner 1979) and its sister theory, self-categorization theory (Turner *et al.* 1987). These are psychological theories commonly used to explain group processes. I explored these theories in the introduction to Part II of this book. I will explore them in further detail in this and the next chapters. As discussed earlier, the root of these theories is the idea that the very existence of a category creates conditions for group behaviour. For example, imagine a room full of strangers. We toss a coin, allocate half the people in the room to 'group A' and the rest to 'group B'. We then measure a number of psychological variables. We find that people in each group report feelings of belonging to their allocated group. We find that people in each group express the belief that people within their own group share important similarities. We find that people in group A, on average, rate people in group A more positively than they rate people in group B. Vice versa for group B. We ask people in each group if they would like to join the other group and find that, on average, the majority say no. All these results are, according to the social identity theory perspective, what we would expect to happen. In short, we can predict that when people belong to a group this has an effect on their feelings and behaviour. For example, when people belong to a group, they engage in 'ingroup' bias. This is to say that they favour the interests of the ingroup over the interests of other groups (that is, 'outgroups'). As in our earlier example, this favouritism has been found to happen even if the group is arbitrary in meaning. An early experiment demonstrated this phenomenon using a setup known as the 'minimal group paradigm' (Tajfel *et al.* 1971). This idea, that merely belonging to a group has important psychological consequences, is the basic premise of social identity theory and self-categorization theory. This led Spong and I to hypothesize that an MP's social categorization predicts the frequency of his/her policy activities. If an MP is inside the social category, he/she will be more active about policies which benefit that social category than an MP who is outside that social category. This hypothesis might seem commonsensical but it needs to be tested empirically.

To test that hypothesis, Abigail Spong and I conducted an archival study. *A priori*, we generated a list of eleven public policy issues. These were based on common policy themes. We then defined what being an 'ingroup' member and an 'outgroup' member meant. This was in terms of each policy issue concerned. For example, as far as a public policy on a specific health issue is concerned, we defined an 'ingroup' member as an MP who has suffered or whose close relative has suffered that particular health issue. As far as public policies about women's issues are concerned, we defined 'ingroup' MPs as female MPs, and 'outgroup' MPs as male MPs. As another example, as far as a public policy on family issues is concerned, we defined an 'ingroup' member as an MP with children. These categorizations might seem like generalizations, but this was the very point that we wanted to investigate. Do such social categorizations have a statistically significant effect on MPs' speech activity in Parliament? If so, this should be early evidence of group processes as drivers of policy agenda.

We then generated a random sample of UK Members of Parliament, for each of the 11 policy issues. The procedure for creating each random sample began by randomly generating a letter from the alphabet, using an online tool. We then referred to the list of MPs in the House of Commons. An MP with a surname beginning with the generated letter was then chosen. To ascertain the group membership of that MP in relation to the given policy issue, we conducted a background search using Google. For example, when we conducted a background search for the 'animal welfare' policy issue, we used search terms such as 'MPs who are vegetarians' and 'MPs who eat meat'. When we conducted a background search for the 'religious policy' issue, we ran searches such as 'MPs who are religious' versus 'atheist/ humanist MPs'. When we conducted a background search for the 'immigration policy' issue, we used search terms such as 'MPs born outside the UK' versus 'MPs born in the UK', and so on, depending on the policy topic. In each instance, we then verified that information from a second source – often the MP's official webpage or some other official information source such as parliamentaryrecord. com. If no second source was available to provide that verification, the MP was not included in the sample for that search topic. This therefore created two groups of MPs for each of the 11 policy topics: those who are 'ingroup members' in relation to that policy topic, and those who are not. The number of MPs sampled for each policy topic, and their group membership, is listed in Table 4.1.

After that, we collected data about each randomly sampled MP's speech activity. Our source was the UK *Hansard,* an online repository of Parliamentary debate transcripts. We counted the number of times that each MP in the random sample spoke about the policy issue in question. We recorded this information then repeated this process for each of the MPs in each of the 11 samples. We compiled this data into a statistical spreadsheet. The data represented 320 MP entries. Across the data, there were 279 unique MPs sampled. This represented 45.69 per cent of the total number of MPs in the UK Parliament.

Let us take a look at the data in Table 4.1 below. The first column names the 11 policy issues. For each policy issue, in the second column of the table, we explain what the 'ingroup' represented. For each policy issue, in the third column of the table, we list the names of the MPs randomly sampled and their political party affiliation. For each policy issue, we report the mean amount of speech activity by the MPs in the 'ingroup' (and the standard error of that mean). We also report the mean amount of speech activity by MPs not in the 'ingroup' (and the standard error of that mean). For example, the table tells that vegetarian MPs raised a mean of 108.5 issues about animal policy in Parliament, based on Hansard records. This was more than non-vegetarian MPs, who spoke a mean of 15.37 times about animal policy in Parliament, based on Hansard records. This implies that vegetarian MPs engage in higher speech activity about animal policy issues than non-vegetarian MPs. Let us consider another example from the table. MPs with children spoke more frequently in Parliament about family policy issues than did MPs without children. The former had a mean speech activity of 21.81, whereas the latter had a mean speech activity of 14.31. As another example, MPs born outside the UK or whose parent/parents were born outside the UK spoke slightly more frequently about immigration issues (M=7.45) than did MPs born in the UK and whose parents were (M=5.35). This sort of pattern was replicated across all policy issues except for men's policy issues and class policy issues. Reasons for these two exceptions will be explored later.

Table 4.1   Spong and Kamau's (2009) analysis of MPs' group motives for public policy instigation

Policy issue	Ingroup motive?	MPs randomly sampled; Mean (*M*) and Standard Error (*S.E.*)
Animal issues	Yes, ingroup motive for raising the issue (eight vegetarian MPs)	Hilary Benn (Labour); Harry Cohen (Labour); Jim Murphy (Labour); Chris Williamson (Labour); Kerry McCarthy (Lib Dem); Jim Fitzpatrick (Labour); Tessa Munt (Labour); David Drew (Labour)
	Amount	M=108.50, $S.E.$=17.81
	No ingroup motive (eight non-vegetarian MPs)	Zac Goldsmith (Conservative); Rt Hon John Gummer (Conservative); Richard Bacon (Conservative); Mark Pritchard (Conservative); Neil Parish (Conservative); Harriet Baldwin (Conservative); Peter Ainsworth (Conservative); Harriet Harman (Labour)
	Amount	M=15.37, $S.E.$=17.81
Women's issues	Yes, ingroup motive for raising the issue (10 female MPs)	Diane Abbott (Labour); Yvette Cooper (Labour); Rosie Cooper (Labour); Mrs Cheryl Gillan (Conservative); Sandra Osborne (Labour); Joan Ruddock (Labour); Linda Roirdan (Labour); Joan Walley (Labour); Jenny Willot (Lib Dem); Lynme Featherstone (Lib Dem)
	Amount	M=4.80, $S.E.$=15.93
	No ingroup motive (21 male MPs)	Rt Hon James Arbuthnot (Conservative); Bob Ainsworth (Labour); Ian Austin (Labour); Christopher Chope (Conservative); Nick Clegg (Lib Dem); David Cameron (Conservative); Tim Yeo (Conservative); George Young (Conservative); Nick Gibb (Conservative; Rodger Gale (Conservative); George Osborne (Conservative); Mr Stephen O'Brien (Labour); Richard Ottaway (Conservative); Jamie Reed (Labour); Bob Russell (Lib Dem); Jeremy Wright (Conservative); Alan Whitehead (Labour); Stephen Pound (Labour); Owen Paterson (Conservative); Eric Pickles (Conservative); James Paice (Conservative)
		M=1.38, $S.E.$=10.99

Policy issue	Ingroup motive?	MPs randomly sampled; Mean (M) and Standard Error (S.E.)
Scotland issues	Yes, ingroup motive for raising the issue (16 MPs of Scottish birth)	Angus MacNeil (Scottish National Party); Alan Reid (Liberal Democrats); Mike Weir (Scottish National Party); Menzies Campbell (Liberal Dem); Sandra Osborne (Labour); Eilidh Whiteford (Scottish National Party); Jim McGovern (Labour); Russell Brown (Labour); Anne Begg (Labour); Anne McGuire (Labour); Cathy Jamieson (Labour); Charles Kennedy (Liberal Dem); David Cairns (Labour); Danny Alexander (Liberal Dem); David Hamilton (Labour); Stewart Hosie (Scottish National Party)
		M=6.50, S.E.=12.59
	No ingroup motive (16 MPs not of Scottish birth)	Stewart Jackson (Conservative); Lyn Brown (Labour); Mark Lancaster (Conservative); John Spellar (Labour); Daniel Rogerson (Liberal Democrats); Caroline Spelman (Conservative); Emily Thornberry (Labour); Joan Walley (Labour); Alan Beith (Liberal Democrats); Tom Brake (Liberal Democrats); Adam Afriyie (Conservative); Adrian Bailey (Labour); David Jones (Conservative); Cheryl Gillan (Conservative); Anne Main (Conservative); Christopher Ruane (Labour)
		M=.12, S.E.=12.59
Religious issues	Yes, ingroup motive for raising the issue (18 MPs with a religious faith)	David Cameron (Conservative); Mohammed Sarwar (Labour); Lee Scott (Conservative); Gary Streeter (Conservative); Steve Webb (Lib Dem); Jon Cruddas (Labour); Caroline Lucas (Green); Khalid Mahmood (Labour); Parmjit Dhanda (Labour); Virenda Sharma (Labour); Alistair Burt (Conservative); Jeffery Donaldson (Democratic Unionist); Desmond Swayne (Conservative); Stephen Timms (Labour); Andrew Selous (Conservative); Sharon Hodgeson (Labour); Simon Hughes (Lib Dem); Andrew Reed (Labour)
		M=4.56, S.E.=11.87
	No ingroup motive (10 MPs who are atheists or humanists)	Nick Clegg (Lib Dem); David Miliband (Labour); Clare Short (Labour); Graham Allen (Labour); Colin Challen (Labour); Charles Clarke (Labour); Julian Huppert (Lib Dem); Kelvin Hopkins (Labour); Michael Connarty (Labour); John Denham (Labour)
		M=1.10, S.E.=15.93

Policy issue	Ingroup motive?	MPs randomly sampled; Mean (*M*) and Standard Error (*S.E.*)
Men's issues	Yes, ingroup motive for raising the issue (25 male MPs)	Tobias Ellwood (Conservative); Don Foster (Lib Dem); Edward Vaizey (Conservative); Ben Wallace (Conservative); Bob Spink (Independent); Lee Scott (Conservative); Jeremy Hunt (Conservative); Russell Brown (Labour); David Blunkett (Labour); Robert Goodwill (Conservative); John Hayes (Conservative); Albert Owen (Labour); Chris Grayling (Conservative); Bruce George (Labour); Rodger Gale (Conservative); Malcolm Rifkind (Conservative); David Wright (Labour); Ronnie Campbell (Labour); Christopher Chope (Conservative); Stephen O'Brien (Conservative); Peter Bone (Conservative); David Clelland (Labour); Simon Hughes (Lib Dem); Angus Robertson (Scottish National Party); David Lidington (Conservative)
		M=.12, *S.E.*=10.07
	No ingroup motive (six female MPs)	Mrs Annette L Brooke (Lib Dem); Maria Miller (Conservative); Margaret Hodge (Labour); Emily Thornberry (Labour); Katy Clark (Labour); Rosie Cooper (Labour)
		M=.50, *S.E.*=20.56
Lawyer/legal issues	Yes, ingroup motive for raising the issue (12 MPs who trained/worked as lawyers)	Jeremy Wright (Conservative); Keith Vaz (Labour); Harriet Harman (Labour); Edward Vaizey (Conservative); Eleanor Laing (Conservative); Dominic Raab (Conservative); Greg Knight (Conservative); Jake Berry (Conservative); Tasmin Qureshi (Labour); Guy Opperman (Conservative); Maria Eagle (Labour); Anne Macintosh (Conservative)
		M=98.17, *S.E.*=14.54
	No ingroup motive (12 MPs with non-lawyer professions)	David Evennett (Conservative); Andrew Turner (Conservative); Vincent Cable (Lib Dem); Helen Goodman (Labour); Michael Gove (Conservative); Norman Lamb (Lib Dem); Peter Luff (Conservative); Tony Lloyd (Labour); Alan Duncan (Conservative); Nick de Bois (Conservative); Sarah Teather (Lib Dem); Micheal McCann (Labour)
		M=15.00, *S.E.*=14.54

Policy issue	Ingroup motive?	MPs randomly sampled; Mean (*M*) and Standard Error (*S.E.*)
Health issues	Yes, ingroup motive for raising the issue (11 MPs affected or with a close relative/spouse affected by a fatal or chronic health issue)	David Lammy (Labour); David Anderson (Labour); Gordon Brown (Labour); Patricia Hewitt (Labour); Iris Robinson (Democratic Unionist Party); Austin Mitchell (Labour); David Ruffley (Conservative); Adrian Sanders (Labour); Fiona Mactaggert (Labour); Andy Burnham (Labour); David Amness (Conservative)
		M=35.45, *S.E.*=15.19
	No ingroup motive health issue (11 MPs – no known public domain information about a fatal/chronic health issue affecting them or a close relative/spouse)	Dan Byles (Conservative); Nigel Dodds (Democratic Unionist); Toby Perkins (Labour); Louise Bagshawe (Conservative); Jim Sheridan (Labour); Teresa Pearce (Labour); John Thurso (Lib Dem); Derek Twigg (Labour); Jane Ellison (Conservative); Julian Lewis (Conservative); Ian Austin (Labour
		M=10.27, *S.E.*=15.19
Family/child issues	Yes, ingroup motive for raising the issue (16 MPs with a child or children, based on information in the public domain)	David Cameron (Lib Dem); Diane Abbott (Labour); Hilary Benn (Labour); Mark Hunter (Lib Dem); Matthew Taylor (Liberal Democrat); Michael Gove (Conservative); Edward Balls (Labour); Yvette Cooper (Labour); David Willets (Conservative); Robert Walter (Conservative); Alison Seabeck (Labour); Valerie Vaz (Labour); Shelia Gilmore (Labour); Gisela Stuart (Conservative); Caroline Flint (Labour); Maria Miller (Conservative)
		M=21.81, *S.E.*=12.59
	No ingroup motive (16 MPs not know to have a child or children)	Hazel Blears (Labour); Mark Francois (Conservative); Steve Baker (Conservative); Clive Betts (Labour); Greg Knight (Conservative); Nick Gibb (Conservative); Martin Caton (Labour); Sammy Wilson (Democratic Unionist); David Laws (Labour); Theresa May (Conservative); Maria Eagle (Labour); Jo Swinson (Lib Dem); Linda Riordan (Labour); Gerald Kaufmann (Labour); Andrea Eagle (Labour); Adrian Saunders (Conservative)
		M=14.31, *S.E.*=12.59

Policy issue	Ingroup motive?	MPs randomly sampled; Mean (*M*) and Standard Error (*S.E.*)
Ethnic minority issues	Yes, ingroup motive for raising the issue (18 MPs from minority ethnic groups in the UK, based on Office for National Statistics groupings)	Diane Abbott (Labour); Adam Afriyie (Conservative); Marsha Singh (Labour); Virendra Kumar Sharma (Labour); David Lammy (Labour); Keith Vaz (Labour); Dawn Butler (Labour); Sadiq Khan (Labour); ShabanaMahmood (Labour); ParmjitDhanda (Labour); Mark Hendrick (Labour); ChukaUmunna (Labour); Helen Grant (Conservative); Ashok Kumar (Labour); Shailesh Vara (Conservative); Priti Patel (Conservative); Kwasi Kwarteng (Conservative); ValerizeVaz (Labour)
		M=2.33, *S.E.*=11.87
	No ingroup motive (18 MPs of white ethnicity, which comprises the majority ethnic group in the UK)	James Brockenshire (Conservative); Sir Stuart Bell (Labour); John Leech (Lib Dem); Dawn Primarolo (Labour); Natascha Engel (Labour); Geoffrey Cox (Conservative); Bob Russell (Lib Dem); Angela Watkinson (Conservative); Rt Hon Tess Jowell (Labour); Malcolm Wicks (Labour); Paul Flynn (Labour); Don Foster (Lib Dem); Michael Fabricant (Conservative); Peter Tapsell (Conservative); Pat Glass (Labour); Adam Ingram (Labour); Siobhain McDonagh (Labour); Jane Ellison (Conservative)
		M=.22, *S.E.*=11.87
Class issues	Yes, ingroup motive for raising the issue (14 MPs who are Eton alumni; attendance of Eton, a private education institution, is often deemed an indicator of an 'upper class' socioeconomic background)	David Cameron (Conservative); John Young (Conservative); Oliver Lewtin (Conservative); Hugo Swire (Conservative); David Tredinnick (Conservative); Bill Wiggin (Conservative); David Heathcoat-Amory (Conservative); Geoffrey Clifton Brown (Conservative); Phillip Dunne (Conservative); John Thurso (Lib Dem); Nicholas Soames (Conservative); Douglas Hogg (Conservative); Boris Johnson (Conservative); James Arbuthnot (Conservative)
		M=1.86, *S.E.*=13.46
	No ingroup motive (14 MPs who did not study at Eton)	David Hamilton (Labour); Rodger Gale (Conservative); Iain Duncan Smith (Conservative); Greg Hands (Conservative); Crispin Blunt (Conservative); Richard Bacon (Conservative); Nia Griffith (Labour); Chris Bryant (Labour); Barbara Keeley (Labour); Gerry Sutcliffe (Labour); Eric Joyce (Labour); Wayne David (Labour); Eric Illsley (Labour); Liam Fox (Conservative)
		M=4.93, *S.E.*=13.46

Policy issue	Ingroup motive?	MPs randomly sampled; Mean (*M*) and Standard Error (*S.E.*)
Migration issues	Yes, ingroup motive for raising the issue (20 MPs born outside the UK or whose mother and/or father was born outside the UK)	Keith Vaz (Labour); Gerald Kaufman (Labour); Shailesh Vara (Conservative); Marsha Singh (Labour); Adam Afriyie (Conservative); Sadiq Khan (Labour); Sajid Javid (Conservative); Yasmin Qureshi (Labour); Richard Spring (Conservative); David Lammy (Labour); Mohammad Sarwar (Labour); Daniel Kawczynski (Conservative); Crispin Blunt (Conservative); Nicola Blackwood (Conservative); Greg Hands (Conservative); Peter Hain (Labour); Tobias Ellwood (Conservative); Alok Sharma (Conservative); Chinyelu Susan Onwurah (Labour); ShabanaMahmood (Labour)
		M=7.45, *S.E.*=11.26
	No ingroup motive (20 MPs born in the UK and whose mother and/or father is not known to have been born outside the UK)	Liam Fox (Conservative); Alistair Burt (Conservative); Edward Leigh (Conservative); Nadine Dorries (Conservative); Malcolm Bruce (Lib Dem); David Heath (Lib Dem); Paul Goggins (Labour); Albert Owen (Labour); Angela Eagle (Labour); Grant Shapps (Conservative); Justine Greening (Conservative); William Hague (Conservative); John Penrose (Conservative); Helen Jones (Labour); Alan Beith (Lib Dem); Sarah Teather (Lib Dem); David Tredinnick; (Conservative); Tim Yeo (Conservative); Alan Williams (Labour); Hazel Blears (Labour)
		M=5.35, *S.E.*=11.26

Let us now consider some examples and case studies from the table.

Some Examples and Case Studies

Before exploring the statistical results, for illustrative purposes, let us consider some examples that elaborate on the procedure leading to Table 4.1 and in the process we will also consider some caveats to assumptions made. The case studies are not exhaustive or systematic, but are instead presented for illustrative purposes.

Animal Issues

The first policy issue, animal issues, included animal welfare and rights, such as in terms of access to veterinary services. For example, the issue could have included questions raised or discussions initiated in Parliament, concerning animals' access to disease detection and treatment. The issue could have also concerned domestic animals or animals in other circumstances, such as zoos or agricultural settings. Questions or discussions concerning animals in agricultural settings concerned conditions for livestock/fisheries, livestock disease outbreaks, and so on. Vegetarianism (including variants such as veganism) can be said to be not just a choice of diet but an attitudinal stance on animal issues. For example, the values of vegetarians can be said to include animal welfare attitudes, beliefs about animals' status in relation to humans, concern for animals' genetic survival, humans' responsibilities to animals, anthropomorphic ideas and so on. Vegetarians might also report greater feelings of identification with animals than non-vegetarians, not simply in the obvious sense of empathizing with animals more, but in the social identity sense. In other words, compared to non-vegetarians, vegetarians might perceive fewer differences between humans and non-human species. Whether or not a given MP is vegetarian was therefore chosen as a means of grouping indicative of his/her group identity in relation to animals.

    Example (case study) Vegetarian MP Hilary Benn (of Labour) raised 61 animal issues in Parliament. For instance, he queried the effectiveness of the Dangerous Dogs legislation in protecting both the public and dogs at risk of abuse. At the time of data collection, Benn was the Secretary of State for Environment, Food and Rural Affairs and so it was unsurprising that he raised issues concerning Foot and Mouth disease and other animal-related aspects of agriculture in the nation. However, looking at the 61 parliamentary records, it seems apparent that Benn's concerns were not just for policies affecting the human public or agriculture *per se*. Benn appeared to place a lot of repeated emphasis on the impact of policies on the animals themselves. It was also notable that he raised issues of access to health facilities for livestock, continuation of funding for research by the Institute for Animal Health, the need for collaboration between it and the Veterinary Laboratories Agency, and the need to alleviate animal suffering through effective detection and treatment of diseases. It is not unreasonable to conclude that Benn's instigation of animal welfare policies was motivated by much more than his ministerial obligations. His being a vegetarian could be, quite reasonably, an overarching driving force for placing animal welfare policy-making high on his agenda.

As Table 4.1 shows, vegetarian MPs, on average, raised seven times as many animal issues in Parliament as non-vegetarian MPs. Being vegetarian itself could be construed as not just a social grouping but as an individual philosophy central to Benn's (or other vegetarian MPs') concepts of self and personal identity. Instigating animal welfare policies therefore becomes a mechanism for self-realization for MPs such as Benn to whom the ideal is important as something which positively distinguishes the self's identity from that of others. In social identity theory (Tajfel and Turner 1979) such notions of the positive distinctiveness are an important motive for group belonging. People therefore desire to belong to groups which contribute to the feeling of esteem. For instance, people could prefer groups with the sorts of values that help set them apart as distinguished individuals.

Women's Issues

This topic involved women's rights, women-specific health issues, women's employment conditions, women's career/other development, such as in terms of women's business entrepreneurship, equality of pay, female lone parent concerns, maternity provisions, conditions for women in prison, gender discrimination and other issues affecting women's quality of life. Whether or not a given MP is a woman was chosen as a means of grouping. Membership of a group is a pre-condition for identification with that group and related feelings or behaviour (self-categorization theory, Turner *et al.* 1987).

Example (case study) Female MP Lynne Featherstone (of the Liberal Democrats) raised 27 issues in Parliament that concerned women. For example, she queried the provision of and the uptake rate for breast cancer screening by primary care trusts. She sought verification on the allocation of £12.5 million of a capital fund intended for female entrepreneurs. She questioned Nottingham City Council's approach to making female employees' pay equal to males'. She raised a query about the government's strategy for dealing with domestic abuse of women. She questioned the government's approach to unequal pay by gender, suggesting mandatory measures. When Labour lost the national elections of 2010 and the English government was led by a coalition of the Conservatives and Liberal Democrats, Featherstone became a minister for equality. Nonetheless, many of the issues sampled pre-dated her time as minister for equality. The instigation of policies advancing women's rights by women MPs is not particularly surprising. The finding that women MPs were more likely than male MPs to instigate policies advancing women's rights is also not surprising, and seems quite in keeping with the hypothesis. As Table 4.1 demonstrates, female MPs raised 3.5 times more women's issues than male MPs.

Scotland Issues

This topic was defined in terms of issues such as reduced fuel duty for occupants of Scottish islands, provisions for the Scottish Gaelic language, procedures affecting the Scottish parliament, the need for inclusion of Scottish sites in world heritage sites lists, child poverty in Scotland, transport links to Scotland, Scottish landscape, transport to Scotland, and so on. We grouped MPs according to whether or not they were born in Scotland.

Example (case study)   MPs with Scottish origin raised 54 times more Scotland-related issues in Parliament than MPs with English, Welsh, or other birth. One 'hitch' with analysing this policy topic is that many of the Scots MPs happened to represent constituencies in Scotland, or had ministerial posts concerned with Scotland (e.g., being the Secretary of State for Scotland). The reason why these MPs raised significantly more issues in Parliament about Scotland was therefore not just because they are themselves Scots. It may therefore be more informative to provide case-studies of the non-Scots MPs randomly sampled. Scotland is a sovereign state that, in 1707, joined the union of the United Kingdom. Since 1999 Scotland has had its own government with 21 ministers, a first minister and 129 members of the Scottish Parliament. The Scottish Government determines Scotland's own policies on agriculture, education, the environment, heritage, the legal system, local government, health, housing and planning, policing, rural affairs, social work, statistics and other records, transport, and a number of other policy areas. However, there are many more 'reserved matters' that remain under the control of the UK's central government (including the House of Commons), House of Lords and monarchy. These reserved matters include: broadcasting, defence, employment, energy, equal opportunities, fiscal/economic issues, foreign affairs, social security, trade and industry, and a number of others. In essence, Scotland's devolved government (1999 onwards) gained control of *some* policies, but not all. This therefore means that there are important reasons why MPs not representing Scottish constituencies could raise questions in Parliament mentioning Scotland. This should be, particularly, if they have ministerial, shadow-ministerial or other such responsibility for one of the reserved matters not devolved to the Scottish government. Despite all the reasons why MPs from the English Parliament *can* speak about Scotland in Parliament because of ministerial or other duties, our analysis showed that MPs with non-Scottish birth raised 54 times *less* issues in Parliament about Scotland than MPs with Scottish birth. This difference supports our hypothesis. Let us look at some examples.

MP Caroline Spelman (Conservative), born in the West Midlands region of England, raised one issue about public loans held by Scottish local authorities in connection with housing. The MP Adam Afriye, born in London (England), raised one issue about whether the Secretary of State for Scotland would apologize further about a postal ballot fiasco that affected areas including Scotland. Spelman and Afriye were exceptions, because none of the remaining 14 non-Scots MPs who were randomly sampled raised any Scotland-related issues in Parliament.

Religious Issues

This topic included issues such as inter-faith dialogue, government funding of religion-related activities, access to religious places of worship, allegations of cult activities, wearing of religious attire, persecution or imprisonment based on religion abroad, discrimination based on religion, tax exemption of religious institutions, and so on. The issues themselves did not need to concern the MP's own religion, nor was it a pre-condition that the MP's question/answer should imply a bias for religion itself or indeed their own religion. The point was that they were participating in a discussion or raising a question in Parliament with implications for policies on religion. As Table 4.1 demonstrates, we randomly sampled MPs who have a religious affiliation. These were the 'ingroup' members, as far as religious policy issues are concerned. We also randomly sampled MPs who are atheists. We then counted the number of times that each of the 28 MPs spoke about a religious policy issue in Parliament. As Table 4.1 demonstrates MPs with a religious affiliation spoke more times in Parliament about a religious policy issue than did atheist MPs.

Examples (case studies)   MPs with a religious faith, according to information in the public domain, participated in parliamentary discussions about religious issues four times more than did atheist or humanist MPs. For instance, Christian MP Alistair Burt (Conservative) highlighted his concern about the imprisonment of seven people in Iran from the Bah'ai group, a religious minority there. He raised the issue of killings of Afghans who converted from Islam to Christianity and in another query he emphasized the need for the Afghan government to implement its own laws safeguarding religious freedom. Christian MP Desmond Swayne (Conservative) raised an issue querying government plans for inter-faith week. Brahmin Hindu MP Virendra Sharma (Labour) questioned the Foreign and Commonwealth department's assessment of freedom of religion in the Maldives. Jewish MP Lee Scott (Conservative) raised an issue about the impact of neo-Nazi parties on rises in anti-Semitism within communities. Sikh Parmjit Dhandha (Labour) raised queries concerning government-funded support for training religious leaders to help combat extremism. He also highlighted the government's inter-faith strategy, and the government's bid for links with religious communities. It was notable that these questions were often about religious freedom in general or the state's support for religion in general, rather than being about their own religion *per se*. Although this might be attributable to a desire to appear fair and balanced, it nevertheless appeared indicative of a desire to protect the interests of people with a religion, and to preserve the state's support or respect for religious practices or institutions.

Statistical Effects

We needed to know whether the differences in the means (see Table 4.1) were statistically significant. Tests of significance are important. We cannot just rely on comparing means by merely looking at the values in Table 4.1. This is because comparing means visually without conducting inferential statistics can lead us to accept a hypothesis for erroneous reasons. Two means could be different for reasons that are not to do with the expected theory-driven hypothesis. Inferential statistics take into consideration factors such as differences in sample size, the variation in values, the presence of outliers, and so on. Inferential statistics also restrict the probability of error to five per cent or below. We therefore conducted statistical analyses to find out not just whether the average amount of issues raised by the MPs differed according to whether they were an 'ingroup' member for that given issue, or not, but also whether the difference was significant with an acceptably low probability of error (that is, a five per cent chance or under).

Was there an overall effect of MPs' group membership (ingroup versus not ingroup)? Yes, there was a statistically significant difference between 'ingroup' MPs and 'other' MPs. An MP was four times more likely to speak about a policy issue in Parliament if he/she was an 'ingroup' member for that policy issue than an MP who was not in the 'ingroup'. On average, across the 320 units of MP data, an 'ingroup' MP spoke 19.28 times about an 'ingroup-relevant' policy issue if he/she was an 'ingroup'. This was in contrast to 'non-ingroup' MPs, who spoke an average of 4.72 issues about the same policy. This supports our hypothesis. A t-test showed that this overall difference in means was statistically significant, with only a three per cent probability (p) that the difference was due to error, $t(318)=2.24$, $p=.026$. This was replicated with a Mann-Whitney Test, which analyses data with non-normal distributions (see explanation below), $U(1)=15277$, $p=.002$.

Was there an effect of MPs' group membership (ingroup versus not ingroup) within each of the 11 policy issues? One could conduct 11 separate t-tests to find out but, in all 11 samples, normal distribution criteria were not met. This means that, in each of the 11 samples, the scattering of values (amount of speech activity in Parliament) deviated greatly from a bell curve shape. Skewness values ranged from 1.79 to 4.69. Kurtosis values ranged from 2.74 to 25.45. Both skewness and kurtosis, in the 11 samples, exceeded twice the standard error of the skewness and kurtosis respectively. Statistics such as t-tests are conducted on data that is normally distributed, which meant that nonparametric tests were needed, rather than a t-test. Mann-Whitney-U Independent Samples tests were carried out for each of the 11 samples.

The results showed that our hypothesis was supported among only the following policy contexts: women's issues, $U(1)=138$, $p=.037$; Scotland issues, $U(1)=222$, $p=.001$; health issues, $U(1)=104$, $p=.004$; and ethnic minority issues, $U(1)=241$, $p=.005$. Among the remaining 7 policy issues, the results of $p>.05$ led us to conclude that group membership predicts MPs' policy activities only if those policies are about women, Scotland, health or ethnic minorities. Why? It could be that these policy contexts involve the clearest inequality or disadvantage, of all 11 policy contexts analysed. People in groups that are quite disadvantaged might display levels of activism that are significantly higher than people not in those groups. This proposition seems plausible as far as women MPs, Scottish MPs, and ethnic minority MPs are concerned. Feminism, Scottish nationalism and ethnic equality are all active campaigns. What about health policy issues? The Mann-Whitney-U test showed that MPs who have suffered a chronic health issue or whose close relative has suffered a chronic or fatal health issue are significantly more likely to speak about health issues in Parliament. The 'rule of thumb' that disadvantaged group members speak out more does not seem to easily explain those results. I will touch upon the explanation for this point later on in this chapter.

In summary, when we ran analyses within each of the 11 samples, our hypothesis was not supported among seven of the 11 samples. When we ran the inferential statistics in each of the 11 samples, we found that the probability of error was higher than five per cent among seven of the 11 samples. The differences in means (in Table 4.1) are therefore not conclusive *if* we wish to make generalizations about what happens in each of the different policy contexts. If, however, we wish to make a generalization about what happens in policy agenda-setting as a whole, overlooking differences among policy contexts, we can conclude that group membership predicts policy agenda.

So the 'Common' Good is not so Common: A Reward Explanation for Group Motives in Public Policy-Making

As discussed in Chapter 1, the notion of the common good is a philosophical ideal. The results of the above archival study suggest that, in reality, the group motives of public policy-makers are sometimes exclusive. As far as particular policy issues are concerned, it can be concluded that the 'common' represents the exclusive social category with which a given public policy-maker identifies in a given policy context, rather than society in general. These findings support the idea that group motives *do* motivate public policy-makers, at least as far as certain public policies are concerned. These findings support the argument that the group motives in public policy-making are more exclusive than the ideal of the 'common good' implies.

Recently, in social psychology, there has been some theoretical discussion about why people engage in group-related behaviour. Why do people join groups, why do they engage in 'ingroup' favouritism, and why do they develop feelings of group identity? Theoretical explanations have emerged beyond social identity theory (Tajfel and Turner 1979) and self-categorization (Turner *et al.* 1987), which emphasize categorization and context (see the introduction to Part II of this book). One compelling explanation is the idea that group-related behaviour is motivated by the desire for rewards (Rabbie, Schot and Viser 1989). For example, people are said to engage in favouritism because they expect that favouring the 'ingroup' will lead to direct or indirect benefits to themselves (Rabbie *et al.* 1989). Another example is the explanation for why people join groups and why they choose some groups and not others. People are said to scope out and join groups which offer the potential for greater rewards than costs (Levine and Moreland 1994). Even after joining a group, people's feelings of group identity can depend on whether rewards outweigh costs (Kamau 2012).

Even if we consider public policy-making as a form of activism, there is evidence that the motives of activism are often reward-oriented. For instance, relative deprivation theory (Runciman 1966) tells us that some people engage in collective action because they have feelings of egoistic deprivation. In other words, they believe that they as individuals are disadvantaged, relative to other individuals. Those who do not feel personally disadvantaged yet engage in activism are said by Runciman's theory to be motivated by the belief that their group is disadvantaged, relative to another group; this is termed 'fraternalistic deprivation'. Even in this case, we can argue that people engaged in activism still anticipate future rewards such as maintaining or increasing their own well-being or safeguarding the well-being of their own offspring, who are likely to belong to the same group affected by the disadvantage. We can therefore apply the argument that group behaviour is driven by the desire to maximize rewards to the self and minimize costs (Rabbie *et al.* 1989). In other words, we can argue that activism via policy-making, like any other form of activism, is driven by the ultimate question: 'how does this policy benefit me?' For example, 'how does this policy benefit me, personally, as a member of a disadvantaged group?' This is not a bad thing and may reflect the reality that individuals navigate group scenarios with the goal of ensuring that the costs of their contributions to groups do not outweigh the rewards. Reward motives may driver each entity within the triad (see Figure 4.1): policy-makers, media organizations and the public. Reward motives may also be the key to reconciling the moral ideal of the common good with the reality of group processes in policy decision-making.

Looking back at the beginnings of public policy, we can find support for the idea that the desire for rewards motivates public policy-making. Let us take early literature on public policy in Britain as an example. We reviewed literature published nearly a century ago or before that, archived in British Library special collections. In reviewing the nature and purpose of public policy in Britain, Ford (1923) discussed Hobbes' notion of the common good as part of the rationale for public policy-making. Ford thus explained the nature and purpose of public policy from the standpoint of moral philosophy. At first glance, Ford's discussion implied that public policy is guided by an ethical duty to serve the public as a whole. Nonetheless, later in the book, Ford considered the individual motives that underpin the notion of the common good. Ford argued that a kind of 'enlightened selfishness', or what psychologists might call 'reward motivation', underpins morality. The idea that a desire for rewards to the self underpins public policy-making is compelling. This is because the question becomes not only how morally worthy a given public policy is, but also how its development might ultimately reward the individuals involved (be they policy-makers, individual media workers or individuals in the public). One way of conceptualizing this notion of individual rewards in policy-making is in terms of self-well-being. As discussed in Chapter 1 the notion of well-being has become a significant driving force for public policy-making today, yet this idea is not new.

For example, Ford (1923) implied that public policy exists because it is part of the path to self-realization. Part I of this book discussed the growth, in government, of the idea that policies should be created to optimize feelings of happiness and other forms of individual well-being among people in the public. We can therefore consider whether such well-being reward motives underpin public policy-making. Do public policy agenda boil down to: how much does the policy benefit the self's basic needs for food, shelter, clothing, the self's cognitive needs for intellectual stimulation, the self's social needs for family, friends, procreation, and the self's aesthetic needs for entertainment, art, travel, culture? This is based on Maslow's (1943) 'hierarchy of needs', a popularly cited taxonomy of human drives – from the basic (e.g., the desire for food) to the complex (e.g., the desire for self-actualization).

It was also notable that Ford's (1923) exploration of public policy tended to be rhetorical and almost manifesto-like, postulating on what public policy *ought* to be rather than on what it is. This point is significant. It explains why public policy decision-making is a process vulnerable to group influences. In other words, Ford's writings give us a good idea of the reasons why public policy decision-making is susceptible to group processes. Public policies can be necessary but in many instances they can be embellishments shaped by group goals and the group decision-making processes surrounding public policy are more than merely functional. This lends weight to our argument that public policy-makers, media organizations and the public are driven by more than functional concerns. If, as our archival study found, public policy-makers are more active about policies which benefit groups to which they belong, it is clear that rewards matter in public policy. It is also clear that public policy decision-making is not simply functional in being driven by the goal of accuracy. This lends weight to the idea that all entities involved are prone to the socio-cognitive group processes introduced earlier in Part II of this book.

Looking at the early literature about what public policy should be it seems apparent that the notion of rewards was inherent in authors' ideas about that. For instance, Ford put forward ideas about what policies should be on crime, social work and poverty. Each idea reinforced Ford's underlying thesis that public policy should be about individual fulfilment. For example, in discussing social work, Ford argued that public policy should ensure that social work is about the development of personality. Let us consider another example.

Group Membership, Reward Motives and the Case of Foreign Policy

Looking at literature archived in the British Library, it appears that early writings about what foreign policy should be hinted at reward motives. Foreign policy was seen as something that should benefit the nation (Wilkinson 1896). Wilkinson's book is a collection of essays aimed at enabling the British Empire to secure its continuity. First, Wilkinson set out an outline of the nation's identity, emphasizing the 'we', 'our', 'us', and discussing Britain relative to other empires. However, Wilkinson did not take a simple nationalistic approach. In reviewing the policies of France, Germany, and Russia, he acknowledged their policy strengths and discussed lessons to be learnt by Britain from them. In fact, one such acknowledgement concerned Bismarck's ideals on German policies and his warning against irrationality as a driving force for public policy:

> (Bismarck) adopts the sound maxim that the policy of a nation ought not to be guided by sentiment, feeling, or passion, but by a stead consideration of its interests (ibid: 51).

Therefore, Wilkinson suggests that public policy should exist to benefit the interests of a nation. In a section titled 'The Defence of British Interests', Wilkinson discusses the need for public policies that enforce the nation's defence of its national interests. This supports the argument presented here concerning the importance of reward motives in public policy-making. Thus, according to Wilkinson, public policy becomes something that is both a service to the public's interests and a defence of the very notion of public interests.

In considering national identity as a form of group identity, it is important to note the special characteristics of national identity. According to Mummendey, Klink and Brown (2001), there are at least two types of national identity: one is nationalism and the other is patriotism. Nationalism is the kind of national identity characterized by derogating national 'outgroups', whereas patriotism is characterized by pride for the national 'ingroup' without necessarily derogating other nations. Where do national interests fit in? The distinction between nationalism and patriotism emphasizes the fact that not every kind of behaviour driven by national identity is underpinned by xenophobia or similar malevolent feelings. Moreover, the desire to serve national interests in public policy-making need not be construed as a nationalistic symptom. Let us remember that serving national interests is not incompatible with serving the interests of groups (e.g., the EU, NAFTA) that include other nations. This difference can help explain how nationalism involves a hostile, derogatory view of 'outgroups' and the belief that one's nation is superior whereas patriotism involves a benevolent pride for one's nation with the possibility of equally acknowledging the positive attributes of other nations. It is feasible that reward motives underpin public policy-making as part of nationalism *or* patriotism.

Looking back at other early writings on UK foreign policy, there is evidence that the notion of national interests was embedded within the rationale for foreign policy. At the time – at the height of the British Empire – it can be argued that the kind of national identity embedded in UK foreign policy was nationalistic. Morris (1885) published a pamphlet called 'The National Policy', which tellingly reflects early evidence of the now intricate relationship between public policy and what is called 'spin'. Likewise, Mackenzie (1984) wrote about the use of such spin by the British Empire. We can extrapolate that the purpose of the spin was to promote national interests. Mackenzie reported that propaganda during the British Empire era was conveyed to the public through photographs, sheet music, short films, church hall displays, posters, leaflets, school textbooks and other media whose readership widened as printing became cheaper over the years. These were intended to keep category differences salient – for example, emphasizing British identity in contrast to other group identities. This also implies that publicity or propaganda about foreign policy is designed to activate group identity and other group processes.

As another example, let us consider Morris (1885). From this early foreign policy pamphlet, we can deduce that rhetoric about social norms is used by policy-makers to emphasize a social category and to make group identity salient or more pronounced. It suggests that public policy proposals – when targeted at voters – tend to overtly conform to social convention in order to please the public and satisfy social identity objectives. Looking at such an early example as that of Morris's pamphlet, we can find evidence of careful impression management. For instance, when Morris made decrees that departed from social convention, he qualified those departures with a reinforcement of social convention. Such strategies typify active group behaviour. That is, the emphasis of collective norms and one's conformity to them is a characteristic of an active social category and a significant group identity. On the rights of women, Morris put forward the policy proposal of 'open(ing) up to women every employment for which they are physically adopted' (ibid: 71), which could be said to have been 'controversial' in advocating more employment rights for women. However, Morris then wrote in the next paragraph: 'There is no immediate need ... for women to sit in Parliament' (ibid.). Morris also wrote several jingoisms in his pamphlet, each tailored to the audience group, e.g., 'the rich people of this country are eminently charitable' (ibid: 108). Such strategies in writings about foreign policy can be used to reinforce feelings of national togetherness and bonds among people within the national category.

Group Membership, Reward Motives and the Case of Regional Policy

A different type of group identity that can drive public policy instigation is regional identity. This idea was written about in Britain, as early as the 19th century, when Dolman (1895) discussed the uniqueness of each region. Dolman considered regions such as Birmingham, Liverpool and Glasgow, and argued that each is unique in terms of things such as land, geographic assets such as waterways, regional debt, and so on. Dolman deduced from these things the kinds of public policies that each region should have. Inherent in Dolman's argument was the assumption that there is a group identity among people living in a given region, and that this regional group identity is what drives municipal public policy-making. To take an example, Dolman wrote that the people of Birmingham are proud of their municipal institutions (e.g., their art gallery, free library), to such a degree that it is a 'pride which so frequently finds expression in gifts and bequests' (ibid: 18). Whether or not the same kind of pride exists in people in other regions does not prevent Birmingham policy-makers from constructing policies that rely on the continuity of that collective pride in municipal institutions. Therefore, for example, they might construct public policies that save those institutions from budget cuts. To consider another example, let us consider what Dolman writes of another region:

> Manchester was the pioneer as regards the collective ownership of gas ... The excess of assets over liabilities now amounts to about £900,000 ... It is the universal opinion in Manchester that the collective ownership of the gas has been a brilliant success (ibid: 34).

This implies that the municipal's astute policy of de-privatizing a service such as gas was not only beneficial for the common good but it was, in itself, an indicator of the region's unique identity, which led it to pioneer such a policy. In summary, Dolman's work provides one of the earliest analyses of public policy-making at the municipal level in Britain. Underpinning these analyses is the view that regional group identity is the driving force for municipal public policy-making. Dolman's ideas about regional identity are compatible with predominant social psychological theories on social identity: Dolman construed regional identity as something unique that fuels strong feelings (e.g., pride) and behaviour (e.g., bequests to the region).

Dolman's conceptualization of regional identity also goes beyond what we ordinarily construe as a social identity in social psychology, since he includes natural resources as part of that regional identity, whereas we tend to define social identity mainly in terms of intangible cognitive (that is, psychological) concepts. The emphasis on resources supports the argument presented here that reward motives (conceptualizing rewards as 'tangible' outcomes of policy) drive public policy-making. Even looking at Britain's regions today, we can easily discover evidence that natural resources, buildings, residents' assets, and other tangible artefacts, are used by municipal bodies as part of their definition of their region's identity. What might limit the pursuit of reward motives in municipal public policy-making, therefore, is what is feasible (based on the region's available capital), what is acceptable (based on regional norms),what is pragmatic (based on what is in the region's best interests) and what is 'legal' (based on public policy set by central government).

Further Questions

In this chapter, I explored the question of what motivates public policy agenda in the first place. Is it really the moral ideal of the common good? I discussed the group motives that drive public policy-makers' decisions about which policies to instigate. We can conclude from this chapter that group processes can explain what is going to be on a given policy-maker's agenda, particularly as far as particular policy contexts are concerned (such as those involving groups suffering high disadvantage). What is the role of media organizations in all this? The role of media as a referee between the public and the government is often explored in Communication Studies literature (e.g., Dearing and Rogers 1996; Yanovitsky 2002). I acknowledge that many authors in Communication Studies argue that the media sets the agenda for policy-makers. The media is said to set this agenda by implying that heavy reportage of a particular issue is indicative of the public's desire for government policy-making concerning that issue (Dearing and Rogers 1996). In other words, there is the idea in Communication Studies literature that the root of public policy instigation is the media, rather than group membership (and related reward motives), as I have discussed in the present chapter. The important question that this raises is whether media organizations and workers 'referee' the type and extremity of group motives that drive public policy-makers. Likewise, do media referee the extent to which reward motives drive public policy-makers? The next chapter will explore these questions.

Some Communication Studies authors argue that media are not always an agenda-setter; they define media as a referee symbiotically connected to both the government and public (Yanovitsky 2002). The next chapter will explore the psychological processes through which media organizations and policy-makers are connected as far as decision-making about policies is concerned. Additionally, the next chapter will explore the psychological reasons for the interdependence: what are the psychological conditions explaining the symbiosis between media organizations and policy-makers when policy decision-making is concerned? Secondly, what psychological conditions explain why policy-makers accept or favourably respond to media organizations, given what we know about group processes? It is clear that we need to consider more than just public policy-makers' perspectives, when understanding the role of media organizations in public policy decision-making. The next chapter will explore the socio-cognitive group processes steering the influence of media organizations on policy-makers. I will argue that media organizations adjudicate psychological decision-making processes among policy-makers. As Chapter 5 and 6 will show, media organizations and media workers are not objective in their adjudication of public policy decision-making. They often engage in faulty decision-making about how to represent public policy matters/opinion.

Conclusion

This chapter tackled the question of whether group membership can indeed predict what is on a given public policy-maker's agenda. By analysing data from the UK Parliament, we can conclude that policy-makers who belong to group X are more likely to propose or participate in discussions about policies that benefit group X, in comparison to policy-makers who do not belong to group X. This supports the argument that the notion of the 'common good' in policy-making is often exclusive. The 'group' in 'group motives' represents, not society in general, but a particular social category with which a public policy-maker identifies. *Which* group will depend on the characteristics of the psychological 'situation': the group memberships of those around, the group relevance of a particular policy issue, the type of policy issue, and so on. In understanding the group motives of public policy-makers, therefore, we need to establish which specific group is concerned.

That conclusion applies if we disregard differences between policy issues. Looking at the effects of group membership per individual policy issue, I can conclude that the effect of group membership is not absolute. Group membership predicts MPs' policy-related activities as far as some types of policy issues are concerned, namely: women's issues, Scotland issues, health issues and ethnic minority issues. This might be because of the extent or intensity of the policy needs associated with these issues. I also suggest that group membership drives some other types of policies not analysed in our study – namely foreign policy and regional policy. In the next chapter, I will further explore the rules of thumb that explain such differences between policy issues. Why are group influences effective for some types of policy decisions but not others? In the next chapter, I will also explore the part played by media organizations in setting the agenda for policy-makers. I will then explore the characteristics of policy decisions that make policy-makers susceptible to media influences.

Chapter 5
Why and When Media Organizations Referee Public Policy Decision-Making

In the Introduction to Part II, I discussed the psychological reasons why umbrella social categories such as the 'media', 'policy-makers' and 'the public' are important. These three categories are the key entities in the triad illustrated in Figure 4.1 (see Introduction to Part II of this book). As Figure 4.1 illustrates, there is continual communication between policy-makers and media organizations/ workers, between media and the public, and between the public and media. Are media organizations the original point of that communication? This chapter will address that question by discussing literature postulating that the media is pivotal in setting the agenda for policy-makers. I will review some studies testing that 'agenda-setter' perspective concerning the role of media and consider whether media organizations sets the agenda for some, but not all, types of policy issues. I will then discuss the idea that media organizations, as a crucial 'actor' in the feedback loop, act as a *de facto* referee between policy-makers and the public. I will discuss the characteristics of the media profession and media organizations which help facilitate their refereeing role in policy-making. In terms of working practices, I will discuss media workers' mental scripts about their profession's public role and the relevance of organizational identity. I will then discuss the characteristics of media organizations that determine whether (and how) they engage in policy refereeing. In particular, I will discuss differences between broadsheet and tabloid organizations, as well as differences between public and private media organizations. This will lead to a consideration of whether the important differences between media organizations involve their level of 'seriousness' (or public accountability) together with their corporate interests. Having considered organizational factors, I will then discuss the psychological circumstances under which policy-makers are prone to media influences. Specifically, I will discuss the use of heuristics in decision-making. I will consider whether policy-makers are most susceptible to media influences when there is ambiguity about the correct policy decision and/ or when the stakes/threats associated with making the wrong decision are low. I will also consider individual differences which makes policy-makers susceptible to media influences, in particular individual differences concerning political ideology and cognitive style in decision-making. Additionally, I will consider whether policy-makers are prone to media influences when specialist knowledge is required to make a policy decision. Under such circumstances, policy-makers can be susceptible to novel information.

Media Organizations' Role in Public Policy-Making: The Agenda-Setter Perspective

The feedback loop model (see Figure 4.1 in the Introduction to Part II) postulates that media organizations and media workers referee public policy-making. However, some previous literature suggests that media are actually the starting point for policy ideas. I will now review this literature.

Some communication scholars argue that public policy-making is reactive, that it is *a posteriori* to media coverage (Dearing and Rogers 1996). Dearing and Rogers defined media as 'agenda-setters' for government policy-making. They argued that media platforms determine what policy-makers think requires policy attention and action. This implies that there is an imbalance of power in the relationship between media organizations and policy-makers. What evidence is there that media organizations set the agenda for public policy-making? Let us take the example of antidrug policies. Dearing and Rogers considered public opinion about whether drugs were the most important problem faced by the US. Dearing and Rogers' data analysis suggested that increments and decrements in public opinion about that, between 1985 and 1992, closely mirrored increments and decrements in the number of media stories about drugs between 1985 and 1992. Dearing and Rogers also noted that US federal spending on antidrug law enforcement in 1987 ($3 billion) was thrice the amount spent in 1981. This supports the idea that the US's antidrug policies increased when media coverage about drugs increased.

At the same time, from correlational data, it is difficult to trace the antidrug policies to the media any more than it is possible to trace the beginning of the policies to policy-makers themselves or the public. One might argue that US policy-makers tested out new antidrug policies in the media shortly before 1985, leading to increments in media coverage about the issue. This in turn might have led to increments in public opinion about drugs. This public opinion might then have been communicated to the media, in turn reaching policy-makers, who then decided to lobby for increased federal spending on antidrug law enforcement. This sequence of events seems plausible, but data analysis methods beyond correlations (such as structural equation modeling) would be needed to test these suppositions.

Let us consider other research testing the idea that media organizations set the agenda for public policy. Yanovitsky (2002) took the issue of drunk-driving policies as an example when researching the agenda-setter perspective. Yanovitsky hypothesized that:

> Heightened policy attention to a public issue will be prompted by increased media attention to the same issue … Following a decrease in media attention to this issue, policy attention to the same issue will decrease as well (ibid: 427).

Yanovitsky (2002) counted the amount of news items solely about drink driving. These were articles published within the following major US news media: the

Associated Press, *New York Times* and *Washington Post*. Yanovitsky counted the number of articles published between 1978 and 1995. Yanovitsky then counted the amount of US Congress hearings on drunk-driving, the amount of US bills proposed on drunk-driving, the amount of US federal money allocated to tackling drunk-driving, and the number of laws adopted by the US concerning drunk-driving. This was all between 1978 and 1995. Yanovitsky's data showed that as media coverage of drunk-driving increased, so did US policy attention towards drunk-driving. For example, when there was an average of 14.8 news stories a month (in 1978–1980), there were five bills and zero hearings on drunk-driving. When the average news stories a month rose to 78.5 (in 1981–1984), there were 25 bills and five hearings. When the average news stories a month rose to 93.4 (in 1985–1988), there were 39 bills and 11 hearings on drunk-driving. Policy actions corroborated that pattern, with Yanovitsky (ibid: 437) noting that 'Between 1984 and 1995, (US) appropriation for (drunk-driving)-related prevention and public education programs more than tripled (from \$33.4 million in 1984 to \$83.4 million in 1995).' This altogether suggests that the media coverage, public opinion and public policy were all inter-related.

Yanovitsky's (2002) findings lend some empirical support to Dearing and Rogers' (1996) conclusion about media roles in US policy-making. However, Yanovitsky (2002) pointed out that media are not the agenda-setter in all or most public policy instances. I similarly argue that one cannot trace the starting point of public policy to media organizations. In some cases (see Chapter 4) the source *could* be traced to policy-makers themselves, rather than media organizations. In most cases, the source of a policy is untraceable because of the continual communication loop tying media organizations, policy-makers and the public (see Figure 4.1). Considering drunk-driving policies, it is actually not so clear that media platforms *were* the starting point. For instance, Dearing and Rogers (1996: 27) noted that the 'designated driver concept' in the US began as a campaign run by Jay A. Winsten, who was a Harvard professor. Winsten was part of a centre in Harvard that endeavoured to highlight the dangers of drink-driving to the public. Winsten is said to have spearheaded public service broadcasts about the issue of drunk-driving during the mid-1980s. Winsten is also said to have encouraged primetime television programmes such as *Growing Pains*, *The Cosby Show*, *Cheers* and *L.A. Law*, to portray the issue drunk-driving.

If we were to categorize Jay A. Winsten and his centre into one of the three entities in Figure 4.1 this entity could be the 'policy-makers' categories. This is because interest groups, campaigners, experts, consultancies and other non-governmental entities often have a pivotal role in public policy-making. Therefore, Winsten and his centre can be classified under the 'policy-maker' umbrella category, rather than under the 'public' or 'media' category. In fact, it appears that Winsten and his colleagues played a pivotal role in not just proposing anti-drunk-driving public policy but in also encouraging media coverage of this proposed policy. We could conclude that Winsten and others communicated the proposed policy to media organizations – rather than media organizations being the originator of the policy. We can note that, around that time, media coverage about drunk-driving increased, as Yanovitsky's (2002) data showed. Following that, the media then communicated the proposed policy to the public. The public responded via the media, which then communicated to policy-makers the idea that the proposal was popular with the public. The proposed public policy then became ratified by the Congress, as policy-makers there had the power to do so. Increments in public spending on anti-drunk-driving followed. In summary, there is more evidence that media organizations refereed the anti-drunk-driving policy than there is evidence that media organizations were the policy's starting point.

There is evidence in support of that extrapolation, and in support of Yanovitsky's (2002) point that a media organization's role varies from policy to policy. In other words, media organizations are not always an agenda-setter in policy-making. Edwards and Wood (1999) tracked the effects of media coverage of public policy issues on the government's policy agenda. Edwards and Woods analysed the government's agenda by focusing on the attention that the US president and US Congress paid to particular policy issues. To quantify the US president's attention to a given policy issue, Edwards and Woods counted the amount of paragraphs in the *Public Papers of the President*. This is the US government's record of the president's public speeches, writings, statements, and so on. To quantify Congress's attention, Edwards and Woods calculated the total number of Congressional hearings on specific policy issues. There were five public policy areas investigated by Edwards and Woods: the Arab-Israeli conflict, crime, education, healthcare, and US-USSR relations. Edwards and Woods restricted their searches to the period between 1984 and 1994. They chose these years as a way of controlling for foreign policy events. Edwards and Woods then calculated the amount of time in minutes that US television network news programmes spent on broadcasts about the five chosen policy issues. Edwards and Woods then analysed the statistical correspondence between the amount of broadcast minutes and the amount of presidential attention towards each policy issue. Edwards and Woods found statistically significant effects of media coverage on the president's attention to three of the five policy issues: the Arab-Israeli issue, the issue of crime and the US-USSR issue. Media coverage of these issues significantly predicted presidential attention towards the same issues, but not vice versa. In other words, presidential attention did not statistically predict media coverage of Arab-Israeli, crime or US-USSR issues. Edwards and Woods thus found evidence of the agenda-setter perspectives as far as three out of five policy areas were concerned.

Edwards and Woods' (1999) evidence therefore partially supports the agenda-setter perspective (Dearing and Rogers 1996). This is in the sense that media coverage predicted policy-makers' attention to foreign policy issues and crime issues. At the same time, Edwards and Woods' evidence shows that media organizations do not set the agenda for all types of public policy. As Edwards and Woods found, education and healthcare policies are not necessarily instigated by media organizations. It therefore seems plausible that media organizations referee – rather than instigate – policies instigated by a different entity in the triad (see

Figure 4.1). As an example, Edwards and Woods found that presidential attention towards healthcare issues had a significant effect on media coverage of healthcare issues. Edwards and Woods also found that presidential attention towards education issues also had a significant effect on media coverage of education issues. In other words, as far as healthcare and education policies were concerned, Edwards and Woods' evidence did not corroborate Dearing and Rogers' view of media as the agenda-setter for public policy. In fact, if we consider the policy areas in Edwards and Woods' research that *did* substantiate the agenda-setter perspective, two out of three concerned foreign policy. There are reasons why foreign policy issues are an exception, not a norm.

Why might foreign policy be an exception, not a norm, as far as public policy decision-making is concerned? Recall that Edwards and Woods (1999) found support for the agenda-setter perspective for three out of five policy issues. Of the three, two were foreign policy issues: the Arab-Israeli issue and the US-USSR issue. It is feasible that policy issues which evoke strong emotional reactions are handled differently from other policy issues. When it comes to foreign policy, we can argue that media organizations have an exceptional role, compared to domestic policy. This is because media within one country are often the only source of information used by people within that country to find out about events abroad. Sharkey (1993) argued that media representations of foreign events often evoke strong emotions when they depict imagery of war situations, kidnappings, or other occurrences abroad. Sharkey therefore argued that foreign policy decisions are often influenced by emotional impulses, such as after the public and policy-makers see disturbing imagery from news reports. Moreover, there can be greater consensus in different media organizations' representations of foreign events, compared to different media organizations' representations of domestic events. For example, the use of the same images or footage of foreign events by different media organizations can create the impression of consensus. As Chapter 6 will show, implying consensus is a fertile condition for polarized opinions. Media portrayals of crime events could likewise evoke strong emotions, explaining media agenda-setting roles in crime policy (Edwards and Woods 1999, see also the next chapter).

What are other examples of policy agenda set by media organizations? Uscinski's (2009) study investigated this. Uscinski analysed US television network news stories that were placed first or second during each programme broadcasted between the years 1968 and 1990. Uscinski then coded each story according to the type of policy issue it concerned. Uscinski then recorded the public's average answers (chartered across time) to a common general survey question. This question asks members of the public to indicate what they believe is the most important problem faced by the nation. Uscinski then analysed the effect of media agenda-setting on the public's opinion about the most important problem. Uscinski found that the unique effect of media agenda-setting was statistically significant if the policy concerned was: defense, federal operations, macroeconomic or about social welfare. At the same time, Uscinski found that media agenda-setting was not statistically significant if the policy issue was agriculture, banking, education, housing, international affairs, science, transport and some others.

Therefore, mixed empirical support for the agenda-setter perspective lends weight to Yanovitsky's (2002) point that the relationship between media and policy-makers is actually symbiotic or mutually advantageous. We can find further support for this idea if we consider the history of the role of media organizations in public policy. For instance, in a historical review of the changing importance of the press to US government from the Roosevelt era onwards, Hess (1984) notes that:

> Pressroom, press conference, press secretary, press office, press release: the development of government mechanisms to service the news media was a product of mutual advantage, not a constitutional responsibility of the (US) Republic (ibid: 2).

In summary, there is some evidence that media organizations set the agenda for particular types of public policy. These include crime policy and foreign policy. However, in many instances of public policy, it is difficult to trace the source of the policy to the media *per se*. More evidence seems to point towards media organizations as a referee in public policy-making, rather than an agenda-setter. At the most basic level, media organizations convey information from policy-makers to the public and vice versa. As well, at the most basic level, media organizations host discussions about public policy. Often, media organizations do not neutrally relay information about public policy, because of a variety of group processes. What are the circumstances under which media organizations plays a refereeing role in policy decision-making? There are characteristics of media organizations, characteristics of policy dilemmas, and characteristics of media working practices that can answer this question.

When does the Media Referee Public Policy Decision-Making? Some 'Rules of Thumb'

I have argued that media organizations referee public policy decision-making by 'standing' between policy-makers and the public. In the following sections, I will consider the circumstances under which this happens. Among others, the media category comprises media staff and media organizations (Part II focuses on these while acknowledging that this definition leaves out informal or 'amateur'/'citizen' media). First, I will explore the role of media working practices, organizational characteristics and corporate interests, as predictors of the refereeing role. I will discuss the idea that whether or not media workers' practices facilitate their organizations' refereeing role depends on the organizations' values/ norms to begin with. I will also discuss the relevance of individual differences in explaining variation among media workers in contributing towards a given media organization's refereeing role. I will discuss the issue of organizational identity among media workers, their mental scripts about the public role of their organization or profession and the public responsibility of each, and other factors such as interpersonal contact with policy-makers.

After that, I will address the question: what is the rule of thumb that can explain which policy decisions are heavily influenced by media organizations and which are not? I will now consider factors ('rules of thumb') which determine when media organizations help shape public opinion about policy issues and policy-making.

A Rule of Thumb: (i) Working Practices within a Media Organization

The first factor that we need to consider involves the working practices of a media organization, in terms of assuming a refereeing role. This is because media organizations vary in the extent to which they expend effort in commenting about policy issues, regulating their representations of public opinion about those issues, and so on. This refereeing role can be shaped by the organization's explicit mission values. It can also be shaped by explicit actions (e.g., by editors) to ensure that the media workers' outputs conform to the organization's overall mission values. Alternatively, or concurrently, the refereeing role can be shaped by implicit psychological processes. Workers within a media organization can conform to implicit norms and values, particularly if they possess strong feelings of social identity as members of that media organization. Through tacit rewards or punishments, workers within a media organization can gauge the normative working practices of that media organization, as far as refereeing the process of public policy is concerned. What evidence is there to corroborate these suppositions?

First, let us consider whether there is evidence of consistency within a media organization in its representations of policy issues, across several years. Wilkinson and McGill (2009) compared *Guardian* newspaper articles about people with learning disabilities, published in 2001 as compared to 1983. They found that the newspaper articles, irrespective of the year published, shared similarities in the way that learning disabilities were represented. Specifically, Wilkinson and McGill found that the newspaper articles from 1983 and 2001 under-played the severity and complexity of learning disabilities. This implies that the *Guardian* newspaper (a broadsheet) made the same erroneous decisions about how to represent learning disabilities, comparing 2001 and 1983. We might speculate on whether this can be attributed to information sampling working practices. *Guardian* staff in 2001 may have used articles from the *Guardian's* own archives when sampling information about learning disabilities as a news issue. They may have referenced the same sort of background information about learning disabilities from the *Guardian* archives. As we will discover, in the next chapter, poor information sampling practices can be detrimental to the quality of a decision made. Likewise, the same ideas or themes about learning disabilities may have been repeated by *Guardian* staff writing in 2001, compared to *Guardian* staff writing in 1983. For example, Wilkinson and McGill noted that the articles' focus remained on learning disabilities among children. This may be attributable to the information sampling explanation.

Interestingly, organizational identity (or membership of an organization) predicts conformity to working practices (McGill and Cummings 1990). A worker's identification with a media organization can predict his/her conformity to erroneous decision-making normative of that media organization. This is consistent with social identity theory (Tajfel and Turner 1979), which explains why people's behaviour and thoughts can be governed by their group's norms, once their self-categorization into that group is activated (see also Turner *et al.* 1987). Is there evidence that media workers' practices depend on their membership of a given media organization? A study by McGill and Cummings (1990) analysed 35 *Guardian* newspaper articles written by either staff reporters or non-staff reporters. All the articles were about the issue of mental handicaps. McGill and Cummings analysed the articles using content analysis, which is a qualitative method. McGill and Cummings found that the *Guardian* articles' representations of mental handicaps depended on whether the reporter was a staff reporter or a non-staff reporter. McGill and Cummings found that staff reporters tended to misrepresent the issue more frequently than did non-staff reporters. The misrepresentations by reporters included conflating the issue of mental handicaps with the issue of mental illness. The difference between staff and non-staff reporters lends weight to my earlier explanation. *Guardian* staff reporters are more likely to identify with the *Guardian* organization than are non-staff reporters. It seems plausible that employees who belong to an organization should report stronger feelings of organizational identity than freelance workers or temporary staff working for the same organization. This supposition is consistent with the social identity perspective (Turner *et al.* 1987; Tajfel and Turner 1979). As we noted in the previous chapter, categorization into a group is a necessary pre-condition for feelings of group identity (see Turner *et al.* 1987). Staff reporters working on an article might therefore be more heavily influenced by organizational identity processes in their decision-making. There is a shortage of empirical evidence about organizational identity among media workers. Moreover, there is little empirical research about the impact of organizational identity among media workers on faulty decision-making. We can surmise, by applying social psychological theories and evidence from other social groups (see the Introduction to Part II of this book), that organizational identity among media workers *is* important.

Research into media workers' organizational identity should explore its relevance for working practices relevant to decision-making, conformity to organizational normative beliefs about policy issues, and so on. From McGill and Cummings (1990), I would extrapolate that workers under contract with a media organization, compared to freelance media workers, are more likely to engage in faulty group decision-making. In order to explain this phenomenon, let us consider information sampling practices, which are a key predictor of the quality of group decision-making (Stasser and Titus 1985). Media workers employed by a given organization might sample more information from the organization's own archives over information from wider sources. This could explain why the 2001 *Guardian* staff reports analysed by McGill and Cummings' represented the issue of mental handicaps in a manner similar to *Guardian* reports published in 1983.As we will find out in the next chapter, poor information sampling is a key antecedent of faulty decision-making. In contrast, non-staff media workers might sample both information sources equivalently. This could be because of practical reasons such as access to multiple information sources. It could also be because of psychological reasons such as a given freelance worker's habit of accessing multiple information sources, or the freelance worker's motivation to access information beyond the commissioning media organization's archives.

The notion of psychological motivation can also explain media workers' choices about how to represent policy issues. Psychological motivation can regulate a media worker's decision to represent a policy issue in a manner that pushes a given agenda, in line with their organization's values. Recalling the importance of reward motives (see Chapter 4), tacit rewards (e.g., approval by colleagues) can create such psychological motivation. Experiments have shown that decision-making depends on not just social cues but also rewards (Evans, Fleming, Dolan and Averbeck 2011).

What research is there exploring decision-making by media workers? Some studies explore instances of faulty decision-making in media workers' choices about how to represent a policy issue, for example poverty and public welfare. Gilens (1996) analysed 214 pictures which accompanied 182 articles published in three American news magazines. All were articles about poverty and public welfare. Gilens found that 62 per cent of the pictures depicted African Americans. This figure misrepresented the percentage of African Americans in poverty (at the time, it was 29 per cent; see Gilens 1996, p 535). To gauge the explanation for this disparity, Gilens interviewed a number of photo editors. Gilens found that the photo editors expressed the motivation to represent poverty in the US fairly. Despite this, as Gilens argued, the photo editors had made decisions to over-select pictures depicting African Americans in poverty:

> Because a photo editor typically has a vastly larger number of pictures available than will be used for publication, the racial composition of the photographs that ultimately appear in the magazine will reflect the selection criteria of the photo editor. A photographer will typically produce anywhere from 400 to 4000 photographs for a single newsmagazine story. Thus even if photographers submit, on average, three pictures of poor African Americans for every two pictures of poor whites, magazine photo editors have the ability to determine the racial mix of the few pictures that find their way into print (ibid: 533).

Gilens' findings therefore emphasize the role of choice in media workers' decision-making about how to represent a public policy issue such as welfare. Gilens argued that the photo editors in the interviews cognitively justified what were actually erroneous decisions, based on stereotypical beliefs about the level of poverty among African Americans.

We should also consider the extent to which media workers' choices about how to represent a policy issue are regulated by their organization's norms and the work settings within the organization. For instance, staff reporters have closer physical proximity to other members of the organization than freelance reporters. This physical proximity to other group members creates a fertile social context for self-categorization and a salient organizational identity (applying Turner *et al.* 1994). Additionally, a media worker's proximity to coworkers within the organization creates opportunities for group discussions about policy issues before they write about them. These could be informal discussions or formal discussions during meetings about the next edition of the organization's output. As we will find out in the next chapter, the mere occurrence of a group discussion before a decision makes members of a group prone to faulty decision-making. For example, opinion polarization often happens after a group discussion, relative to no group discussion (Wallach, Kogan and Bem 1962). Opinion polarization happens because talking about a decision in a group setting leads people to conform to other group members' opinions, it leads people to strengthen their initial attitudes towards the decision after hearing other people expressing/repeating the same opinion, and ultimately a shift to a more extreme version of one's original attitudes (see e.g., Isenberg 1986; Kamau and Harorimana 2008, for a review of literature about this).

Even beyond media workers' feelings and actions driven by their organizational identity, media workers could possess mental 'scripts' about what being a media worker entails. Hanitzch (2005) conducted research alluding to this concept of mental scripts by interviewing 385 journalists in Indonesia. Hanitzch asked them a series of questions to gauge their perceptions about what being a journalist entails. Hanitzch then subjected the survey results to factor analysis, a statistical technique. The results suggested that journalists construe the roles of journalists as follows: 'public-oriented news journalism, popular service journalism, critical watchdog journalism, objective precision journalism and opinion-oriented news journalism' (ibid: 493). For instance, Hanitzch (2005) found that constructions of objective precision journalism involved workers placing high importance on accuracy and neutrality in their reporting. Such mental scripts about one's professional role as a media worker has interesting consequences for one's working practices.

There is evidence that media workers' mental scripts about their profession's role predispose them to the kind of faulty decision-making which we discussed earlier. Richards and Rees (2011) interviewed 40 people associated with the journalist profession. Some were journalists, some were people involved in journalism education and others were experts on journalism. Richards and Rees explored the role of emotions in a journalist's role as someone who interviews people. Richards and Rees found that there was confusion among journalists about what constitutes objectivity. Richards and Rees found that not all journalists defined objectivity in terms of political impartiality. Some defined it in terms of emotional detachment. Nonetheless, the absence of a consistent notion of objectivity in the profession could mean that journalists are prone to the group processes we discussed earlier, in their decision-making. Not feeling obliged to be objective, or not adhering to objectivity in its real sense, can mean that media workers are not 'inoculated' against groupthink, polarization, and other kinds of faulty decision-making.

There is some evidence suggesting that media workers' mental scripts about their profession's role vary according to the kind of media organization that they work for. There is some evidence that the type of media organization interacts with the 'mental scripts' discussed above. Hanitzch (2005) analysed the effect of the type of media organization that the journalists worked for, and the amount of importance that the journalists placed on each type of journalism. Hanitzch found that working for a radio organization was associated with placing lower importance on objective precision journalism. This corroborates Machill and Beiler (2009), who found that, of all journalists, radio journalists spent the least amount of time (4.8 per cent) doing fact checking/cross-research. We can explain such findings by considering how radio organizations construe their public role, relative to other types of media organizations.

Moreover, there is evidence that media workers' mental scripts about their profession's public role can depend on culture. Seo (2011) found evidence that journalists' beliefs about their professional roles can vary according to their cultural origin. Seo surveyed 90 journalists who had written news reports on talks about North Korea's nuclear programme. Of these 90 journalists, 45 were South Korean, 24 were from the US and 21 were European. Seo found that South Korean journalists agreed more with the statement 'journalists become active participants in the process of the diplomatic negotiations' (ibid: 475) than did US or European journalists. This difference between the South Korean and US/European journalists was statistically significant. However, we do not know whether this was because of South Korea's geographic/historical proximity to North Korea and – perhaps – South Korean journalists' view of their own role as 'intermediaries' between their northern neighbours and the rest of the world. Therefore, cultural values in a country can moderate the mental scripts which media workers possess about their profession's refereeing role.

In addition, there is evidence that some media workers adhere to particular mental scripts about their profession's role more than others. Hanitzch (2005) found that journalists with lower formal education held stronger beliefs that their professional role should involve critical watchdog journalism. Hanitzch likewise found that the more formally educated the journalist, the greater the importance he/she places on objective precision journalism. These findings imply that media workers' mental scripts about their profession's role as a public referee are minimized by professional training. Interestingly, Hanitzch also found that journalists who had existing interpersonal relationships with politicians or policy-makers were more likely than other journalists to believe that critical watchdog journalism is important. This illustrates the individual differences which exist among media workers, in terms of their mental scripts about their profession's public role.

There is also evidence that media organizations 'vet' the incidence of individual differences among their workforce. This is in the sense that a media organization selects prospective employees who will uphold its norms and values. Hollifield, Kosicki and Becker (2001) explored the idea that each media organization has a 'culture' comprising a set of values, norms, social identity, and so on. Hollifield *et al.* conducted an archival analysis of survey data. The data were from a 1996 US national survey of 318 television news directors, a 1996 US national survey of 735 newspaper editors, and a 1996 US survey of 2383 media graduates. Hollifield *et al.* explored whether organizational culture shapes each media organization's hiring practices. They hypothesized that media organizations hire staff who will echo the organization's culture. Hollifield *et al.* found that staff making hiring decisions in the media organizations evaluated applicants' personality traits from the point of view of the organization's values. This implies that the selection practices in media organizations minimize the sorts of individual differences (e.g., particular personality traits) which might undermine the organization's norms and values. Such 'vetting' of individual differences in a group context can be a symptom of groupthink (see the next chapter). It can also be a symptom which exacerbates other symptoms of faulty decision-making, such as self-censorship and opinion conformity (see Kamau and Harorimana 2008 for a review of the symptoms).

In summary, working practices within a media organization determine and facilitate the organization's role as a referee in public policy-making. These working practices are defined by the media organization's values and norms. For example, media organizations often have political ideologies that determine their construal of public policy news, their interest in certain public policy issues over others, and their ideas about what they should be doing (as an organization) about public policy. Additionally, media organizations often have corporate goals. Therefore, market forces regulate their investment in public policy news/ features over other kinds of news/features. A media organization's values and norms become absorbed by workers explicitly or implicitly. They can be absorbed explicitly during formal editorial meetings, informal team discussions, reading the organization's mission values, and so on. The values and norms can also be absorbed implicitly when workers are tacitly rewarded for conforming to them. Likewise, values and norms can be absorbed implicitly when workers read or view their colleagues' outputs, and so on. Exactly what are the norms and values of different media organizations? There is a lack of psychological research about this. In particular, there is a lack of psychological research about the relationship between norms/values in media organizations and decision-making practices when staff handle public policy news. This kind of evidence would tell us a lot about media organizations' refereeing role in public policy-making. There is also a scarcity of research into working practices within media organizations and the concept of organizational identity among media workers. The research reviewed in this section suggests that (semi)permanent employees of a media organization are more prone to faulty decision-making processes in their representation of news than are freelance workers. Individual differences among media workers are also important. Some media workers are more prone to faulty decision-making processes than others, because of a lower level of professional training or higher intensity of interpersonal relations with policy-makers.

Something else that is important, in determining media workers' practices and a media organization's characteristics (relevant to refereeing public policy) is the type of media organization in question.

A Rule of Thumb: (ii) Tabloid vs. Broadsheet Organizations and Corporate Interests

In the UK and some countries, print media are thought of as either 'broadsheets' or 'tabloids'. Originally, these labels were based on the size of the newspaper. Coincidentally, we can say that there are often stark differences between 'broadsheet' and 'tabloid' media, in terms of their 'seriousness'. For example, UK broadsheets such as the *Telegraph*, *Independent*, or the *Financial Times* can be said to comprise a greater proportion of political news stories and commentary about public policy. This is in comparison to tabloids such as the *Sun* or *Express*, which comprise a greater proportion of celebrity stories, sensationalized or playful reportage, and so on. In recent years, many publishers of broadsheet newspapers decided to adopt the print size of tabloid newspapers. Nonetheless, the thematic differences between the two categories remained.

We can formulate some hypotheses about the relevance of this distinction. Whether a given print medium falls under the 'serious' or 'playful' category could govern the parent organization's refereeing role in policy-making. The labels 'broadsheet' and 'tabloid' will be used here to refer to any print newspapers commonly described that way, irrespective of their current print size. Considering studies that explore the differences between print media on the basis of their 'seriousness', we can deduce that there are important differences between these two types of print media organizations. This can be in the extent to which each type of media organization financially invests in reportage and commentary about public policy issues. The difference between broadsheets and tabloids can also be in what the refereeing involves. Specifically, the question is: how is a policy issue represented and what kind of information is sampled in representing that policy issue? Additionally, the difference between broadsheet organizations and tabloid organizations can be in the type of policy issues that each organization chooses to referee. I will now explore some research which will help investigate these hypotheses.

Consider, for example, evidence from Hallam (2009) about the differences in the content of broadsheet newspapers, relative to tabloid newspapers. Hallam searched a database of newspaper articles published between 1992 and 2000.

Hallam focused on articles about three crime cases, all of which involved individuals with mental disorders. Hallam suggested that broadsheet newspapers reported the cases more frequently than did tabloid newspapers. Hallam also suggested that the reportage had the effect of creating an imbalanced debate about mental health policy issues, such as policies on care in the community. This implies that broadsheet newspapers play a greater refereeing role in public policy-making, compared to tabloid newspapers; at least as far as mental health policy is concerned. This corroborates research by Foster (2006) about different newspapers' impact on the re-drafting of the UK Mental Health Bill. I will explore the impact of media refereeing on mental health policy in further detail in the next chapter.

Let us consider research exploring differences between broadsheets and tabloids in terms of their coverage of particular types of issues. Shepherd and Seale (2010) qualitatively analysed 3583 UK newspaper articles about eating disorders. They used the qualitative method of content analysis. Shepherd and Seale found that broadsheets reported eating disorder research stories more frequently than did tabloids. This implies that broadsheet organizations place stronger emphasis on health reportage than do tabloids. There is other evidence of differences between broadsheets and tabloids in their reporting of health issues. Williams *et al.* (2008) qualitatively analysed newspaper articles about snoring and insomnia. They found that broadsheets and tabloids differed in the way in which they represented snoring and insomnia as medical issues. They also varied in the extent to which they represented snoring and insomnia as conditions prevalent in one gender. These findings imply that broadsheet organizations and tabloid organizations assume different levels of social responsibility in their coverage of health issues. Tabloids are also often accused of sensationalizing health issues. For example, Corcoran (1998) of the Family Planning Association complained about one UK tabloid's coverage of the use of contraceptives by teenagers:

> The *Daily Mail* has been trying to raise public anxiety over teenagers, sex and the contraceptive pill to reckless levels …The Daily Mail is opposed to the provision of family planning counselling and argues that all family planning advice is a conspiracy of the Left. The publication recently devoted its front page to a story claiming that 10% of girls take oral contraception by reaching age 15 years. This study was based upon 13 words in a 13-page Department of Health document published weeks earlier which stated that an estimated 10% of resident women aged 14–15 years attended family planning clinics (Corcoran 1998: 23).

Do broadsheet organizations assume a clearer refereeing role than tabloids, as far as public health policies are concerned? There is some evidence that broadsheet organizations assume a stricter or more critical role in their representations of health issues. Pieters, De Gucht and Kajosch (2003) conducted a survey of broadsheet and tabloid newspaper article headlines. All of these headlines were selected from a one-month period in a Dutch-speaking region of Belgium. Pieters *et al.* compared newspaper headlines about psychiatric issues with newspaper headlines about non-psychiatric medical issues. They analysed the extent to which the headlines represented the issue in a negative or positive tone. Pieters *et al.* found a difference between tabloids and broadsheets in the sum negativity of the headlines. Broadsheet articles about medical issues (be they psychiatric or not) were more negative than tabloids. Recalling the notion of mental scripts that we discussed earlier, Pieters *et al.*'s findings suggest that workers in broadsheet organizations have stronger mental scripts about 'critical watchdog journalism' (Hanitzch 2005), as far as health issues are concerned.

There is other evidence that broadsheet organizations represent health issues in more objective ways than tabloid organizations. For example, Joffe and Harhoff (2002) analysed 48 UK newspaper articles about Ebola, a rare but very dangerous virus. Joffe and Harhoff found that tabloids represented Ebola in a more stereotypical manner than did broadsheets. Specifically, Joffe and Harhoff found that tabloids drew on stereotypical ideas about Africa, where Ebola outbreaks occurred, to a greater extent than did broadsheets. Such stereotyping is something which tabloids such as the UK *Daily Mail* are often accused of. For example, Ibrahim (2011) argued that the *Daily Mail* represented Calais (France), a town near the Channel Tunnel associated with illicit immigration, as a 'jungle'. This implies differences between tabloids and broadsheets, in terms of their adherence to norms of political correctness or in terms of their political ideologies. There is similar evidence of differences between tabloid and broadsheet readers. Joffe and Harhoff supplemented their analysis of the tabloid/broadsheet newspaper articles with a study in which they interviewed 50 newspaper readers. Of these 50, 30 were broadsheet newspaper readers and 20 were tabloid newspaper readers. Joffe and Harhoff concluded that the readers' beliefs about Ebola echoed the kind of newspaper that they read (tabloid versus broadsheet). These findings can be said to demonstrate the ideological differences between broadsheet organizations and tabloid organizations. In particular, they hint at ideological differences between tabloids and broadsheets in the incidence (or characteristics) of their policy refereeing role.

There is evidence similar to that by Joffe and Harhoff (2002) showing that broadsheet organizations adhere to norms of political correctness more than do tabloid organizations. Clement and Foster (2008) conducted a study in which they rated the quality of 1196 newspaper articles about schizophrenia. These were articles from five UK national newspapers published in either 1996 or 2005. Clement and Foster found that tabloid articles in 2005 used the term schizophrenia as a metaphor more than did tabloid articles in 1996. In contrast, Clement and Foster found that broadsheet articles in 2005 used the term schizophrenia as a metaphor less than did broadsheet articles in 1996. Beyond the categories 'broadsheet' and 'tabloid', there is some evidence that 'serious' media engage in more socially responsible reporting than 'playful' media. For example, Mason, Darnell and Prift (2010) found that 63.41 per cent of media news articles sampled portrayed the issue of aging positively, whereas 73.33 per cent of cartoons portrayed the issue negatively. We could infer that the important characteristic is a medium's constructions about its own social responsibility.

Nevertheless, evidence of differences between broadsheets and tabloids is not unequivocal. For instance, Pieters *et al*. (2003) found that both tabloids and broadsheets were similar in the way in which they represented psychiatric issues, relative to non-psychiatric medical issues. Pieters *et al*. found that negative articles about psychiatric issues tended to focus on the patient, irrespective of whether the articles were published by broadsheet organizations or tabloid organizations. Likewise, Pieters *et al*. found that negative articles about non-psychiatric medical issues tended to focus on the doctor as well as the patient. Similarly, Bell and Seale (2011) found no differences between broadsheets and tabloids in the way in which they represented cervical cancer news. Bell and Seale concluded that the use of in-depth celebrity case studies by tabloid organizations benefited the quality of their representations of cervical cancer. This was because the celebrity case studies presented by the tabloids often included detailed information about symptoms, risk factors and screening. Additionally, Clement and Foster (2002) found that in both broadsheets and tabloids there was no improvement in the quality of reports about schizophrenia, comparing 2005 with 1996. Clement and Foster found that the newspaper articles in the two years did not differ in describing schizophrenia in a manner that stigmatized it.

This leads us to consider differences among media organizations beyond their 'broadsheet' or 'tabloid' nature, in terms of their corporate interests. We have noted that the important characteristic is a media organization's construction of its level of social responsibility. We can extend the inferences made in this section to explain differences between publically funded non-print media (e.g., BBC television, radio) and privately funded non-print media (e.g., Sky television, Fox television). These can differ in their constructions of their public accountability because market forces or corporate financial interests can regulate a media organization's decisions about whether (and how) to engage in public policy refereeing. For these reasons, we can expect differences between organizations with different corporate financial concerns. This is in terms of their observance of responsible reporting, political correctness, and so on.

How do private media organizations compare with public media organizations? We can draw some inferences about this by considering differences between public and private organizations in general. Consider research by Özbilgin and Tatli (2011), who investigated whether the prevalence of individualist values over collectivist values depends on an organization's private or public status. Collectivist values, compared to individualist values, emphasize social accountability, social interdependence, and so on. When people make decisions about how to evaluate group concerns, collectivist values may become psychologically activated (Kamau, Giner-Sorolla and Zebel, in press). Özbilgin and Tatli interviewed 66 employees working within the field of equality and diversity from a variety of public and private organizations within the UK. Özbilgin and Tatli interviewed each employee for up to an hour then they thematically analysed the transcripts. Özbilgin and Tatli found that individualist values were more prevalent among private sector employees. Applying these sorts of findings to media organizations, we can surmise that publically owned media espouse collectivist values to a greater extent than do privately owned media. This could be explained by not just a difference in accountability to the public, but also by a difference in consideration of commercial gains.

There is also evidence that collectivist or individualist values within an organization determine the kinds of public lobbying tactics used by the organization. Barron (2010) researched the impact of corporations' values on their contributions to public policy-making. Barron proposed that the prevalence of individualist or collectivist cultural values determines a corporation's preferred lobbying tactics. Barron interviewed British and French government affairs managers working in companies based in Brussels. Barron concluded that cultural values have some relevance for the kinds of lobbying tactics used by corporations. Specifically, Barron found that collectivist/individualist values determine whether an organization seeks to influence policy-making via individual political action, or via building community relations.

Corroborating that, there is evidence that culture can determine policy decisions. In a study of corporate policy-making, Janssens, Brett and Smith (1995) proposed that employees' levels of individualism and collectivism have important ramifications for policy-making. Janssens *et al.* sampled 693 employees working at a US multinational corporation. The sample comprised employees of American nationality, Argentine nationality, and French nationality. Janssens *et al.*'s rationale was that these three nations differ in their prevalence of individualism and collectivism. Based on Hofstede (1980), American culture is said to have a high prevalence of individualism, French culture a medium prevalence of individualism and Argentina a high prevalence of collectivism. Janssens *et al.*'s survey found that both employees and management personnel construed the importance of policies differently, depending on their cultural values (individualism or collectivism). Janssens *et al.* also suggested that cultural values have an impact on the extent to which employees feel the need to participate in policy-making.

Exploring that point further, it is plausible that the surrounding culture determines media workers' beliefs about what a public policy should be. For instance, Gallagher (2011) proposed that an emphasis on individual entitlement and patient autonomy in US healthcare is reflective of individualist cultural values in the US. Likewise, Kaplan (1987) discussed the proliferation of individualist attitudes in some health policies. For example, Kaplan attributed attitudes of 'victim blaming' (ibid: 353) in the media to individualist values. This victim blaming is connected to a 'lifestyle theory' (ibid: 351) about the causes of chronic illnesses, meaning that patients with illnesses such as cancer are often directly or indirectly blamed in the media.

As well as considering the relevance of cultural values and corporate interests, we need to consider whether the impact of one media organization's outputs varies according to the type of medium in question. For example, how do different types of media (e.g., print versus online media) influence public opinion? This might be an unintended consequence of the psychology of media consumption, for example, in comparing consumption of print media with the consumption of online media. Some tentative evidence in this respect comes from Althaus and Tewksbury (2002). They conducted an experiment in which they divided people into three conditions. Each contained roughly 44 people. In condition#1, participants went to a laboratory five days in a week to read the New York Times website. In condition#2, a different set of participants went to a classroom to read the *New York Times* newspaper. In condition#3, the control condition, a different set of participants simply showed up on the sixth day. All participants were then asked to recall the stories that had appeared in the *New York Times* over the preceding five days. Althaus and Tewksbury found that participants who read the print version had a better memory of published stories, compared to participants who read the online version or who were in the control condition. It may be that audiences consume online media differently. Alternatively (or additionally), it may be that online versions of the same content are accompanied by extraneous content such as advertisements or links which divert readers' attention and therefore reduce their memory for the content. However, Althaus and Dewksbury found no statistically significant differences among online readers', print readers' and control participants' beliefs about the importance of policy issues in line with the *New York Times'* policy 'agenda-setting'. In other words, the print version of the newspaper did not have more or less of an impact on readers' beliefs about a policy's importance, relative to the online version or none. This might be because the influential aspects of a newspaper's content, such as the headlines, remain constant across different types of media (print, online). Therefore, even if readers do not recall the online content of articles as well as the print content of the same articles, they may recall the headlines just as well. The headlines may be sufficiently influential as agenda-setters.

Section Summary

In summary, there are some differences between tabloid organizations and broadsheet organizations, in terms of their public policy refereeing activities. The two types of organizations can differ in the extent to which they invest in reportage or commentary about public policy. The two types of organizations can also differ in the types of policies that they choose to referee. Additionally, the two types of organizations can differ in how they referee policy-making. Nevertheless, I have reviewed evidence showing that differences between broadsheets and tabloids are limited. The categorizations 'broadsheet' and 'tabloid' are more useful in giving us a general indication of a media organization's sense of social responsibility. Additionally, we can conclude that public and private media organizations engage in policy refereeing in different ways (be they more intense or less intense), depending on the policy issue, and depending on commercial interests. From this section we can conclude that a media organization's 'seriousness' and its commercial interests can help predict its refereeing role in public policy-making.

Having considered factors associated with media organizations and their working practices let us now consider factors associated with policy-makers' susceptibility to media influences. Media organizations and media workers can assume a refereeing role for a given policy, but the impact of that refereeing will depend on the characteristics of the policy decision in question.

A Rule of Thumb: (iii) Decision Characteristics and Susceptibility to Media Influences

Media organizations play a successful refereeing role when some types of policy decisions are being made. What are the likely characteristics of these decisions? When people are making decisions about something, they sometimes refer to heuristics (Dhami 2003). They resort to heuristics under certain circumstances. Firstly, people resort to heuristics to make a decision when they are unsure about the correct decision (Stewart and Stasser 1998). Moreover, people making a decision in a group setting often defer to other people in the group when they need to make a decision but they perceive ambiguity in identifying the correct decision (ibid.):

> if group members do not believe there is sufficient information to identify one demonstrably superior option, they may approach the task as a matter of collective judgment... This prediction is consistent with social comparison theory (Festinger, 1954) which suggests that when a task lacks an objectively correct answer group members will rely on comparisons with each other to decide if they have reached an acceptable answer (ibid: 98).

This leads us to extrapolate that public policy-makers are prone to the media's refereeing influences when there is ambiguity about the correct policy decision.

For example, imagine that council policy-makers in England need to make a decision about whether to buy and store large quantities of snow gritters before the next winter begins. Imagine that they need to make this budgetary decision well in advance of the winter, meaning that reliable weather forecasts are not yet available. The decision to use the budget could be correct, but only *if* there will be heavy snow in the region. If there will not be heavy snow, then the decision will be incorrect. Imagine that weather experts are unsure about what decision to make. Imagine that they encounter numerous commentaries in the media about the issue. Many of these media commentaries are arguing that councils should buy more snow gritters in preparation for the next winter. Based on the evidence that we discussed earlier (Stewart and Stasser 1998), we can predict that the council policy-makers will be very susceptible to media influences in this instance. This is because the correct decision is ambiguous.

Secondly, heuristics are used when there is a low level of threat associated with the decision or its outcome (Astorino-Courtois 2002). For instance, if policy-makers are faced with a dilemma whose consequences are not serious, they may defer to heuristics to make a decision about that policy. This creates a fertile opportunity for media organizations to assume a refereeing role. Astorino-Courtois conducted an experiment involving 140 students as participants. The participants were divided into four conditions, each requiring the participant to solve a particular hypothetical foreign policy dilemma. Astorino-Courtois manipulated the extent to which each dilemma involved high or low stakes, and high or low threat. For example, a 'high stakes' and 'high threat' foreign policy dilemma involved a scenario whereby a country known to have sponsored international terrorism had just gained access to uranium. Astorino-Courtois found some support for the idea that the decision-making depended on the level of threat in the dilemma, although the statistical differences between the four experimental conditions were not significant to a satisfactory probability level. Nonetheless, such a simulation policy experiment provides an interesting illustration of the kinds of decision-making processes that happen among public policy-makers when they are considering dilemmas of varying stakes.

Recall the fictitious example of the council needing to make a decision about the purchase of snow gritters. Imagine that the council policy-makers need to make a decision about whether to increase the anti-snow budget from 10 per cent of the council's overall budget to 12 per cent. In such an instance, the financial stakes are low. Imagine that the council policy-makers are repeatedly exposed to media commentaries calling for councils across the country to spend more money preparing for the winter. Due to the low stakes, the policy-makers will probably acquiesce and make the decision to increase the anti-snow budget to 12 per cent. However, imagine an instance whereby the council policy-makers need to make a decision about whether to double the anti-snow budget, to increase it to 24 per cent of the council's annual budget. In this instance, the financial stakes are high. We would expect that the council policy-makers will be much less susceptible to media influences in this instance.

Related to the above notion of threat and stakes in public policy-making is the notion of a policy's relevance to the majority. A policy which is of low direct relevance to the majority could be construed as being low in threat and stakes. In such a case, policy-makers may be highly susceptible to media influences. Policy issues deemed to be low in importance could include those which seem to have few direct ramifications for the immediate public audience, such as atypical issues.

Thirdly, there is evidence that some people are more likely to use heuristics to make decisions than other people, because of their political ideology or cognitive style (Tetlock 2000). Tetlock surveyed 259 middle-managers in public sector organizations by measuring their world-view and their cognitive style. Tetlock measured the managers' world view in terms of their liberal/conservative beliefs. Tetlock measured the managers' cognitive style using an adaptation of a questionnaire known as the 'Need for Closure Scale' constructed by Kruglanski and Webster (1996). This scale requires participants to indicate their agreement with items such as 'I dislike questions that can be answered in many different ways.' It is a scale which gauges participants' psychological tolerance for ambiguity (Tetlock). Tetlock found that the managers' political ideology, together with their cognitive style, predicted a variety of outcomes. For instance, 'conservative managers with strong preferences for cognitive closure were most likely ... to defend simple heuristic driven errors' (ibid: 293). Therefore, we would expect party-political differences among public policy-makers, in terms of their susceptibility to media influences that present heuristics about particular policy decisions. Additionally, we would also expect individual differences among public policy-makers based on their cognitive styles as far as ambiguity in decision-making is concerned. Recall the fictitious example of the council making a decision about increasing its anti-snow budget. A regional council run by a conservative party might subscribe to the ideology that individuals should be responsible for clearing snow in the areas around their own homes. For that reason, policy-makers within that council might resist media pressure to increase the council's anti-snow budget.

Fourthly, susceptibility to heuristics and media influences can depend on the knowledge needed to make a policy decision. In explaining when the media *does* referee public policy-making, we need to consider the complexity or technicality of the policy issue. Policy issues that require specialist background knowledge might be prone to the media's refereeing role. In other words, the media can become the condenser of such background information. This media refereeing role can be treacherous if the background information is misunderstood by the media workers. Martinez-Cajas *et al.* (2008) investigated the impact of journalists attending HIV/AIDS conference programmes specifically run to help train journalists for their reportage of HIV/AIDS issues. The conferences were organized by the National Press Foundation and the content was presented by HIV/AIDS researchers. Martinez-Cajas *et al.* argued that 'Journalists need to have basic tools to be able to identify overtly false science, which can be a common and widespread cause of public misinformation' (ibid: 3). Martinez-Cajas *et al.* surveyed some of the journalists who attended the conferences. Martinez-Cajas *et al.* also gauged feedback from conference records and concluded that such preparatory conferences help journalists improve the quality of their reportage on scientific issues. For example, one journalist said: 'Honestly, without the J2J training, I would have spent half of my time at the IAS conference referring to either a science dictionary or Googling up certain complicated scientific phrases' (ibid: 6). Their findings demonstrate the benefits of training journalists to process scientific research information in a way that prevents them from misinterpreting the results or relaying unrepresentative results.

What does that mean for public policy-makers making decisions? There is evidence that when people are about to make a decision about something which requires specialist knowledge, they are easily influenced by novel information

(Vinokur *et al.* 1985). It is therefore plausible that public policy-makers are influenced by novel information presented by media, when they do not have expertise in the policy issue concerned. For example, media reports about the dangers of a new vaccine may disproportionately influence a public policy-maker. This is in comparison to media reports about a public health issue that policy-makers may be more familiar with (e.g., the issue of restricting public access to antibiotics).

Let us revisit our fictitious example of the council policy-makers. They need to make a decision about whether to increase their anti-snow budget. Imagine that the council policy-makers in the previous examples are given complicated weather forecast information. They would need to analyse a series of probabilities associated with different meteorological factors that are used by specialists in their forecasting of snow. Just then, a weather expert X is interviewed in the media. He/she claims that the best factor to use in the prediction of snow is the average daily temperature that year. If the council were to ask weather experts what they think of X's claim, they might disagree with X's claim and point to empirical research in meteorological journals that shows the limitations of X's claims. Nonetheless, to a lay reader, expert X's claim seems plausible. The council policy-makers might therefore look at the average daily temperature that year, conclude that snow is likely, and decide to increase the council's anti-snow budget that year.

In summary, public policy-makers are susceptible to media influences under certain circumstances. We can make some general assumptions about these circumstances, based on previous literature. We can assume that media representations exist all the time, and they present continual 'heuristics' about given policy decision. The heuristic could be 'policy X is a sensible policy' or 'policy Y should be abandoned' or it could be more specific, for example 'councils should permanently increase their anti-snow budgets'. Whether or not the heuristic is adopted by policy-makers depends on a number of things. Whether or not media refereeing is successful depends on the characteristics of the policy issue and the characteristics of the policy-makers. From a psychological point of view, what makes policy-makers susceptible to media influences is: (i) ambiguity about the correct policy decision; (ii) the threats and/or stakes associated with different policy decisions; (iii) the policy-makers' ideology and cognitive style; and (iv) the specialist knowledge needed to make the policy decision.

Conclusion

We can conclude that media workers' organizational identity motivates them to perpetuate their organization's public policy refereeing role. This is in the sense that organizational identity predicts workers' adherence to organizational norms and values relevant to public policy refereeing. As a consequence of a variety of group processes, media workers can develop mental scripts about what to do (for example, what information to sample) and what to write (for example, in conformity to what other staff in the organization wrote), when handling public policy news. We can also conclude that key individual differences among media workers explain variation in their contribution to media refereeing roles. In particular, there are differences among media workers in their constructions of their profession's public role. There are also differences among media workers in terms of their professional training. For example, a lower level of professional training can exacerbate beliefs about critical watchdog journalism being normative of the journalistic profession. Additionally, individual differences exist among media workers in their level of interpersonal contact with public policy-makers. There is some evidence that interpersonal contact with politicians can exacerbate media workers' beliefs about their profession's public role. There is also evidence that media organizations engage in recruiting practices which regulate the extent of individual differences among their staff.

I then discussed evidence of differences among media organizations. I also reviewed evidence of similarities between tabloid and broadsheet media organizations. From this, it is concluded that what is important is the extent to which a print medium invests in 'serious' output. This includes political commentary and public policy lobbying. I can also conclude that tabloid/broadsheet media organizations differ in their regulation of their outwardly expressed attitudes. In other words, these two types of organizations differ in their level of involvement with public policy refereeing. They also differ in the types of policy issues that they choose to referee and also in how they go about refereeing public policy. All in all, it is important to consider a media organization's construal of its public accountability, in considering whether (and how) it referees public policy-making. Public media organizations may invest more in refereeing policy-making than private media organizations. This can be because of the prevalence of collectivist values in public media organizations, compared to private media organizations. It can also be because of greater concerns about market forces and financial interests, in the case of private media organizations.

I can also concluded that, as well as exploring media organizations (and their working practices) as determinants of the nature of media influences in public policy-making, we also need to consider the characteristics of policy decisions most susceptible to media influences. One important characteristic is the ambiguity of a potential policy decision, in terms of its correctness. Another characteristic of a decision that makes policy-makers susceptible to media influences is the level of threat or stakes associated with the policy decision. A third predictor of policy-makers' susceptibility to media influences is their political ideology and their cognitive style. Fourthly, something else which predicts policy-makers' susceptibility to media influences is their expertise in a given policy issue. All in all, the influence of media organizations on public policy-makers depends on the psychological characteristics of the policy decision in question, the characteristics of the media organization and the characteristics of media workers involved.

Chapter 6
Group Processes Among Media Workers, Faulty Decision-Making Processes and Effects on Public Opinion about Policy

In the previous chapter, I discussed the influences of media organizations on policy-makers. I will now discuss the influences of media organizations, through their employees, on public opinion. In the previous chapter I introduced the notion of media working practices and discussed some of the ways in which they help facilitate media organizations' policy refereeing role. I will now discuss practices associated with media workers' decision-making in more detail; this is because the decision-making aspects of media organizations' practices have important consequences for the media's policy refereeing role. They are the basis of media representations and media effects, which I will discuss in this chapter. Media workers therefore facilitate their organizations' values, norms and missions through these decisions. Additionally, media workers are influenced by other group processes – some associated with the umbrella group identity of being a media worker, and some associated with the public sphere. This means that, in certain policy instances, media workers from different organizations are subject to the same group influences and therefore we can observe patterns of faulty group decision-making processes across the media. In this chapter I will discuss how media organizations (focusing on media workers) contribute to polarization in public opinion about policy issues. I will then discuss how the public's consumption of media transitions into private discussions about policy issues, thus facilitating media organizations' policy agenda-setting or refereeing. I will explore two case studies that illustrate these processes at work: the Case of the Mental Health Bill and the case of UK national health policy. I will then take a deeper look at some working practices which contribute to faulty decision-making among media staff, such as poor information sampling practices and simplistic representations of outgroups' policy needs.

Why Media Workers' Professional Identities are Important

One of the consequences of belonging to a social category is that one possesses feelings of identification with that category (self-categorization theory, Turner *et al.* 1987). Tajfel and Turner (1979) described this notion of a social category aptly:

> We can conceptualize a group, in this sense, as a collection of individuals who perceive themselves to be members of the same social category, share some emotional involvement in this common definition of themselves, and achieve some degree of social consensus about the evaluation of their group and of their membership of it (ibid: 100).

The feeling of identifying with a particular social category is known as a social identity or a group identity (see also Turner 1996). If the social category is a profession, then the group identity can be called a professional identity. For example, people working in the media who identify with the media profession as a social category possess a media professional identity. The basic, essential characteristics of this group identity are the same as the basic characteristics of group identity as a generic concept (see social identity theory, Tajfel and Turner 1979; Turner 1996; Introduction to Part II of this book). To determine the most essential characteristic of group identity, Tropp and Wright (2001) synthesized various theoretical perspectives, including social identity theory. Through three empirical studies, Tropp and Wright statistically analysed the psychometric properties of different measures of group identity. Tropp and Wright concluded that the most essential characteristic of group identity is the inclusion of the category into one's sense of self. In other words, the most important indicator of group identity is the inclusion of the group in question into one's self-concept. The classic method of finding out what is in someone's self-concept is to ask them to respond to the question 'Who am I?' with descriptors that are of highest importance to them (Aronson, Wilson and Akert 2002). For example, if 'Gerard' works in the media and he has a strong group identity associated with the media profession, he might answer the question by including the professional descriptor in his answer: 'I am witty, sporty, a media professional, a father and I support the Green Party'. Note that the other descriptors represent identities that are also important to Gerard – his personal traits, his parental status and his political affiliation. Of course, the 'Who am I?' method is not the only method of measuring group identity that we should use. Tropp and Wright's literature review and empirical findings tell us that we should ask Gerard to estimate the psychological distance between him and other members of the media profession (see also an instrument, by Aron, Aron and Smollan 1992, used in a variety of settings, including laboratory research, Kamau, 2012; and field research, Kamau, Giner-Sorolla and Zebel, in press). This would corroborate the conclusion that Gerard possesses a strong media professional identity. What are the consequences of possessing a media professional identity?

We know from the social identity literature that group identity has a variety of consequences (see Brown 2000 for a literature review). For example, Brown concluded from his review that group identity determines members' stereotyping of their own group and also their stereotyping of other groups. In other words, the strength of one's group identity predicts one's beliefs about the homogeneity of the 'ingroup' or the homogeneity of the 'outgroup' Applying this example to media workers, we can say that the stronger their feelings of identification with the media profession, the stronger their beliefs about homogeneity within the media professions. For instance, given that he has a strong group identity, Gerard's perception of the homogeneity the media profession could include the belief that there is strong similarity in the values and norms amongst different media workers (e.g., journalists versus photographers; CNN employees versus ITV employees). Secondly, the stronger a media worker's professional identity, the stronger his/her beliefs about the homogeneity of any given 'outgroup'. For instance, Gerard might believe that public policy-makers are very similar to each other, regardless of their political affiliation. Thirdly, applying self-categorization theory (Turner *et al.* 1987), a strong media professional identity will be associated with greater perceptions of the differences between the 'ingroup' (i.e., the media profession) and 'outgroups' (e.g., public policy-makers, the public, other professions). For instance, Gerard might perceive very stark differences between the values and norms of media professionals compared to the values and norms of public policy-makers.

Aside from stereotyping, there are other consequences of group identity. If we divide the consequences of group identity into mental (i.e., thought-based) consequences, and behavioural consequences, the latter are particularly important in explaining how/why media group identity impacts on media workers' handling of public policy issues. One little explored behavioural consequence of group identity is decision-making in a group context. We know from a large, empirically robust body of evidence, that group decision-making is prone to faultiness (see Kamau and Harorimana 2008 for a literature review). For example, group discussions skew individual group members' opinions, leading to a polarized decision (see e.g., Isenberg 1986 for a meta-analysis of the causes). Individuals making a decision in a group setting suffer from groupthink, which is characterized by reduced objectivity, opinion conformity, self-censoring of dissent, defensive avoidance of contrary opinions and other symptoms (Janis and Mann 1979; Janis 1982). The extent to which a group member is prone to these faults is likely to depend on the strength of their identification with the group in question. For example, it is plausible that a media worker who ranks his/her professional identity high in his/her self-concept is more prone to media groupthink than a media worker whose ranks his/her professional identity low in his/her self-concept. Why? One simple explanation could be the extent to which a strong group identifier engages in self-stereotyping in conformity to group norms and practices, compared to a weak group identifier.

What are the implications so far? One implication is that individual media workers are prone to faulty group decision-making to a varying extent, depending on subjective factors. One subjective factor that we have discussed so far is the extent to which the individual media worker feels a sense of identification with others in the media profession. How strongly does he/she feel they belong to the media profession, to what extent does he/she conform to the norms/values of the media profession, to what extent does he/she emulate prototypical or exemplary members of the media profession such as Jon Snow? Remembering self-categorization theory (see the previous chapter's discussion of it), we note that a related subjective factor is the immediate context in which a particular decision is being made. Different public policy issues and different circumstances or situations in media professionals' working moments constitute different subjective contexts. This point is important because the psychological salience or relevance of one's membership of a given group varies from situation to situation (Turner *et al.* 1987).

In an immediate context whereby the group identity salient *is* the media group identity, then yes the media worker will be prone to the faulty group decision-making processes to be discussed in this chapter. If, in an immediate context, the media group identity is not psychologically salient, or a different group identity is salient (e.g., the media worker's gender, nationality, religion or other), then the faulty processes discussed in this chapter will not necessarily apply. The media worker might still be prone to faulty processes affecting those other group memberships. I acknowledge, as I discussed in the Introduction to Part II, that people belong to different groups, and as far as a particular group is concerned people self-categorize according to the psychological characteristics of a given situation. For example, let us consider one situation whereby a media worker is making decisions about how to represent a recent environmental policy. The decisions could be: 'What shall I write about this policy, shall my piece be purely factual or shall I include commentary?'; 'Shall my piece echo what other newspapers have written about this policy?'; 'Which background information about the environmental issue shall I include in the piece: where shall that information come from; what criteria shall I use to select that information?' Let us now consider a variety of plausible contexts in the following fictitious examples:

Table 6.1   An illustration of different policy situations, different salient group identities and different decision consequences for journalists

Policy situation?	Relevant group identity?	Consequence (vis-à-vis decision-making)
A journalist at a newspaper receives a press release from the UK's environmental government department (DEFRA). The press release is being discussed on an online forum by journalists from a variety of different media organizations across the UK. The policy is about DEFRA's plans to increase funding for environmental research.	The group identity likely to be salient in this situation: media group identity.	If the journalist's feelings of media group identity are strong, his/her reportage of the policy is likely to conform to other journalists' reportage. If the journalist has a strong media group identity, he/she will conform to other journalists. For example, he/she might interview the same academic expert as a source of background information about the policy, or publish the same quotes. If other journalists seem to have consensus in, say, being sceptical about the policy, then the journalist might decide to source or selectively include background research demonstrating the policy's limitations.
A journalist at a newspaper receives a press release from the UK's environmental government department (DEFRA). There is not much being said or published in media about the policy. The policy is about DEFRA's plans to increase funding for environmental research.	The group identity likely to be salient in this situation: none or public identity.	The journalist would probably report the policy factually, with little or no commentary. The journalist would probably source and include balanced background information (showing the advantages and disadvantages of the policy).
A journalist at a local newspaper in England receives a press release from the government indicating the UK's environmental policy on fishing in all waters between France and England. The newspaper is based in a region not far from the Channel. The local population relies heavily on income from the fishing industry.	The group identity likely to be salient in this situation: regional identity.	The journalist might first consider the region's norms and values vis-à-vis the fishing industry. The journalist's regional group identity will also matter. The journalist might also gauge local sentiment about the policy, such as from his/her experience of the region. Suppose that the policy would be detrimental to the region's economy and the journalist has a strong regional identity. His/her decisions would therefore be to include commentary when reporting the policy and to select background information that highlights the policy's limitations.

Policy situation?	Relevant group identity?	Consequence (vis-à-vis decision-making)
A journalist at a local newspaper in England, receives a press release from the government indicating the UK's environmental policy on global climate change. The newspaper is based in a region very far from the Channel. The journalist takes a coffee break and chats casually with some colleagues about the policy. They start discussing the policy's relevance to the issue of national sovereignty. After the break the journalist discovers that other newspapers have published commentaries discussing the policy in that very manner. There appears consensus, across different media even those with varying political leanings about the issue.	The group identity likely to be salient in this situation: media group identity (and, potentially, national identity).	The journalist's media group identity will influence his/her decisions. If he/she has a strong media group identity, then his/her commentary would mirror the consensus of opinion in other media. The commentary may reflect a small but significant shift towards a stronger version of the opinion believed to be the consensus amongst the media. The journalist might also selectively report background information that highlights the policy's implications for national sovereignty.
A journalist at a national newspaper receives a press release from an environmental campaign group with branches across the UK. The group is lobbying for a policy forcing landowners with unused farmland to let locals wanting an allotment to use it. Such issues of wealth distribution and interference by the state have traditionally divided national newspapers, according to their left-wing or right-wing leanings.	The group identity likely to be salient in this situation: organizational identity.	As with other situations, the strength of the journalist's group identity will determine his/her actions. In this instance, the strength of the journalist's identification with his/her employing organization will be relevant. If he/she does not identify strongly with the organization, his/her decisions will mirror the second example in this table. The piece will lean towards the factual and background research will be relatively balanced. Of course, his/her editor might exert pressure that will cause him/her to act as though he/she has a strong organizational identity. Whether under pressure or because of real identification, the journalist might alternatively conform to the organization's political ideology.

In summary, media workers' self-categorizations into the media profession are the first step towards their sense of group identity. In a media worker's day-to-day working moments, the psychological salience or relevance of his/her media group identity will vary from situation to situation. As far as representing policy news is concerned, this caveat is important in further explaining why there is variation in media agenda-setting roles as far as public policy decision-making is concerned (see Chapter 5). This caveat is also important because it explains individual differences among media workers (see Chapter 5). Different individuals in the media have different levels of media group identity. Subsequently, some media workers will be more prone to group processes associated with the media profession than other media workers. The strength of a media worker's feelings of group identity – their professional identity – has a variety of behavioural consequences. Of particular interest, in this chapter, is the behavioural consequence concerning decision-making. When media workers are making decisions about how to represent public policy news, the outcomes of their decision-making are important to the process of public policy decision-making. The media has the powerful capacity to shape public opinion about policy issues.

The Power of Media Decisions: Media Effects on Public Opinion

Why are media workers' decisions about how to represent public policy news important? Media organizations often help the government and public decide whether a public policy about a given issue is needed. This is the 'agenda-setting' perspective explored in Chapter 5. Media organizations also help the government and public decide whether a proposed policy should be pursued or not pursued, amended, if so how or why and so on. In other words, media workers' decisions about how to represent policy news are a pivotal part of the public policy-making process. Put differently, in the public policy decision-making process, media platforms become the meeting point for the public, media workers and policy-makers to discuss potential policies. As discussed earlier on in this chapter, media organizations and the discussion facilities they provide are not just a meeting space but also a context for a variety of group processes. What we know about the psychology of groups, group identities and group decision-making can tell us a lot about what happens when media workers referee the meeting space and the policy decisions.

In fact, the government often uses media platforms as a place to test out new public policies, as I will explore later on in this chapter. Platforms presented by media organizations become the place where group discussion about a given public policy takes place. Price (1988) presented the idea that public opinion is the result of a discussion that takes place via mass communication. Price thus viewed mass communication as the means through which the public 'see' (ibid: 670) a debate about an issue. What the public 'sees' about the policy issue is the outcome of decision-making by media workers. As I will explore later on in this chapter, certain faulty processes often affect that decision-making. Before we explore those processes, let us consider why media workers' decision-making about policy news is important to the public.

At the very basic level, we know that mere exposure to media reports has an effect on public attitudes and behaviours. This phenomenon has been demonstrated repeatedly in the 'media effects' literature. For example, exposure to media reports influences attitudes and behaviours relating to crime. Nabi and Sullivan (2001) surveyed 257 students by asking them questions about their crime-prevention behaviours (e.g., locking windows at night) and their beliefs about the incidence of crime in New York. Nabi and Sullivan also asked the students about their consumption of television. Nabi and Sullivan found statistically significant evidence that the higher the number of hours spent watching television, the stronger the beliefs about the incidence of crime. Likewise, they found that the higher the number of hours spent watching television, the higher the students' engagement in crime-prevention behaviour. Media exposure is also known to influence the public's beliefs about crime policies. For example, as far as the effects of media exposure on crime policy agenda are concerned, Beale (2006) argued that the US media skews public opinion about crime. Beale also argued that the US media plays a significant part in setting the agenda for US policies on crime. Therefore, media accounts influence not just the public's crime-prevention behaviour but also their opinions about crime policies.

Another example of evidence showing the effects of media reports on crime attitudes is the experimental research by Niven (2002). Niven divided 564 participants into three conditions. Participants in condition#1 read a newspaper article portraying the death penalty as something with popular support. Participants in condition#2 read a newspaper article portraying the death penalty as something with mixed support. Niven then asked the participants a variety of questions. Hidden among these were questions gauging the participant's support for the death penalty. Niven found that 85 per cent of participants in condition#1 indicated that they supported the death penalty, whereas 62 per cent of participants in condition #2 indicated that they supported the death penalty. This corroborates the idea that what media organizations say about a given crime policy can shape the public's opinion about that policy. It also highlights the fact that media workers' decisions about how to represent crime policies are consequential, as far as public opinion is concerned.

Let us consider another area of public policy. Media effects have been demonstrated as far as health issues are concerned. For example, Cook *et al.* (1983) conducted a naturalistic experiment in which they telephoned members of the public. Cook *et al.* asked roughly half of the people they telephoned to watch a TV programme on a health issue. Cook *et al.* asked the rest of the people to watch a TV programme on an issue unrelated to health. Cook *et al.* then later telephoned all the people in the study and they asked them a series of questions relating to health policy. Cook *et al.* concluded from analyses that exposure to the TV programme about the health issue influenced the sampled public's beliefs about the importance of particular healthcare issues. This shows that public opinion about whether a particular public health policy is required is influenced by exposure to media reports. The way in which media workers frame news about a given health policy proposals is therefore consequential in shaping the public's belief's about that health issue's importance.

Media effects have likewise been demonstrated in a related topic – vehicle safety issues. Feigenson and Bailis (2001) investigated the issue of public opinion about the dangers of vehicle air bags, relative to their benefits. Feigenson and Bailis pointed out that public opinion about the risks of air bags contradicted the reality that airbags saved the lives of approximately 97 per cent of people involved in low speed crashes. Feigenson and Bailis also pointed out that public opinion about the risks of air bags contradicted the reality that of the 43 per cent of people injured by airbags, 96 per cent of injuries were cuts and bruises. To investigate this issue, Feigenson and Bailis analysed 533 newspaper articles on the topic. These were articles published between 1993 and 1997. Feigenson and Bailis found that newspapers articles were four times more likely to present the idea that air bags endanger lives, than the idea that air bags save lives. In other words, the newspaper articles presented a skewed opinion about this issue. Feigenson and Bailis then conducted an experiment using 151 participants divided into several conditions. The conditions varied in terms of the qualities of the newspaper article provided, for example a biased article versus a neutral article. Feigenson and Bailis then asked the participants a variety of questions. Among these were questions gauging the participants' opinions about the safety of airbags. Feigenson and Bailis found that participants exposed to biased newspaper articles were statistically significantly less likely to report the opinion that airbags should be installed in all new cars. These participants were also more likely to believe that drivers have the option of switching off installed airbags. This demonstrates another reason why media workers' decisions about how to represent public policy news are consequential. How media workers represent a proposed policy's benefits or risks influences public opinion about that.

Similar evidence of media effects has been found in the context of immigration policy issues. For example, Dunaway, Branton and Abrajano (2010) searched a database of US newspaper articles on the issue of immigration, published in 2006. Dunaway *et al.* calculated the amount of media coverage about immigration issues in the months within that year. Dunaway *et al.* then accessed opinion poll data collected at different points that year. This data included responses to the question 'What is the most important problem facing this country today?' Dunaway *et al.* found that there was a statistically significant correlation between the amount of media coverage on immigration issues and the public's opinion about the issue's importance. Dunaway *et al.* tracked the month-to-month variation in both media coverage and public opinion and found similar patterns. The correlation remained significant even if Dunaway *et al.* controlled for potential confounding factors such as geographical location (proximity to the US border), demographic context (ethnic composition of the local population) and individual differences within the public (e.g., political affiliation). This demonstrates the influence of the media on public beliefs about the importance of immigration issues. The fact that the influence varies from one time period to another time period shows the consequentiality of media workers' decisions about whether/how to represent immigration issues.

Media effects have also been demonstrated as far as government policy agenda are concerned. What is reported in media platforms one month has an effect on the government's policy agenda the next month. This was demonstrated by Van Noije, Kleinnijenhuis and Oegema (2008). Van Noije *et al.* scanned the *Times*, *Independent* and *Guardian* newspapers for articles about European Union (EU) policy from the period 1988 to 2003; this yielded 2349 days of coverage about the issue. Van Noije *et al.* also scanned British parliamentary records (i.e., *Hansard* records) for debates about EU policy during the same period of 1988 to 2003. Van Noije *et al.* then used a statistical technique known as structural equation modelling to explore the month-to-month effects. Van Noije *et al.* concluded that media coverage had a significant effect on the incidence of parliamentary debates about EU policy.

This demonstrates yet another reason why media workers' decisions about how to represent public policy issues are important. They have an impact on politicians' decisions about the need to debate those issues. As Van Noije *et al.*'s evidence shows, when media coverage about policy issue X increases one month, there is an incremental effect on parliamentary debates about issue X the next month. When media coverage about issue X decreases, then the next month there is a decrease in parliamentary debates about issue X. Such evidence demonstrates the consequences of media workers' decisions about how much space they will allocate to representations of a particular policy issue (say, broadcast time, newspaper column inches, number of articles, etc.). These decisions impact on the amount of attention that policy-makers subsequently spend on those same policy issues.

In summary, this section has explored the reasons why media workers' part in representing policy news is consequential. I have explored the consequences for public opinion. I have also explored the consequences for the opinions and agenda of public policy-makers (see also Chapters 4 and 5). I did this by discussing evidence spanning a number of policy areas – crime, health, safety, immigration, EU policy and US foreign policy areas. The way in which I have discussed these media effects so far has been general. For example, I have discussed the impact of media exposure on public opinion, but exactly how does this phenomenon work?

Media Effects and the Polarization of Public Opinion about a Policy

As we learnt in the previous section, how much coverage media workers give to a particular policy issue influences public opinion about that issue's importance. We learnt that how much coverage media workers give to a particular policy issue influences the agenda of public policy-makers: how much priority they give to that issue and how much time they spend debating it. We also learnt in the previous section that what media reports say about a given policy issue influences public opinion about that issue, for example: is a policy needed and what should that policy be? Another phenomenon I discussed in the previous section was the correspondent variation between media coverage and public opinion, or between media coverage and policy-makers' agenda. When media coverage about a policy increases one month, there is a correspondent increase in the public's beliefs about that issue's importance. When the media coverage decreases, there is a correspondent decrease in the public's opinions about that issue's importance. The question that we will now explore is: how exactly, in the psychological sense, does media exposure influence public opinion about policy issues?

At first glance, media effects seem to work in a manner that can be explained simply. The more an audience is exposed to an opinion in the media, the greater the influence. For instance, media exposure has been found to have an effect on public opinion about health risks. A literature review by Vasterman, Yzermans and Dirkzwager (2004) provides evidence that repeated media exposure amplifies the public's perceptions about the riskiness of a particular vaccine, the presence of toxicity in a foodstuff, and so on. In fact, the influence of media reports can extend to physical reactions among audiences (with a psychosomatic basis). Vasterman *et al.* reviewed evidence that repeated exposure to media reports about health or disaster issues can lead to physical symptoms in audiences. This issue of repeated exposure is important for a number of reasons.

One reason is that the repeated media representation of a policy-related opinion implies that there is consensus about the opinion or that there will be convergence towards consensus. For example, if media reports repeatedly present the opinion that a proposed policy to fluoridate water should be dropped the repetition implies that there is agreement about fluoridation being bad among concerned entities (media, public, experts, etc.). Repetition is an opportunity to broadcast voices from these different entities, therefore strengthening the idea that the same opinion is being echoed by people from different segments of society. Repetition can therefore build the argument's persuasiveness (see e.g., Isenberg 1986). The repetition also implies that the policy issue is of paramount public importance and that, perhaps, policy-makers are ignoring the public's united opinion or the experts' uniform stance. In the psychology of group decision-making, all this is part of a process called group polarization (Isenberg 1986).

The more an audience is exposed to an opinion in media reports, the more polarized the audience's opinion becomes, in the direction of the opinion presented by the media. Brauer, Judd and Gliner (1995) provide evidence corroborating this idea that repeated exposure to a message results in a polarized opinion. Brauer *et al.* conducted a laboratory experiment using 140 participants who were divided into groups of four. These participants engaged in discussions about a variety of US public policy issues, such as equality legislation, funding of employment programmes, drug legalization, increasing taxes, decreasing the military budget, and so on. Brauer *et al.* found that participants who repeatedly expressed an opinion about an issue held that opinion more strongly by the end of the discussion. In other words, they displayed a polarized opinion by the end of the discussion. As well, Brauer *et al.* found that the greater the number of different people heard expressing a given opinion, the greater the chance of polarization towards that opinion. This supports the earlier point that repeated media coverage about a policy issue strengthens the media's influence on public opinion. Consensus about the policy issue is implied and the persuasive powers of the argument represented by media reports (e.g., 'the policy should be dropped') increase.

In the laboratory, an audience member is a passive recipient of repeated media exposure. Outside of the laboratory, audience members are often active participants in their own media consumption. Applying Brauer *et al.*'s findings, we would expect opinion polarization to happen among members of the public who read about the same opinion in different media sources, or who read about the same opinion expressed by different voices in media platforms. In other words, the fact that the same opinion is expressed by different sources makes opinion polarization among the audience all the more likely. The fact that people are not passive in their media consumption strengthens the likelihood of opinion polarization. Brauer *et al.*'s findings suggested that hearing repeated expressions of an opinion builds one's own repeated expression of that opinion, further creating a polarized opinion of that issue. For example, imagine that across several months or years, a member of the public 'Marissa' is 60 per cent supportive of the opinion that government building planning policies should be relaxed. In the UK, these policies regulate activities such as if/how one can build a house extension, if/how one can build a new house on a plot of land, how tall a fence can be, in some cases whether one can paint the outside of one's house or change the windows, and so on. In the morning, Marissa watches a breakfast television programme featuring a guest urging the government to relax planning policies. An hour later, while driving to work, Marissa hears a radio broadcaster espousing the relaxation of planning policies. During Marissa's lunch break, she reads a newspaper online column calling on the government to relax planning regulations. Comments by members of the public, posted under the column, include a mix of views. Among them are people agreeing that planning policies should be relaxed. In the evening, Marissa watches a television news feature on the issue of building planning policies implying that the policies should be relaxed. The broadcast includes a variety of guests, ranging from an architect, a retired planning officer and a house owner, all of whom were denied planning permission. That evening, if we measure Marissa's opinion about government planning policy, what is it going to be? Evidence from the psychological literature leads us to predict that Marissa will no longer have an opinion 60 per cent supportive of the relaxation of planning policies. She will now be more fervently (say, 80 per cent) in support of the relaxation of planning policies. Opinion polarization will have happened because Marissa was repeatedly exposed to others' opinions about that policy issue. In fact, even if Marissa was only 51 per cent supportive of the opinion in the beginning, opinion polarization would most likely still happen.

What is more, the more repeated the media exposure to an opinion about a policy issue, the greater its familiarity, and therefore the more one thinks that others share that opinion. This effect has been robustly demonstrated, for example through six experiments conducted by Weaver, Garcia, Schwarz and Miller (2007). Weaver *et al.* found that polarization happens even if the opinion is being repeated by the same source. Weaver *et al.* concluded that the phenomenon happened because the opinion in question becomes more psychologically accessible than competing opinions. Recalling the fictitious Marissa, we would expect that by the time she retires to sleep that night she will not only be more strongly in support of relaxed building planning policies but she will also hold the belief that majority of the public share the same opinion. From a mass communication perspective Price (1988) argued that because of feelings of social identity, the norms of the group concerned (i.e., the public as a group) become exaggerated in people's minds.

As well, the more repeatedly one is exposed to an opinion, the more likely one is to talk to others about it. This is in the sense of repeating the same opinion to others (Brauer *et al.* 1995). This sort of evidence leads to us to predict that the more audiences are repeatedly exposed to an opinion about a public policy in the media, the more likely those audiences are to re-enact discussions about the policy in their social interactions. Consider, for example, Schuster *et al.*'s (2006) telephone survey of 503 people. Schuster *et al.* found that that there was a statistically significant effect of the respondents' memory for an anti-tobacco advertisement and the extent to which the respondents talked about the ad with friends, colleagues and/or relatives. In line with Brauer *et al.*'s evidence, the probability is that expressing the opinion repeatedly will make polarization towards that opinion all the more likely.

In summary, the public's discussions and decision-making about policy issues are shaped by the media. Media effects on the public, as far as public opinion about policy issues are concerned, increase as the public's exposure to relevant media reports increase. We can extrapolate that those members of the public whose original opinions lean towards the consensus implied by media are most prone to polarization. If someone in the public is initially moderately supportive of a particular proposed policy, repeated exposure to media espousing support for that policy inflates his/her support for that policy. If someone in the public is initially moderately disapproving of a proposed policy, repeated exposure to media espousing disapproval for that policy will increase his/her disapproval for that policy. What is more, the more exposed a member of the public is to the same opinion from different media sources, the greater the likelihood of polarization. Repeated media exposure to a particular opinion also increases the likelihood that a member of the public will initiate discussions about the opinion in his/her private life, with friends, relatives, colleagues and others. This in turn can lead to further opinion polarization. Let us explore how this happens in more detail.

**From Media Consumption to Media Participation and Private Discussion:
How Opinion Polarization Happens in the Public**

I have explored the impact of media reports on opinion polarization in the public.
I have discussed some evidence that media consumption behaviour determines
who will be prone to polarization. I have also noted the importance of taking
into account individuals' original opinions about a policy issue. What I will now
explore is the complex interaction between the individual's original opinion and
the characteristics of media that he/she consumes. How much time and effort
does the individual invest in finding media that portray a particular policy issue?
How reflective is the chosen media of the individual's initial opinion? How much
interaction is there between the individual and the media, for example can his/her
comments be published by that media online or offline?

We can deduce the answers to these questions from evidence such as that
demonstrated by Baldassari and Bearman's (2007) research. Baldassari and
Bearman argued that, in natural settings, group polarization of political attitudes
happens among certain combinations of individuals, but not other combinations.
Baldassari and Bearman proposed a theoretical model postulating that opinion
polarization happens when there is the least spatial distance among individuals.
Baldassari and Bearman's theoretical model also postulated that opinion
polarization happens when people choose to interact with other people who hold
similar beliefs. Baldassari and Bearman tested their theoretical model using
computer simulation methodology. In this simulation there were 100 hypothetical
actors, each of whom began with their individual opinion about a public policy. This
individual opinion was represented by a number between -100 and $+100$, whereby
-100 denoted an opinion totally against the public policy and $+100$ denoted an
opinion totally for the public policy. Baldassari and Bearman set the parameters of
the computer simulation in such a way that each individual actor had a particular
amount of interest in the policy issue. This is because, aside from the degree of
one's approval or disapproval of a policy issue, different people have different
degrees of interest in particular policy issues. Baldassari and Bearman gave each
hypothetical actor a number to represent the actor's level of interest in the public
policy issue. This number was anywhere between -100, denoting total disinterest
in the policy issue, to 100, denoting total interest in the policy issue. Baldassari
and Bearman's rationale was that the stronger a person's interest in a public policy
issue the more prone he/she is to opinion polarization. Baldassari and Bearman
then calculated the ideological distance between each pair of hypothetical actors
among the 100 hypothetical actors in total. To calculate this distance, Baldassari
and Bearman used a mathematical calculation method producing a value known
as 'Euclidean distance'. This enabled Baldassari and Bearman to gauge the
probability of any given pair of actors interacting with each other. They gauged
this probability while taking into account similarities in actors' opinions about
the public policy and also while taking into account the actors' level of interest in
the public policy. Subsequently, this enabled Baldassari and Bearman's computer

simulation to show if and where (in the sample of hypothetical actors) opinion polarization took place. What was additionally valuable about Baldassari and Bearman's computer simulation method was that it simulated discussions between as many pairs of actors as was allowed by the variables (interest, opinion). This simulated what would happen in reality. It allowed the computer to simulate polarization where within the sample of actors it was likely to happen, and in what direction. If there was a shift to extremity of opinion, what direction was the shift?

How can we apply Baldassari and Bearman's (2007) results in our understanding of media effects and polarization of public opinion? Firstly, Baldassari and Bearman results showed that the stronger a given actor's interest in a given policy issue, the more likely he/she is to engage in biased information sampling. For example, a person will only read the articles of media commentators who share similar views. A person will only listen to radio or TV programmes featuring interviewees saying things about the issue that echo his/her own views, and so on.

How can we apply Baldassari and Bearman's notion of spatial distance, in our understanding of how individuals' relationships with media determine the likelihood of opinion polarization? We can think of spatial distance as the extent to which the individual member of the public feels 'close' to a given medium. For example, can he/she post a comment to a newspaper's article about the policy issue? Most media organizations' websites contain most or all of their non-online content, with additional blogs or comment pages that give the public the opportunity to 'publish' their opinions. Another interesting question is, can a member of the public express his/her opinion about a policy issue by clicking 'like', 'recommend', 'e-mail to a friend' or some other indicator which contributes to media organizations' portrayal of that issue's importance? For instance, the BBC website publishes live information about the most e-mailed BBC articles. The BBC website's discussion pages allow users to indicate their approval of other users' comments by clicking on a '+' sign, or to indicate their disapproval by clicking on a '−' sign. This results in comments being ranked according to the approval that they gather. A similar example is the *Guardian* newspaper's website, which allows browsers to 'recommend' comments. By someone in the public e-mailing an article to a friend, or clicking on an 'approve' or 'recommend' button, this serves some interesting purposes as far as opinion polarization is concerned. Firstly, the member of the public becomes a contributor to the media; his/her voice becomes one of the voices portrayed by the media as holding a given opinion on a given policy issue. Secondly, additional media consumption happens. Rather than, say, reading a BBC website article and closing the browser, he/she additionally reads the public's comments about the article on the same or linked page. In so doing, the member of the public is repeatedly exposed to a particular opinion. Let us recall our example of fictitious 'Marissa' from early on in this chapter. In the example, Marissa was repeatedly exposed to the same opinion about a proposed public policy concerning the relaxation of building regulations. This exposure happened when Marissa watched breakfast television, listened to the radio in her car, read a newspaper website blog at lunch time, and so on. Let us imagine that, after reading the website blog, Marissa reads comments underneath the blog, posted by members of the public. Some of them say they agree with the proposed policy of relaxing building regulations. Without reading those comments, Marissa would have been exposed to N sources expressing the same opinion. After reading those comments, Marissa exposure has increased; she will have been exposed to $N+x$ sources expressing the same opinion. As we learnt earlier, this makes opinion polarization all the more likely. If in the first example Marissa's opinion shifted from 60 per cent support to 80 per cent support for the relaxation of planning policies, with yet more media exposure the shift might be to 90 per cent support.

If Marissa posts her own comment about the policy issue on the newspaper blog, her comment becomes yet another source of the same opinion. The fact that she is a member of the public might have an impact on the extent to which other people consuming given media are persuaded. Moreover, an important question is whether the member of the public can interact with other members of the public who comment on the policy issue – can he/she respond directly to their comments or private message them? Most websites allow commentators to 'quote' other commentators. Some allow commentators to contact each other privately. These sorts of functions help transform media consumption to not just participation in media communications but also private discussions about the policy issue. These sorts of opportunities further increase the risk of opinion polarization about particular policy issues. Frau-Meigs (2000) suggested that online discussions about political issues are likely to descend into a 'lynch mob' (ibid: 237) mentality. This implies that the group dynamics of online discussions, such as in terms of the degree of interactivity that they afford users, makes participants all the more prone to opinion polarization.

In summary, this section has discussed the way in which opinion polarization happens among members of the public. I discussed how members of the public go from having an initial opinion about a policy issue to media consumption, to revising their opinions about the policy issue. This shift in opinion is known as polarization when the shift in opinion is a shift in the direction of the consensus implied by the media. As well, this section discussed the ways in which members of the public go from being media consumers to being active participants in the media. For example, most media organizations' websites now allow members of the public to 'publish' their opinions. Technology on these websites also allow members of the public to contribute to the media's agenda-setting, such as in the sense of contributing to media rankings showing which policy issues are most interesting to the public or what opinion is most representative of public opinion. I will now consider some examples of opinion polarization in specific policy areas.

An Example of Opinion Polarization via Media: The Case of the Mental Health Bill

To understand how opinion polarization about policy issues occurs, let us consider some case studies. The first example concerns UK public policy on mental health. Foster (2006) used software to content-analyse 256 UK newspaper editorials, articles and letters published between 2001 and 2004. Foster searched for items containing the phrase 'Mental Health Bill'. This bill was in draft stage at the time, having been first proposed by the UK government in 2001 as a revision of the 1983 Mental Health Act. Through the revision, the government proposed to increase definitions of mental disorders and to increase powers of detaining people. Foster found some unanimity in media opinion towards the bill. Foster found evidence of this unanimity amongst local and national newspapers, with 63.05 per cent of newspaper items expressing an entirely negative or mostly negative view of the Mental Health Bill. The notion of a majority in group decision-making can make group polarization worse, as discussed earlier. This is because polarization often happens when there is an identifiable majority of group members sharing an opinion. How did media workers build this picture of consensus about the proposed mental health policy?

Foster (2006) noted that the newspaper items tended to quote the same text or phrases from the Mental Health Alliance, an organization which opposed the bill. Empirical evidence – see Kamau and Harorimana (2008) for a review– shows that an important symptom of faulty decision-making is the recurrent sampling by group members of the same, shared information. This selectivity in the information chosen constitutes biased information sampling. The bias tends to favour the group's prevailing viewpoint. Foster noted:

> For example, the Mental Health Alliance referred to the Bill soon after its publication as 'draconian'. Many newspapers picked up on this adjective, and adopted it as an assessment of the Bill without attributing it to the MHA (ibid: 291).

This is an interesting illustration of how group polarization occurs. A particular opinion, in the early stages of a discussion, is taken up by some group members, repeated by other group members, and by the end of the discussion that opinion will take a more extreme form than when it began. There was other evidence that group polarization was happening in media portrayals of the Mental Health Bill. Foster found that the newspaper items treated information contradicting the prevailing media viewpoint differently from how it treated information supporting media disapproval of the proposed policy. Foster found that media accounts did not 'own' or envelope such information. For instance, media reports of contradictory information remained in quotation marks. Foster noted:

> In fact, the use of quotation marks when citing governmental statements could even come across as sceptical, or even scathing, of the views expressed. This did not seem to be the case when the views of those who oppose the Bill are discussed (ibid: 292).

It is interesting to note that some sections of the media exert considerable influence on public policy-making, irrespective of their audience share. Foster (2006) found that most media coverage about the UK Mental Health Bill was by newspapers with the smallest audience share. For example, there were 35 items in the *Guardian* 83 items in the *Independent/Independent on Sunday* and nine items in the *Daily Telegraph*, compared to one item in the *Sun*; five items in the *Daily Mail*; two in the *Daily Star* and two in the *Express*. Taking the example of the *Guardian,* the number of people who buy it represent 0.005 per cent of the UK adult population and 0.02 per cent of newspaper buyers (279,308 daily out of approximately 10 million newspapers bought daily; Audit Bureau of Circulation, 2011).This shows that 'minority' media organizations (minority in the sense of audience share) can have a disproportionate impact on opinion polarization as far as public policy is concerned. On the other hand, there is the argument that such newspapers tend to be the ones regarded as 'quality' newspapers in comparison to tabloids; therefore their influential capabilities might be a good thing. For instance, the *Guardian* is regarded as a respectable newspaper, which might explain why public policy-makers would be more swayed by content in it than in the tabloids. The organization's identity as a serious medium would also explain why it might cover serious public policies more intensely (see also Chapter 5). All the same, the point to note is that policy-makers' construal of public opinion about particular policies might reflect opinion that originated in a small section of media.

Therefore, media representations implied that there was public consensus about the proposed Bill. Specifically, media accounts implied that there was widespread disapproval for the Bill. This false consensus was powerful in propelling further opinion polarization. If one believes that their fellow group members hold homogenous opinions about an issue, this strengthens one's own beliefs/actions in line with the same opinion (Anastasio, Rose, and Chapman 1999). Anastasio *et al.* found that participants in an experiment led to believe that there was consensus within their 'ingroup' conformed to that belief. This was in comparison to participants led by Anastasio *et al.* to believe that there was heterogeneity within their group in terms of group members' opinions about the issue. Media representation of 'consensus' about the need for a policy about issue X is therefore paramount. In the case of the Mental Health Bill, the false consensus implied by the media was powerful. In actual fact, people might have had inconsistent opinions about the Bill, many were probably indifferent, there might have been no majority opinion about the issue, and the experts quoted might have been unrepresentative.

The consequence was that the government abandoned its initial draft of the Mental Health Bill, made amendments and a revised draft was passed in

Parliament in November 2006 (see Department of Health, 2007). The revised Mental Health Act received royal assent in 2007. In summary, the purpose of this section was not to comment on whether the initial draft of the Mental Health Bill was good or bad, or whether media workers' and media organizations' influential role in this instance was for the common good or not, but rather to discuss the fact that influence happened. As Foster's (2006) research found, it can be concluded that media organizations/workers had an influential role. Media representations presented increasingly polarized opinions about the proposed Mental Health Bill. This played a significant part in the UK government's decisions to amend that Bill.

An Example of Opinion Polarization via Media: The Case of UK National Health Policy

Let us consider another example of media workers' role as catalysts in the polarization of public opinion about policy issues. This time, the example is a case study illustrating a different aspect of this catalyst process: focusing on the most extreme or sensationalist details about a policy. Davidson, Hunt and Kitzinger (2003) described media as integral to health policy-making in the sense that policy-makers release proposals to the media to 'test the water'. Davidson *et al.* proposed that what transpires in media coverage has ramifications for policy-makers' continued pursuit of a particular policy. In earlier sections, we noted the reasons why media representations of policy proposals become a catalyst for opinion polarization.

Davidson *et al.* (2003) selected four government documents about proposed health policies over a 17-month timeframe. Davidson *et al.* then qualitatively analysed national newspapers' articles about these policy documents. The general gist of the government documents was to propose public policies aimed at improving national health. The documents contained titles such as '*Our Healthier Nation: a Contract for Health*' and '*Working Together for a Healthier Scotland: a Consultation Document*'. In contrast to such relatively modest titles, the newspaper headlines about comprised sensationalized phrases like '*Four goals for healthier Britain could save 15,000 lives*' (*Independent*); '*Dobson pledges to cut illness gap*' (*Guardian*); '*Now nanny backs off in health war*' (*Daily Express*); '*Living in Glasgow takes 5 years off your life*' (the *Scotsman*); '*More money on table for under-age sex clinics*' (*Daily Mail*). Davidson *et al.*'s content analysis showed that many of the newspaper headlines exaggerated the government press releases. The newspapers implied the presence of a political controversy that was not really there.

In summary, media representations of proposed policies are often sensationalized in a manner symptomatic of group polarization. In other words, even if there is little or no controversy about a proposed policy, media working practices appear to be geared towards instigating group polarization. Having discussed media effects and group polarization in public opinion about policy issues, and having discussed media representations of policy issues, let us now consider other examples of faulty processes in media decision-making about public policy issues.

Faulty Processes in Media Workers' Practices: Poor Information Sampling and Background Research Practices

In the psychology of group decision-making, we know that people tend to select information in a biased manner that supports the group's prevailing viewpoint (see Kamau and Harorimana 2008 for a review of the evidence). For example, people use psychological defence mechanisms to avoid information which contradicts the group's prevailing view. They might think of such information as poorer in quality than information supporting the group's prevailing view. Another example is that people making a decision in a group setting tend to focus on shared information rather than unshared information. People have the tendency to use information that is already available to most group members, rather than fully utilizing the available information pool (Stasser and Titus 1985). Poor information sampling affects the quality of the decision made by the group because, with incomplete information, the decision is not objective or necessarily the best decision. In the context of media decision-making about public policy issues, shared information can constitute public opinion polls released to the press, interviews of the same experts, quotes or letters selected for publication, and so on. Media workers often re-use the same broadcast clips and quotes from their own archives. Media workers also often use the same news sources, such as the same news aggregator companies or the same public relations contacts. As well, a shared social history within one nation contributes other shared information, such as that concerning which public policy decisions were effective in the past. Other sources of shared information can include stereotypic beliefs. Whatever the type of sharing at work, the important point to note is that the greater reliance on shared background information over unshared background information creates fertile conditions for opinion polarization within one media organization and/or across media organizations.

Such issues have been investigated by Machill and Beiler (2009), who investigated journalists' background research practices. Machill and Beiler postulated that 'the increased self-referentiality in journalism and the "Google-ization" of research represent a cause for concern to journalism' (ibid: 178). Machill and Beiler sampled 235 journalists from 34 media organizations in Germany. These media organizations included newspapers, television stations and online media. Machill and Beiler observed each journalist for about eight hours. This produced nearly 2000 hours whereby journalists were observed while doing research activities. Machill and Beiler reported that the average journalist spent nearly half his/her working day doing research. Half of that time was spent finding news topics, assessing the relevance of incoming news, and so on. Very little time (5.5 per cent of the time spent) was spent cross-checking research – only 0.6 per cent was spent cross-checking a source. Additionally, Machill and Beiler found that only 4.7 per cent of the time spent on research by journalists was spent fact checking. About 29.3 per cent of the time spent on research by journalists was spent finding additional information. We can extrapolate that this is fine, but if the original information was polarized, then the additional information is likely to be likewise skewed. Of all journalist categories, television editors engaged in the highest frequency (9.3 per cent) of fact checking, compared to job categories such as newspaper journalists (6.5 per cent). In terms of the research tools used, a very small proportion (2.3 per cent to 4 per cent) comprised databases and archives. These would be where scientific research is likely to be reported. Machill and Beiler additionally found that journalists had even less reliance on documents/writings (0 to 2 per cent).

Machill and Beiler also highlighted the problem of 'self-referencing' from another angle. This is when a media worker references research, articles and other information archived within his/her media organization. This creates a further problem, as far as the quality of the information pooling is concerned. This is also an example of how people in groups focus on shared, rather than unshared information. It also denotes a spiralling cycle of polarization. For example, one polarized source, if never fact-checked, can be reported as a newspaper article or described as background research in that article. The newspaper article is then stored in the organization's archive. Weeks, months or years later, a different journalist researching the same theme comes across the archived article and cites the background information. What is more, the journalist looks for more information corroborating the archived background information, potentially missing information contradicting it. In other words, skewed research builds upon already skewed research. This problem is compounded by the finding by Machill and Beiler (2009) that 'scientific establishments' comprised less than one per cent of the research tools used by the journalists sampled. Although research in science databases is not the only empirically robust research, it would seem essential for background information on many public policy topics, such as health, energy, crime, education, environment, and so on.

Another reason why media workers' background information sampling is often sub-optimal concerns the lack of optimum access to academic experts. Some may argue that the kinds of academic experts who respond to media requests for opinion are seldom the most credible experts in the field, in terms of their research expertise. Some might also argue that 'most' academics regard the media with the suspicion; therefore those academics who heed media requests might not always be representative as academics. As well, many academic researchers within a given field could argue that media reportage of their own subject is often inaccurate because media workers' sampling of information on that subject is often poor. For example, Hyde-Lay (2010) surveyed 48 delegates at an academic conference on asthma/allergy research. Of these, 70.8 per cent said that they rated media representations of asthma/allergy research as accurate only some of the time. 95.7 per cent rated the quality of allergy/asthma research evidence cited by the media as mid-quality or poor-quality. Despite the discrepant or inaccurate media reports (inaccurate in part or in whole) on asthma/allergy issues, 62.5 per cent of these experts believed that media reports shape public policy on asthma/allergy issues. This is consistent with the evidence reviewed and discussed earlier in this chapter. Hyde-Lay also discussed the impact of media reports on public policies concerning medical research, arguing that media practices compromise the independence and scientific integrity of the process of policy-making on medical issues. As well, Hyde-Lay discussed the impact of media reports about allergies/asthma on public opinion and behaviour, citing evidence that large percentages of people alter their eating behaviour because of media representations. This corroborates our earlier conclusion that media reports exert influence on both opinion-based consequences and behaviour-based consequences.

Let us consider another example of poor information sampling: when media workers rely on one-sided information about a topic, or when media workers concentrate on the most extraordinary details about a policy news piece. We discussed an example of this symptom earlier, in reviewing media influence on the amendment of the UK's Mental Health Bill. Caulfield and Bubela (2004) expressed concern that media reports sensationalize biomedical news. They asked coders with a scientific background to rate the accuracy of 597 newspaper headlines about genetic research. Caulfied and Bubela found that only 6.8 per cent of the headlines mentioned controversy within the given area of genetics research. They also found that only 15 per cent of articles about genetic discoveries mentioned the 'opposite side of the coin': the risks associated with applying a given research finding. Caulfield and Bubela also found that newspaper articles reporting research from specialist medical journals were more likely to contain exaggerations than newspaper articles about research from generic medical journals. This demonstrates how novel information can have a disproportionate impact on group decision-making (see research into this phenomenon by Vinokur, Burnstein, Sechrest and Wortman 1985).

A related example is the impact of novel information on media representations of climate change issues in recent years. Young and Dugas (2011) content-analysed 897 items about the issue of climate change in two Canadian newspapers. Young and Dugas found that in 1988/9, media articles cited academic experts nearly twice as they cited environmental groups (26 per cent and 12 per cent respectively). In 1998/9 media articles on climate change, environmental groups were cited slightly more than academic experts (24 per cent of citations were of environmental groups, and 18 per cent of academic experts). A similar difference was observed in 2007/8 (21 per cent and 18 per cent respectively). Therefore, campaign groups were given a greater voice by media organizations and media workers during the 1990s and 2000s, compared to the 1980s. This shows that information from environmental campaign groups, once regarded as 'extreme' groups, is now regarded as normative. One explanation could be that there has been convergence in the information provided by environmental campaign groups and climate change scientists. Together, their influence on media representations may have increased. Another explanation could be that new climate science evidence has emerged, and therefore environmental campaign groups have intensified their activities. Nonetheless, Young and Dugas found that only 16 per cent of newspaper items contained 'an identifiable rebutter' of the thrust of the climate-change item. The implication is that the opinions presented in media reports about climate change are quite imbalanced – they are polarized.

Some claim that climate change scepticism has been suppressed by media organizations and workers, with the alleged collusion of academic experts engaged in research about climate change (Taranto 2010). 'Climategate' was a fiasco that began when a hacker gained access to approximately 4000 documents/e-mails from the Climatic Research Unit of the University of East Anglia. The hacker(s) copied the files to the internet and they alleged that the files contained evidence of scientists suppressing research results that contradicted the idea of global warming. The idea that global temperatures are rising has come to be regarded as a 'fact' not to be challenged within mainstream media. It was therefore interesting that the allegations were regarded by many media representations as a 'smear campaign'. The hacker(s)' allegations of a conspiracy or fraud among climate scientists were not upheld by various investigations. At the same time, commentators such as Taranto, a *Wall Street Journal* columnist, claimed that there was evidence of opinion conformity and suppression of dissenters, through a 'corrupt' peer review process. For instance, Taranto claimed that some climate scientists suggested a boycott of an academic journal which published a climate-sceptical article, and Taranto claimed that other climate scientists avowed not to cite climate-sceptical journal articles. Furthermore, Taranto wrote about angry correspondence from some climate scientists directed at a *New York Times* blog writer because of his unfavourable reportage. Even before Climategate, the writer claimed to be under fire from 'global warmists' for failing to suppress inconvenient information (Taranto 2010). If these accounts are accurate, they suggest that academic experts can have a disproportionate impact on the content of media reportage.

In summary, there is evidence that media workers' background research practices are sub-optimal. The information pooling tends to be poor in the sense that there is an imbalanced reliance on shared information (e.g., in-house archives) over unshared information (e.g., scientific bibliography search results). For example, on medical issues, the quality and accuracy of background research cited by journalists is judged sub-optimal by academic experts. An additional issue concerns media organizations' access to neutral academic experts, and whether academic experts who feature often in media are necessarily representative (for instance, have their research results been corroborated elsewhere). A related point is the extent to which novel information, such as that provided by academic experts, sways the media representations about the correct opinion about a given policy issue. One emerging example of this involves media representations of climate change issues whereby (as in other examples of polarization discussed earlier), opinions contradicting climate change experts' views are often suppressed. Having discussed information sampling practices, I will now consider other examples of faulty processes in media decision-making about policy issues.

Other Faulty Processes in Media Decision-Making: Simplistic Representations of Outgroup Policy Needs

According to Janis (1982), groups suffering from groupthink have a simplistic view of other groups (that is, 'outgroups'). This symptom of groupthink could involve imagining that the policy concerns of the 'ingroup' (e.g., one's nation, region, class) are more complex and more important than the policy concerns of 'outgroups' (e.g., foreign nations, minority groups, other regions, classes). Consider media workers' coverage of policy issues concerning minority communities, in comparison to coverage concerning majority communities. Atuel, Seyranian and Crano (2007) analysed Dakota and Californian newspaper headlines referring to the majority population versus headlines referring to the minority population. Atuel *et al.* found that most headlines about the majority population were about political issues, whereas most headlines about the minority population were about social issues. Atuel *et al.* argued that this is because there is more power at stake with political issues, compared to social issues. Atuel *et al.*'s findings also suggest that 'important' policy issues were discussed by media workers with reference to the concerns of the majority group.

A related symptom of groupthink is the perpetuation of stereotypes about 'outgroups' which portray them in a simplistic way. Consider media workers' reports about people with autism spectrum disorders. Jones and Harwood (2009) searched a database for news reports about autism and Asperger's between 1996 and 2005. Jones and Harwood suggested that the media reportage perpetuated simplistic stereotypes, portraying people with autism or Asperger's as either unloved/neglected or dangerous. We can argue that these simplifications have policy implications, in the sense that media workers are likely to report or support policies which address issues that can be easily categorized using common stereotypes.

Another example is media workers' coverage of other nations' policies. Willnat and Weaver (2003) sampled 153 journalists working as foreign correspondents in 52 countries. Willnat and Weaver found that only 32 per cent of foreign correspondent journalists thought it is 'extremely important' to 'stay away from stories where factual content cannot be verified' (ibid: 415). This contrasted with 49 per cent of US journalists who were not foreign correspondents but thought that the same value was 'extremely important'. This implies that journalists 'lower' their objectivity standards when they are dealing with foreign ('outgroup') issues – a classic illustration of groupthink. In other words, when groupthink is happening, people reduce information or simplify information about 'outgroups'.

Similar conclusions apply when media representations concern ethnic minority groups. To explore conservative attitudes and attitudes towards affirmative action,

Reyna, Henry, Korfmacher and Tucker (2005) analysed 893 white Americans' responses to the General Social Survey of 1996. Reyna *et al.* also surveyed 184 white Chicago residents. Reyna *et al.*'s results led them to conclude that whites' attitudes towards affirmative action for African-Americans were indicative of stereotyping or prejudice rather than indicating objective beliefs about the fairness of affirmative action policies. For instance, Reyna *et al.* found that the whites sampled were more receptive to affirmative action policies for women, compared to affirmative policies for African-Americans. The implication is that media representations of public policies concerning ethnic minority groups may not be rational representations of public opinion. The representations could be symptomatic of faulty processes such as groupthink.

In summary, this section explored symptoms of faulty decision-making beyond poor information sampling and polarization. I explored faulty processes in media workers' representations of outgroups' policy needs as an illustration of groupthink. We will now recap the present and previous chapters by summarizing, in the figure on the next page, the faulty processes that encroach upon media workers' decision-making about how to represent public policy issues.

Conclusion

As we can deduce from the below hypothetical example (Figure 6.1), the refereeing role of media organizations and media professionals does not necessarily begin at the outset. As often happens at the beginning of group discussions, people in the group do not necessarily know other group members' opinions. In the first stage, the potential policy issue is presented by media workers either factually, as news, or accompanied by a variety of opinions. At that stage, the public and/ or policy-makers have the opportunity to shape what media workers believe is the popular or 'correct' opinion about the policy. Additionally, media organizations' mission values have the opportunity to shape media workers' construal of the 'correct' opinion about the policy. Moreover, media workers' own beliefs (either as individual citizens or as members of a relevant group) shape their construal of the 'correct' policy. Following that, as step 2 in Figure 6.1 shows, one or more psychological processes begin to work. For example, media workers can misrepresent the majority's policy needs; media workers can place too much emphasis on an expert's views about the correct policy; media workers can reiterate information used before or cite information already known but not seek supplementary information; media workers can overestimate or underestimate a risk associated with adopting the policy; media workers can censor or unduly disparage information contradicting the emerging 'popular' opinion; media workers can selectively publish comment articles, readers' letters, and other outputs which reinforce, rather than contradict, the emerging 'popular' opinion. Simultaneously, as I have discussed in this chapter, the public's consumption of the media transitions from relatively passive consumption to active integration of

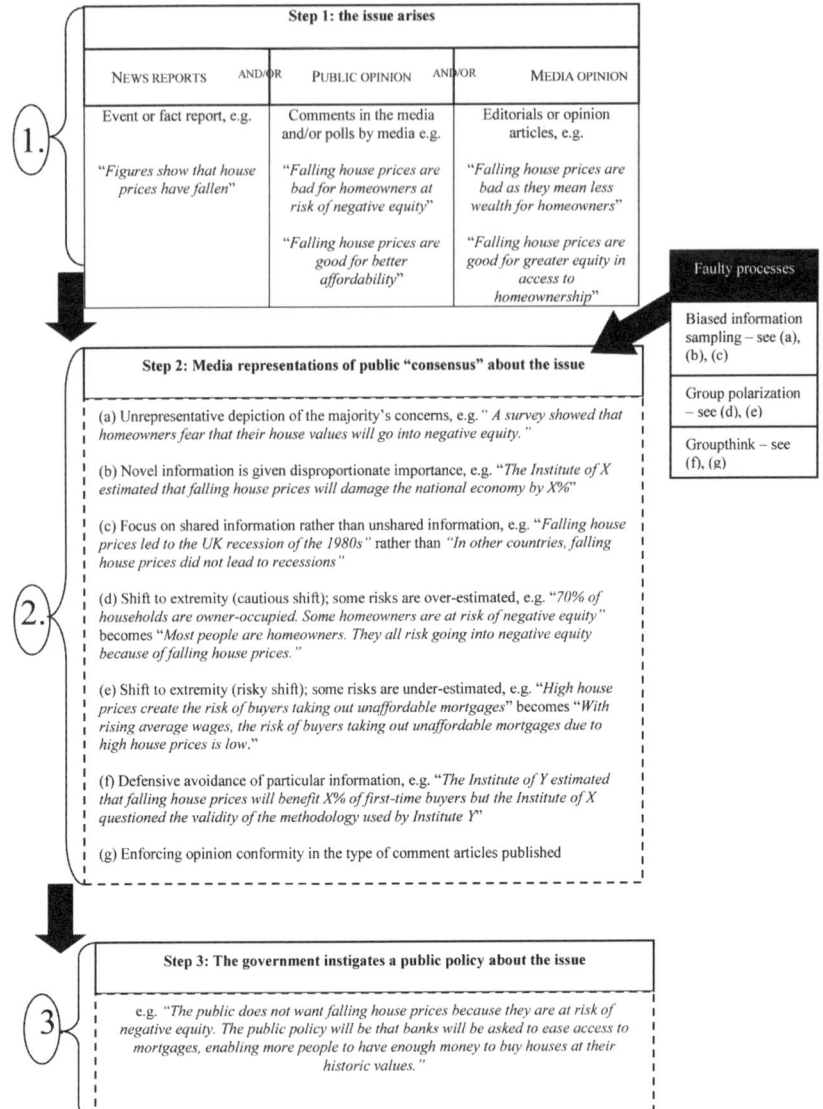

Figure 6.1   How faulty processes in decision-making shape media representations about public policy issues

the ideas presented by media workers into private opinions. The boundary between the public and media organizations/workers therefore becomes blurred, as far as the ownership of the opinion is concerned. The boundary is also blurred as far as repetition of the opinion about the policy is concerned. The picture that then emerges, as I have discussed in this chapter (see also step 3 in Figure 6.1), is one whereby there appears to be consensus about the 'correct' policy for public policy-makers to adopt. The example in Figure 6.1 is a conveniently simple example which excludes differences between media organizations and types of policies (see Chapter 5). Additionally, the example in Figure 6.1 does not illustrate the policy-makers' own initiatives or roles in the policy-making process (see Chapter 4). As I discussed in Chapter 4, policy-makers are themselves driven by group processes which can be inserted into Figure 6.1 as a step parallel to steps 1–2.

All in all, my conclusion is that socio-cognitive group processes play an important part in the policy-making process. These psychological processes shape policy-makers' agenda (see Chapters 4 and 5).They also explain the role of media organizations and media workers in representing and refereeing public policy. We can also conclude that group processes at the level of social cognition shape when and how media organizations and media workers referee public policy-making.

References

Abrams, D., and M. A. Hogg, 1999. *Social Identity and Social Cognition*. Malden, MA, US: Blackwell Publishers.

Alasuutari, P., 1995. *Researching Culture: Qualitative Method and Cultural Studies*. London: Sage.

Althaus, S. L., and D. Tewksbury, 2002. 'Agenda setting and the "new" news: Patterns of issue importance among readers of the paper and online versions of the *New York Times*'. *Communication Research*, 29(2), 180–207.

Altheide, D. L., 1976. *Creating Reality: How TV News Distorts Events*. New York: Sage.

Alvesson, M., and K. Skoldberg, 2000. *Reflexive Methodology: New Vistas for Qualitative Research*. London: Sage.

Anastasio, P. A., K. C. Rose and J. Chapman, 1999. 'Can the media create public opinion? A social identity approach'. *Current Directions in Psychological Science*, 8(5), 152–155.

Ang, I., 1991. *Desperately Seeking The Audience*. London: Routledge.

Aristotle, 1967. *Politics*. Translation by H. Rackham. London: Heinemann.

Aristotle, 1975. *Nichomachean Ethics*, Books I–X. Translation by H. Rackham. London: Heinemann.

Aron, A., E. N. Aron and D. Smollan, 1992. 'Inclusion of other in the self scale and the structure of interpersonal closeness'. *Journal of Personality and Social Psychology*, 63(4), 596–612.

Aronson, E., T. D. Wilson and R. M. Akert, 2002. *Social psychology*. 4th edition. Upper Saddle River, NJ, US: Prentice Hall.

Astorino-Courtois, A., 2000. 'The effects of stakes and threat on foreign policy decision-making'. *Political Psychology*, 21(3), 489–510.

Atuel, H., V. Seyranian and W. D. Crano, 2007. 'Media representations of majority and minority groups'. *European Journal of Social Psychology*, 37(3), 561–572.

Audit Bureau of Circulations, 2011. National Newspapers and Bulk Distribution (November 2011). http://www.abc.org.uk/Certificates-Reports/Latest-Reports/.

Baldassarri, D. and P. Bearman, 2007. 'Dynamics of Political Polarization'. *American Sociological Review*, 72(5), 784–811.

Barthes, R., 1973. *Mythologies*. London: Paladin Books.

Barthes, R., 1988. *The Semiotic Challenge*. Oxford: Blackwell.

Beale, S. S., 2006. 'The news media's influence on criminal justice policy: How market-driven news promotes punitiveness'. *William and Mary Law Review*, 48(2), 397–481.

Bell, L. L., and C. C. Seale, 2011. 'The reporting of cervical cancer in the mass media: A study of UK newspapers'. *European Journal of Cancer Care*, 20(3), 389–394.

Bennett, W. L., 1993. 'Constructing publics and their opinions'. *Political Communication* (10), 101–120.

Berger, A. A., 2000. *Media Research Techniques*. 2nd edition. London: Sage.

Berger, P. L., and R. J. Neuhaus, 2003. 'To Empower People: From State to Civil Society', in M. Emirbayer (ed.). *Émile Durkheim: Sociologist of Modernity*. Oxford: Blackwell.

Bills, D. B., 2004. *The Sociology of Education and Work*. Oxford: Blackwell.

Bobbio, N., 1987. *Which Socialism?* Translation by Roger Griffin, edited and introduced by Richard Bellamy. Minneapolis: University of Minnesota Press.

Bogason, P., 2000. *Public Policy and Local Governance: Institutions in Postmodern Society*. Cheltenham: Edward Elgar Publishing Limited.

Bourdieu, P., 1993. *The Field of Cultural Production*. Oxford: Polity Press.

Brauer, M., C. M. Judd and M. D. Gliner, 1995. 'The effects of repeated expressions on attitude polarization during group discussions'. *Journal of Personality and Social Psycho logy*, 68(6), 1014–1029.

Brown, R. J., 2000. 'Social identity theory: past achievements, current problems and future challenges'. *European Journal of Social Psychology*, 30(6), 745–778.

Brown, R. J. and J. C. Turner, 1979. 'The criss-cross categorization effect in intergroup discrimination'. *British Journal of Social and Clinical Psychology*, 18(4), 371–383.

Brown, R. J., H. Tajfel and J. C. Turner, 1980. 'Minimal group situations and intergroup discrimination: Comments on the paper by Aschenbrenner and Schaefer'. *European Journal of Social Psychology*, 10(4), 399–414.

Brülde, B., 2007. 'Happiness and the Good Life: Introduction and Conceptual Framework'. *Journal of Happiness Studies*, 8(1), 1–14.

Caulfield, T. and T. Bubela, 2004. 'Media representations of genetic discoveries: Hype in the headlines?' *Health Law Review*, 12(2), 53–61.

Chambers, I., 1994. *Migrancy, Culture and Identity*. London: Routledge.

Chomsky, N., 1998. *The Common Good*. London: Pluto.

Clayton, J., 1992. *Journalism For Beginners: How to Get into Print and Get Paid for it*. London: Piatkus Publishers.

Clement, S., and N. Foster, 2008. 'Newspaper reporting on schizophrenia: A content analysis of five national newspapers at two time points'. *Schizophrenia Research*, 98(1–3), 178–183.

Connerton, P., 1989. *How Societies Remember*. Cambridge: Cambridge University Press.

Cook, F. L., T. R. Tyler, E. G. Goetz, M. T. Gordon, D. Protess, D. R. Leff, and H. L. Molotch, 1983. 'Media and agenda setting: effects on the public, interest group leaders, policy makers, and policy'. *Public Opinion Quarterly*, 47(1), 16–35.

Corcoran, C., 1998. 'The *Daily Mail* has been trying to raise public anxiety over teenagers, sex and the contraceptive pill to reckless levels'. *Nursing Times*, 94(9), 23.

Cottingham, J., 1996. *Western Philosophy: An Anthology*. Oxford: Blackwell.

Davidson, R., K. Hunt and J. Kitzinger, 2003. '"Radical blueprint for social change"? Media representations of New Labour's policies on public health'. *Sociology of Health and Illness*, 25(6), 532–552.

Davis, C., and N. Raynor, 2000. 'Reproducing consciousness: what *is* Indonesia', in D. Berry (ed.). *Ethics and Media Culture: Practices and Representations*. Oxford: Focal Press.

Deacon, D., M. Pickering, P. Golding and G. Murdock, 1999. *Researching Communications: A Practical Guide to Methods in Media and Cultural Analysis*. London: Arnold.

Dearing, J. W., and E. M. Rogers, 1996. *Agenda-setting*. Thousand Oaks, CA: Sage.

Department of Health, 2007. Mental Health Bill: Draft secondary legislation and statements of intent. http://www.dh.gov.uk/en/Healthcare/Mentalhealth/DH_063139.

Dhami, M., 2003. 'Psychological models of professional decision-making'. *Psychological Science*, 14(2), 175–180.

Diener, E., 2006. 'Guidelines for National Indicators of Subjective *Well-Being* and *Ill-Being*'. *Journal of Happiness Studies*, 7(4), 397–404.

Diener, E., and K. Ryan, 2009. 'Subjective well-being: an overview'. *South African Journal of Psychology*, 39(4), 391–406.

Dolman, F., 1895. *Municipalities at Work: The Municipal Policy of Six Great Towns and its Influence on their Social Welfare.* London: Methuen & Co.

Dunaway, J., R. P. Branton and M. A. Abrajano. 2010. 'Agenda setting, public opinion, and the issue of immigration reform'. *Social Science Quarterly*, 91(2), 359–378.

Durkheim, E., 1964. *The Rules of Sociological Method.* Translation by S. A. Soloway and J. H. Mueller, New York: Free Press.

Durkheim, E., 1976. *The Elementary Forms of Religious Life.* Translation by J. W. Swain. London: Allen and Unwin.

Edelman, M. J., 1993. 'Contestable categories and public opinion'. *Political Communications*, 10(3), 231–242.

Edwards, G. C. and B. D. Wood, 1999. 'Who influences whom? The president, congress and the media'. *The American Political Science Review*, 93(2), 327–344.

Elliot, P., 1970. 'Selection and Communication in a Television Production: A Case Study'. J. Tunstall (ed.). *Media Sociology: A Reader*. London: Constable.

Entman, R. M., 1993. 'Framing: Towards clarification of a fractured paradigm'. *Journal of Communication*, 43(4), 51–58.

Epstein, E., 1973. *News From Nowhere: Television and the News*. New York: Random House.

Evans, S., S. M. Fleming, R. J. Dolan and B. A. Averbeck, 2011. 'Effects of emotional preferences on value-based decision-making are mediated by mentalizing and not reward networks'. *Journal of Cognitive Neuroscience*, 23(9), 2197–2210.

Fairclough, N., 1995. *Critical Discourse Analysis*. London: Longman.

Feigenson, N. R. and D. S. Bailis, 2001. 'Air bag safety: Media coverage, popular conceptions, and public policy'. *Psychology, Public Policy and Law*, 7(2), 444–481.

Festinger, L., 1954. 'A theory of social comparison processes'. *Human Relations*, 7(2), 117–140.

Fisher, K., 1997. 'Locating frames in the discursive universe'. *Sociological Review Online*, 2(3), retrieved from http://www.socresonline.org.uk/2/3/4.html.

Fishman, M., 1980. *Manufacturing the News*. Austin, TX: University of Texas Press.

Floud, J., 1968 'The Sociology of Education', in A. T. Welford, M. Argyle, D. V. Glass and J. N. Morris. *Psychological Problems and Methods of Study*. London: Routledge & Kegan Paul.

Ford, J., 1932 (ed.). *Social Problems and Social Policy*. Boston: Ginn & Company.

Foster, J. L. H., 2006. 'Media presentation of the mental health bill and representations of mental health problems'. *Journal of Community and Applied Social Psychology*, 16(4), 285–300.

Frau-Meigs, D., 2000. 'A cultural project based on multiple temporary consensus: Identity and community in Wired'. *New Media Society*, 2(2), 227–244.

Gaertner, S.L., J. F. Dovidio, P. A. Anastasio, B. A. Bachman and M. C. Rust, 1993. 'The common ingroup identity model: Recategorization and the reduction of intergroup bias', in W. Stroebeand and M. Hewstone (eds). *European Review of Social Psychology*, 4. Chichester: Wiley.

Gallagher, S. M., 2011. 'Individualism and collectivism: Impact on outcome and effectiveness research, policy, and bariatric patient care'. *Bariatric Nursing and Surgical Patient Care*, 6(1), 11–14.

Galtung, J., and M. Ruge, 1965. 'The structure of foreign news'. *Journal of Peace Research* 2(1), 64–90.

Gamson, W. A., and A. Modigliani, 1987. 'The changing culture of affirmative action', in R. G. Braungart and M. M. Braungart (eds). *Research in Political Sociology*, (3), 137–177. Greenwich, CT: JAI Press.

Gans, H. J., 1979. *Deciding What's News*. New York: Free Press.

Gerston, L. N., 2008. *Public Policymaking in a Democratic Society: A Guide to Civic Engagement*. 2nd edition. New York: M. E. Sharpe.

Gerston, L. N., 2010. *Public Policy Making: Process and Principles*. 3rd edition. New York: M. E. Sharpe.

Gilens, M., 1996. 'Race and poverty in America: Public misperceptions and the American news media'. *Public Opinion Quarterly*, 60(4), 515–541.

Gitlin, T., 1980.*'The Whole World is Watching': Mass Media in the Making and the Unmaking of the New Left*. Berkeley: University of California Press.

Glasgow Media Group, 1980. *More Bad News*. London: Routledge and Kegan Paul.

Goffman, E., 1974. *Frame Analysis: An Essay on the Organization of Experience*. Cambridge, MA: Harvard University Press.

Golding, P., and P. Elliot, 1979. *Making The News*. Harlow: Longman.

Goodin, R. E., 1982. *Political Theory and Public Policy*. Chicago: University of Chicago Press.

Grey, T. C., 1976. 'Property and need: The welfare state and theories of distributive justice'. *Stanford Law Review*, 28(5), 877–902.

Gunter, B., 2000. *Media Research Methods*. London: Sage.

Habermas, J., 1995. *The Theory of Communicative Action, Volume Two, Lifeworld and System: a Critique of Functionalist Reason* . Cambridge: Polity Press.

Hall, S., C. Critcher, T. Jefferson, J. Clarke and B. Roberts, 1978. *Policing The Crisis: Mugging, the State, and Law and Order*. London: Macmillan.

Hallam, A., 2009. 'Media influences on mental health policy: long-term effects of the Clunis and Silcock cases'. *International Review of Psychiatry*, 14(1), 26–33.

Hanitzsch, T., 2005. 'Journalists in Indonesia: educated but timid'. *Journalism Studies*, 6(4), 493–508.

Harre, R., 1981. 'Philosophical Aspects of the Macro – Micro Problem', in K. K. Cetina and A. V. Cirourel (eds). *Advances in Social Theory and Methodology*. Boston: Routledge and Kegan Paul.

Hausman, C., 1990. *The Decision Making Process in Journalism*. Chicago: Nelson-Hall.

Hegel, G. W. F., 1967. *Hegel's Philosophy of Right*. Translation by Thomas M. Knox. Oxford: Oxford University Press.

Herman, E., and N. Chomsky, 2002. *Manufacturing Consent: the Political Economy of the Media Mass*. New York: Pantheon.

Hess, S., 1984. *The Government/Press Connection: Press Officers and their Offices*. Washington, DC: Brookings Institution Press.

Hill, M. J., and P. L. Hupe, 2006. *Implementing Public Policy: Governance in Theory and Practice*. Sage: London.

Hofstede, G., 1980. *Culture's Consequences: International Differences in Work Related Values*. Beverly Hills, CA: Sage.

Hogg, M.A., and D. Abrams, 1988. *Social Identifications: A Social Psychology of Intergroup Relations*. London and New York: Routledge & Kegan Paul.

Hollifield, C.A., G. M. Kosicki and L. B. Becker, 2001. 'Organizational vs. professional culture in the newsroom: Television news directors' and newspaper editors' hiring decisions'. *Journal of Broadcasting and Electronic Media*, 45(1), 92–117.

Hornig-Priest, S., 1996. *Doing Media Research: An Introduction*. London: Sage.

Hyde-Lay, R., 2010. 'Media representations of allergy and asthma issues, policy and research: views from the AllerGen Research Community'. *Health Law Review*, 18(3), 24–29.

Ibrahim, Y., 2011. 'Constructing "the Jungle": Distance framing in the *Daily Mail*'. *International Journal of Media and Cultural Politics*, 7(3), 315–331.

Isenberg, D. J., 1986. 'Group polarization: A critical review and meta-analysis'. *Journal of Personality and Social Psychology*, 50(6), 1141–1151.

Kress, G., 1990. 'Critical discourse analysis'. *Annual Review of Applied Linguistics*, 11, 84–89.

Janis, I. L., 1982. *Groupthink: Psychological Studies of Policy Decisions and Fiascos*. Boston: Houghton Mifflin.

Janis, I. L., and L. Mann, 1979. *Decision Making: A Psychological Analysis of Conflict, Choice and Commitment*. Free Press: Collin MacMillan, London.

Janssens, M., J. M. Brett and F. J. Smith, 1995. 'Confirmatory cross-cultural research: Testing the viability of a corporation-wide safety policy'. *Academy of Management Journal*, 38(2), 364–382.

Joffe, H., and G. Haarhoff, 2002. 'Representations of far-flung illnesses: The case of Ebola in Britain'. *Social Science and Medicine*, 54(6), 955–969.

Jones, S. C., and V. Harwood, 2009. 'Representations of autism in Australian print media'. *Disability and Society*, 24(1), 5–18.

Kamau, C., 2012. 'What does being initiated severely into a group do? The role of rewards'. *International Journal of Psychology*, dx.doi.org/10.1080/002075 94.2012.663957.

Kamau, C., and D. Harorimana, 2008. 'Does knowledge sharing and withholding of information in organizational committees affect quality of group decision making?' *Proceedings of the 9th European Conference on Knowledge Management*. Reading: Academic Publishing, 341–348.

Kamau, C., R. Giner-Sorolla and S. Zebel, in press. 'Reconciliation responses, blame and expressions of guilt or shame'. *Journal of Applied Social Psychology*.

Kaplan, M. S., 1987. 'Implications of individualism in public health policy'. *Journal of Economic Issues*, 21(1), 349–356.

Kruglanski, A. W., and D. M. Webster, 1996. 'Motivated closing of the mind: "Seizing and freezing"'. *Psychological Review*, 103(2), 263–268.

Lakoff, G., and M. Johnson, 1980. *Metaphors we live by*, at http://www.metaphor. org.uk, accessed November 2005.

Lang, K., and G. Lang, 1955. 'The inferential structure of political communications'. *Public Opinion Quarterly*, 19(2), 168–183.

Lascoumes, P., and P. Le Gales, 2007. 'Introduction: understanding public policy through its instruments – from the nature of instruments to the sociology of public policy instrumentation'. *Governance: An International Journal of Policy, Administration and Institutions*, 20(1), 1–21.

Lazenby, J. M., 2006. *The Early Wittgenstein on Religion*. London: Continuum.

Lehning, P. B., 2009. *John Rawls: An Introduction*. Cambridge: Cambridge University Press.

Lerman, C. L., 1983. 'Dominant Discourse: the Institutional Voice and the Control of the Topic' in H. Davis and P. Walton (eds). *Language, Image, Media*. Oxford: Blackwell.

Lester, M., 1980. 'Generating newsworthiness: The interpretive construction of public events'. *American Sociological Review*, 45, 984–994.

Levine, J. M., and R. L. Moreland, 1994. 'Group socialization: Theory and research', in W. Stroebeand and M. Hewstone (eds), *European Review of Social Psychology*, 5, 305–336. New York, NY: Wiley.

Lewin, P., 2007. 'Facts, values and the burden of proof'. *The Independent Review*, XI(3), 503–517.

Locke, J., 1990. *Two Treatises of Government*. London: J. M. Dent & Sons Ltd.

McChesney, R. W., 1997. *Corporate Media and the Threat to Democracy*. New York: Seven Stories Press.

McCombs, M., D. L. Shaw and D. Weaver, 1997 (eds). *Exploring the Intellectual Frontiers in Agenda-setting Theory*. London: Lawrence Erlbaum Associates.

McGill, P., and R. Cummings, 1990. 'An analysis of the representation of people with mental handicaps in a British newspaper'. *Mental Handicap Research*, 3(1), 60–69.

Machill, M. and M. Beiler, 2009. 'The importance of the internet for journalistic research'. *Journalism Studies*, 10(2), 178–203.

Mackenzie, J. M., 1984. *Propaganda and Empire: the Manipulation of British Public Opinion, 1880–1960*. Manchester: Manchester University Press.

McQuail, D., 1993. *Media Performance: Mass Communication and the Public Interest*. London: Sage.

Martín-Barbero, J., 1993. *Communication, Culture and Hegemony: From Media to Mediations*. London: Sage.

Martinez-Cajas, J. L., C. F. Invernizzi, M. Ntemgwa, S. M. Schader and M. A. Wainberg, 2008. 'Benefits of an educational program for journalists on media coverage of HIV/AIDS in developing countries'. *Journal of the International AIDS Society*, 11(2), retrieved from http://www.jiasociety.org/content/1/1/2.

Marx, K., 1967. *Capital*. Volume 1. New York: International Publishers.

Maslow, A. H., 1943. 'A theory of human motivation'. *Psychological Review*, 50(4), 370–396.

Mason, S. E., E. A. Darnell and K. Prifti, 2010. 'Stereotypes and representations of aging in the media'. *Journal of Instructional Psychology*, 37(2), 189–190.

Morris, J. C., 1885. The National Policy: Being a Series of Addresses Delivered through the Press to the 5,000,000 Electors of the United Kingdom, and More Especially to the New Voters. London: Allen.

Morrison, D. E. and M. Svennevig, 2002. 'The Public Interest, the Media and Privacy'. A Report for British Broadcasting Corporation, Broadcasting Standards Commission, Independent Committee for the Supervision of Standards of Telephone Information Services Independent Television Commission, Institute for Public Policy Research, The Radio Authority, March.

Mummendey, M., A. Klink and R. Brown, 2001. 'A rejoinder to our critics and some of their misapprehensions'. *British Journal of Social Psychology*, 40(2), 187–191.

Nabi, R. L., and J. L. Sullivan, 2001. 'Does television viewing relate to engagement in protective action against crime? A cultivation analysis from a theory of reasons action perspective'. *Communication Research*, 28(6), 802–825.

Nederman, C. J., 2003. 'Community and self-interest: Marsiglio of Padua on civil life and private advantage. *The Review of Politics*, 65(4), 395–416.

Negrine, R., 1994. *Politics and the Mass Media in Britain*. London: Routledge.

Niven, D., 2002. 'Bolstering an illusory majority: The effects of the media's portrayal of death penalty support'. *Social Science Quarterly*, 83(3), 671–689.

Nozick, R., 1974. *Anarchy, State and Utopia*. New York: Basic Books.

Oakes, P., and J. C. Turner, 1986. 'Authors' rejoinder to Jahoda and Tetlock'. *British-Journal of Social Psychology*, 25(3), 257–258.

Oakes, P. J., S. A. Haslam and J. C. Turner, 1994. *Stereotyping and Social Reality*. Oxford, UK and Cambridge, MA: Blackwell.

Oliver, P. E., and H. Johnston, 2000. 'What a good idea: Frames and ideologies in social movements research'. *Mobilisation*, 5(1), 37–54.

Ott, J., 2010. 'Happiness, economics and public policy: A critique'. *Journal of Happiness Studies*, 11(1), 125–130.

Ouweneel, P., 2002. 'Social security of the unemployed in 42 nations'. *Journal of Happiness Studies*, 3(2), 167–192.

Özbilgin, M. and A. Tatli, 2011. 'Mapping out the field of equality and diversity: Rise of individualism and voluntarism'. *Human Relations*, 64(9), 1229–1253.

Pan, Z., and G. M. Kosicki, 1993. 'Framing analysis: An approach to news discourse'. *Political Communication*, 10(1), 55–75.

Petley, J., 2012. 'Jürgen Habermas: The Modern Media and the Public Sphere', in D. Berry (ed.). *Revisiting the Frankfurt School: Essays on Culture, Media and Theory*. Aldershot: Ashgate Publishing.

Pieters, G., V. De Gucht and H. Kajosch, 2003. 'Newspaper coverage of psychiatry and general medicine: Comparing tabloids with broadsheets'. *Psychiatric Bulletin*, 27(7), 259–260.

Plato, 1903. *Crito*. Edited with Introduction by J. Adam. Cambridge: Cambridge University Press.

Plato, 1966. *The Republic*. Edited by I. A. Richards. Cambridge: Cambridge University Press.

Price, V., 1988. 'On the public aspects of opinion: Linking levels of analysis in public opinion research'. *Communication Research*, 15(6), 659–679.

Prior, L., 1997. 'Following in Foucault's Footsteps: Texts and Contexts in Qualitative Research', in D. Silverman (ed.). *Qualitative Research: Theory, Method and Practice*. London: Sage.

Rabbie, J. M., J. C. Schot and L. Visser, 1989. 'Social identity theory: A conceptual and empirical critique from the perspective of a behavioural interaction model'. *European Journal of Social Psychology*, 19(3), 171–202.

Rawls, J., 1971 (reprinted 2008). *A Theory of Justice*. Cambridge, Mass: Belknap Press.

Reyna, C., P. J. Henry, W. Korfmacher and A. Tucker, 2005. 'Examining the Principles in Principled Conservatism: The Role of Responsibility Stereotypes as Cues for Deservingness in Racial Policy Decisions'. *Journal of Personality and Social Psychology*, 90(1), 109–128.

Richards, B., and G. Rees, 2011. 'The management of emotion in British journalism'. *Media Culture and Society*, 33(6), 851–867.

Roscho, B., 1975. *Newsmaking*. Chicago: University of Chicago Press.

Rothstein, B., 2010. 'Happiness and the welfare state'. *Social Research*, 77(2), 441.

Runciman, W. G., 1966. *Relative Deprivation and Social Justice*. Berkeley: University of California Press,.

Ryan, A., 2010. 'Happiness and political theory'. *Social Research*, 77(2), 421–440.

Sacks, J., 2000. *Radical Then, Radical Now: On Being Jewish*. London: Continuum.

Salazar, J. M., 1998. 'Social Identity and National Identity', in S. Worchel, J. F. Morales, D. Paezand and J. C. Deschamps, (eds). *Social Identity: International Perspectives*. London: Sage, 114–123.

Scheufele, D., 1999. 'Framing as a theory of media effects'. *Journal of Communication*, Winter, 103–122.

Schimmel, J., 2007. 'Development as happiness: The subjective perception of happiness and UNDP's analysis of poverty, wealth and development'. Published online. *Springer Science + Business Media B.V.*, 9 June.

Schlesinger, P., 1978. *Putting 'Reality' Together*. London: Methuen.

Schulman, P. R., 1975. 'Non-incremental policymaking: Notes towards an alternative paradigm'. *The American Political Science Review*, 69(4), 1354–1370.

Schuster, D.V., T. W. Valente, S. N. Skara, M. R. Wenten, J. B. Unger, T. B. Cruz and L. A. Rohrbach, 2006. 'Intermedia processes in the adoption of tobacco control activities among opinion leaders in California'. *Communication Theory*, 16(1), 91–117.

Schutz, A., 1964. *Collected Papers*, *2 volumes*. The Hague: Nijhoff.

Seo, H., 2011. 'Media and foreign policy: A comparative study of journalists' perceptions of press-government relations during the six-party talks'. *Journalism*, 12(4), 467–481.

Sharkey, J., 1993. 'When pictures drive foreign policy'. *American Journalism Review*, 15(10), 14.

Shepherd, E., and C. Seale, 2010. 'Eating disorders in the media: The changing nature of UK newspaper reports'. *European Eating Disorders Review*, 18(6), 486–495.

Sigelman, L., 1973. 'Reporting the news: an organisational analysis'. *American Journal of Sociology*, 79(1), 132–151.

Simon, B., C. Hastedt and B. Aufderheide, 1997. 'When self-categorization makes sense: The role of meaningful social categorization in minority and majority members' self-perception'. *Journal of Personality and Social Psychology*, 73(2), 310–320.

Smith, D. M., K. M. Langa, M. U. Kabeto and P. A. Ubel, 2005. 'Health, wealth, and happiness: Financial resources buffer subjective well-being after the onset of a disability'. *Psychological Science (Wiley-Blackwell)*, 16(9), 663–666.

Smith, E. R., and S. Henry, 1996. 'An ingroup becomes part of the self: Response time evidence'. *Personality and Social Psychology Bulletin*, 22(6), 635–642.

Sparks, C., 1998. *Communism, Capitalism and the Mass Media*. London: Sage.

Spears, R., B. Doosje and N. Ellemers, 1997. 'Self stereotyping in the face of threats to group status and distinctiveness: The role of group identification'. *Personality and Social Psychology Bulletin*, 23(5), 538–553.

Splichal, S., 1994. *Media Beyond Socialism*. Boulder: Westview Press.

Spong, A., and C. Kamau, 2009. *'Who Raises Which Policy Topic in Parliament? An Analysis of MPs' Group Motives'*. Faculty Funded Research Project: Faculty of Media Arts and Society, Southampton Solent University.

Stasser, G., and W. Titus, 1985. 'Pooling of unshared information in group decision making: Biased information sampling during discussion'. *Journal of Personality and Social Psychology*, 48(6), 1467–1478.

Stewart, D. D., and G. Stasser, 1998. 'The sampling of critical, unshared information in decision-making groups: the role of an informed minority'. *European Journal of Social Psychology*, 28(1), 95–113.

Stutzer, A., and B. S. Frey, 2010. 'Recent advances in the economics of individual subjective well-being'. *Social Research*, 77(2), 679–714.

Tajfel, H., M. G. Billig, R. P. Bundy and C. Flament, 1971. 'Social categorization and intergroup behaviour'. *European Journal of Social Psychology*, 1(2), 149–178.

Tajfel, H., and J. Dawson, 1965. *Disappointed Guests: Essays By African, Asian and West Indian Students*. London: Oxford University Press.

Tajfel, H., and J. C. Turner, 1979. 'An Integrative Theory of Intergroup Conflict', in S. Worcheland and W. G. Austin (eds). *The Social Psychology of Intergroup Relations*. Monterey, California: Brookes/Cole.

Taranto, J., 2010. 'Peer pressure'. *The American Spectator*, February.

Tetlock, P. E., 2000. 'Cognitive biases and organizational correctives: Do both disease and cure depend on the politics of the beholder?' *Administrative Science Quarterly*, 45(2), 293–326.

Theobald, J., 2000. 'Radical mass media criticism: elements of a history from Kraus to Bourdieu', in D. Berry (ed.). *Ethics and Media Culture: Practices and Representations*. Oxford: Focal Press.

Thompson, J. B., 1990. *Ideology and Modern Culture: Critical Social Theory in the Era of Mass Communication*. Cambridge: Polity Press.

Tiberius, V., 2004. 'Cultural differences and philosophical accounts of well-being'. *Journal of Happiness Studies*, 5(3), 293–314.

Tiffen, R., 1989. *News and Power*. Australia: Allen and Unwin.

Tönnies, F., 2002. *Community and Society*. Newton Abbot: David & Charles.

Tracey, M., 1977. *The Production of Political Television*. London: Routledge and Kegan Paul.

Tropp, L. R., and S. C. Wright, 2001. 'Ingroup identification as the inclusion of ingroup in the self'. *Personality and Social Psychology Bulletin*, 27(5), 585–600.

Tuchman, G., 1978, *'Making News': A Study in the Construction of Reality*. New York: The Free Press.

Tunstall, J., 1972. 'News Organisation Goals and Specialist Newsgathering Journalists', in D. McQuail (ed.). *Sociology of Mass Communications*. Harmondsworth: Penguin.

Turner, J. C., 1982. 'Towards a cognitive redefinition of the social group'. *Cahiers de Psychologie Cognitive/Current Psychology of Cognition*, 1(2), 93–118.

Turner, J. C., 1996. 'Henri Tajfel: An Introduction', in W. P. Robinson (ed.). *Social Groups and Identities: Developing the Legacy of Henri Tajfel*. Oxford: Butterworth Heinemann.

Turner, J. C., M. A. Hogg, P. J. Oakes, S. D. Reicher and M. S. Wetherall, 1987 (eds). *Rediscovering the Social Group: A Self-Categorization Theory*. Basil Blackwell: Oxford.

Turner, J. C., P. J. Oakes, S. A. Haslam and C. McGarty, 1994. 'Self and collective: Cognition and social context'. *Personality and Social Psychology Bulletin*, 20(5), 454–463.

Turner, J. C., I. Sachdev and M. A. Hogg, 1983. 'Social categorization, interpersonal attraction and group formation'. *British Journal of Social Psychology*, 22(3), 227–239.

Uscinski, J. E., 2009. 'When does the public's issue agenda affect the media's issue agenda (and vice-versa)? Developing a framework for media-public influence'. *Social Science Quarterly*, 90(4), 796–815.

Van Dijk, T., 1988. *News As Discourse*. London: Lawrence Erlbaum Associates.

Van Dijk, T., 1991. *Racism and the Press*. London: Routledge.

Van Noije, L., J. Kleinnijenhuis and D. Oegema, 2008. 'Parliament as media's puppet on a string. Is this the price we pay for European integration? A Longitudinal and cross-sectional analysis of agenda building in the United Kingdom and the Netherlands'. *British Journal of Political Science*, 38(3), 455–478.

Vasterman, P., C. J. Yzermans and A. J. E. Dirkzwager, 2004. 'The role of the media and media hypes in the aftermath of disasters'. *Epidemiologic Reviews*, 27(1), 107–114.

Vinokur, A., E. Burnstein, L. Sechrest and P. M. Wortman, 1985. 'Group decision making by experts: Field study of panels evaluating medical technologies'. *Journal of Personality and Social Psychology*, 49(1), 70–84.

Wallach, M. A., N. Kogan and D. J. Bem, 1962. 'Group influence on individual risk taking'. *Journal of Abnormal and Social Psychology*, 65(2), 75–86.

Weaver, K., S. M. Garcia, N. Schwarz and D. T. Miller, 2007. 'Inferring the popularity of an opinion from its familiarity: A repetitive voice can sound like a chorus'. *Journal of Personality and Social Psychology*, 92(5), 821–833.

Weiss, G., and Wodak, R. 2002 (eds). *Critical Discourse Analysis: Theory and Interdisciplinarity*. Basingstoke: Palgrave Macmillan.

Wexler, P., 1991. *Social Analysis of Education: After the New Sociology*. London: Routledge.

Whale, J., 1970. 'Journalist news'. *The Listener*, October, 510–512.

Wilkinson, P., and P. McGill, 2009. 'Representation of people with intellectual disabilities in a British newspaper in 1983 and 2001'. *Journal Of Applied Research In Intellectual Disabilities*, 22(1), 65–76.

Wilkinson, S., 1896. *The Nation's Awakening: Essays Towards a British Policy*. British Library Collection.

Williams, S. J., C. Seale, S. Boden, P. Lowe and D. Steinberg, 2008. 'Medicalization and beyond: The social construction of insomnia and snoring in the news'. *Health: An Interdisciplinary Journal for The Social Study Of Health, Illness And Medicine*, 12(2), 251–268.

Willnat, L., and D. Weaver, 2003. 'Through their eyes: The work of foreign correspondents in the United States'. *Journalism*, 4(4), 403–422.

Winter, J., 1997. *Democracy's Oxygen: how Corporations Control the News*. Montreal: Black Rose.

Yanovitzky, I., 2002. 'Effects of news coverage on policy attention and actions: A closer look into the media-policy connection'. *Communication Research*, 29(4), 422–451.

Young, N., and E. Dugas, 2011 'Representations of climate change in Canadian national print media: The banalization of global warming'. *Canadian Review of Sociology*, 48(1), 1–22.

Index